Table of Contents

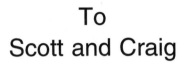

To
Scott and Craig

Preface

"All the world loves a winner" is one of the most enduring proverbs on the American landscape, transcending many fields of endeavor, including the stock market. Finding a winner, in spite of all the fancy stock market theories individual investors are supposed to follow, such as "capital asset pricing" and "asset allocation" and the like, still provides the ultimate satisfaction.

Every investor who is reading this book has probably come up with a couple of winners now and then. We all have probably had the thrill of what Peter Lynch calls a "ten bagger."

For most investors, the winners have come along sporadically. Many investors searching for winners can relate to Ben Hogan's description in his classic, *Five Lessons, The Modern Fundamentals of Golf.* Here Hogan states, "When the average player gets ready to hit a shot, some days, purely by accident, he does one or two things correctly. He hasn't the faintest idea what these key things are, but he does them and consequently he plays quite well. On most days, however—on nearly all days, for that matter—he feels very uncomfortable and unconfident as he addresses the ball and is completely baffled when he tries to figure out the remedies that will give him that sense of rightness."

In his "Five Lessons," Hogan goes on to explain the principles of golf. The techniques of successful investing can be learned and practiced as well. Instead of a hit-or-miss approach to investing, the common-sense principles set forth in *Finding Winners Among Depressed and Low-Priced Stocks* will improve investor success in the stock market.

We'll start by exploring the world of low-priced and depressed stocks. Low-priced and depressed stocks are largely ignored by today's investment community for a variety of reasons. We are constantly being lectured by "those in the know" that "you get what you pay for," implying that investing in low-priced and depressed stocks is tantamount to getting your hands dirty.

Yet, year in, year out, the best stock market gains come from low-priced stocks, stocks selling under $20, often less than $10, and sometimes under $5. Wall Street conditions the investor to buy high-priced stocks, but the best returns invariably arise from low-priced and depressed stocks. As they say, "every dog has its day."

Or many, but not all, dogs, I should add. Some low-priced stocks become lower priced. Some low-priced stocks remain low-priced for years. Some low-priced stocks end up worthless. Investing in low-priced and depressed stocks is not a matter of throwing darts. Instead, keeping track of how well stocks are acting, whether they are under accumulation or distribution, whether the trend is bullish or bearish, in other words, technical analysis, is what gives investors the winning edge.

Finding Winners discusses the characteristics of the type of stocks most likely to be big winners, and develops a system that will tell investors when and how to buy them. Good investing!

About the Author

Richard L. Evans, a Registered Investment Advisor and the principal of Richard L. Evans Investments, is a manager of individual investment and retirement portfolios. Evans is a graduate of Northwestern University's prestigious Kellogg Graduate School of Management, a recognized Dow Theorist, and formerly President, Chief Market Strategist, Director of Research, and an owner of *Dow Theory Forecasts*, one of the best-known investment letters.

Periodically quoted in nationally recognized publications such as *Barron's*, *The New York Times*, *The Wall Street Journal*, *Forbes*, *The Chicago Tribune*, *Money* Magazine, and *Investor's Business Daily*, Evans has been featured at length in *Money* Magazine's "Money Profile-Advice from a Pro" and was asked to select a *Money* Magazine "Stock of The Month" feature. Evans has participated in and won one of the monthly stock-picking contests in *The Wall Street Journal*'s "Your Money Matters" and has been interviewed at length by *Barron's* Kathryn M. Welling for his market views.

On television Evans hosts and produces a biweekly "Your Investments" program on PBS WYIN-Channel 56. Evans appeared on Terry Savage's WBBM-CBS TV's "Money Talks," Ira Epstein's "Stocks, Options, and Futures," WCIU's Channel 26 "Stock Market Observer," and on CNBC-FNN. On radio Evans has been quoted by WBBM News Radio 78's Financial Editor Len Walter and WMAQ's Alan Crane and gives occasional interviews across the country.

As a speaker, lecturer, and author Evans keynoted several Charles Schwab Investor Conferences, addressed chapters nationwide of the American Association of Individual Investors, gave presentations for Chicago Rotary One and similar organizations, and frequently speaks at programs sponsored by various financial institutions. On a professional basis Evans has lectured for The Financial Analysts Federation, The Investment Analysts Society, and Indiana University School of Finance. He has written for *Technical Analysis of Stocks & Commodities*, is the technical analysis contributing editor for the *AAII Journal*, and periodically writes a stock market column for daily newspapers. Evans was also a contributing author to *The Individual Investor's Guide to Winning On Wall Street*.

List of Figures and Tables

Section I

FINDING WINNERS

· 1 ·

Low-Priced and Depressed Stocks: Philosophy and Merit

The Performance Advantage

Low-priced and depressed stocks can be extremely profitable opportunities for the individual investor. *Finding Winners* offers a spectrum of concepts, theories, opinions, statistics, technical tools, and case studies on the whys, hows, and whens of these opportunities. The best gains, year in and year out, are in low-priced and depressed stocks. With some knowledge of how the markets operate, the average investor is in an excellent position to achieve above-average gains in these stocks.

My interest in low-priced stocks began as a result of a personal experience. I first started buying stock in the late 1960s. I was going to college at the time and working during the summers. Whenever I had accumulated some funds, I marched down to the local brokerage office and bought stock in odd-lots. I did not buy just any stock. I bought stock in a Wall Street consensus favorite—Magnavox.

Magnavox at the time was the epitome of the growth stock to buy. During the late '60s the nifty-fifty craze was becoming vogue. The nifty-fifty was a one-decision-type issue. That is, all an investor had to do was buy stock in companies with solid earnings and the capital gains took care of themselves.

I remember those fancy Kidder-Peabody reports on high-quality grey paper. I was taking finance in college and planning a career in the investment business. Those reports impressed me. I thought that if highly paid Wall Street experts said that glamour was the way to buy stocks, it must be so. They never said that their ability to predict earnings was far less impressive than the appearance of their research reports.

I don't remember if Magnavox was on the list of the "50", but the firm certainly had all the qualifications—an outstanding reputation, solid earnings, an excellent dividend record, double-digit profit margins, low debt, and top-of-the-line products. Magnavox also followed one of the keys to success professors were teaching me at Northwestern's Kellogg Graduate School of Management—a defined "corporate mission" in servicing the electronics market.

Magnavox marketed to a broad segment of the electronics market. Its consumer products included color televisions, radios, phonographs, and hi-fi and stereophonic sound equipment. It served the business market with its Minicard and Magnacard systems, and the firm was moving into facsimile transmissions under the name Magnafax. It also had a wide range of products in military electronics, such as UHF communication systems, sonar detection devices, and navigational equipment. In high-margin, high-quality consumer products, specifically consoles, the Magnavox name was premier. As part of its "synergy," another buzzword from Kellogg, Magnavox had brought Baker, one of the premier names in furniture, into the fold.

Magnavox had developed a full line of "integrated" products, specializing in the high end of the market. It had even integrated distribution through a direct-to-dealership network.

Magnavox was doing everything right. I felt confident every time I bought 20 or 30 shares of this Rolls-Royce of the industry at $40, $50, $60 a share and higher. Because the firm was based in Fort Wayne, Indiana, the stock was exempt from Indiana personal property tax. I was even beating the tax man!

Unfortunately, glamour does not necessarily convert into profits, except, perhaps, for the printers of those glossy annual reports. Wall Street abounded with positive opinions and earnings expectations when the stock was at its highs, but analysts quickly cut and run as their estimates prove wrong. Wall Street expert opinion is more part of a selling effort than it is true analytical work.

A friend of the family, a pharmaceutical chemist, had a very different approach. The chemist ran a thriving family business, but he always liked to "play" the market. An old-fashioned stock picker, he had little use for the "consensus" stocks adorning the top of the Kidder-Peabody reports.

The chemist believed in buying low, buying cheap, buying depressed stocks. Instead of taking brokerage house recommendations, he browsed through the stocks making the list of new lows, the stocks languishing at the bottom of the bin. One of these, Texas Gulf Sulphur, made the chemist millions.

Texas Gulf Sulphur was one of the largest producers of sulphur in the world. About 90% of its sulphur was produced by four mines in Texas: Boling, Spindletop, Moss Bluff, and Fannett. Texas Gulf mined potash in Utah and had phosphate fertilizer operations in North Carolina. It also owned Kidd Creek Mine in Canada, a producer of copper, lead and zinc concentrates, and silver. Kidd Creek Mine would make the difference.

When the chemist was buying the stock in the early '60s few Wall Street analysts were interested in Texas Gulf. The favored evaluation method on Wall Street and among MBA types was the buy decision based on earnings. Texas Gulf, with flat sales and declining earnings, was languishing in the teens. Texas Gulf Sulphur was low priced and truly depressed.

The chemist, though, was a buyer, accumulating his initial 10,000 share position during the summer of '62 around the 12 level. When the firm cut its dividend a few weeks later, he bought another 5,000 shares.

The chemist bought Texas Gulf on the combination of price, value, and activity. The stock was low. The leverage on a $10 stock is many times greater than the leverage on a $100 stock. Value was present in that the stock was selling low on earnings. At a price/earnings (P/E) ratio of 5:1, the chemist figured that he would be paid back for the price of the stock in five years. Finally, the stock was acting well. The stock price was actually higher at the time of the dividend cut.

The chemist was buying assets in the ground. The stock seemed cheap in relation to past price levels as well as fundamentals. He was buying in anticipation that Texas Gulf would return to "normal" price levels at some point. The inflationary days of Lyndon Johnson's Great Society administration were just around the corner and so were accelerating commodity prices.

The chemist's net worth grew as Texas Gulf Sulphur moved from 15 to 20, then to 25, then to 50, then to 100, then to 150. Meanwhile, I watched in disbelief as Magnavox, one of Wall Street's darlings, begin to sink into oblivion, from 50 to 40, then to 30, 20, 10, and then to under 5, only to be bought out at distressed prices by North American Philips.

The chemist scored big with his low-priced stock. Eventually, Societe Nationale Elf Aquitaine offered 56 per share for Texas Gulf. Reflecting several splits, the chemist owned 90,000 shares. His cost basis was around 2. He still carries around the copy of the $5,002,932.80 check he received for selling the stock.

The comparison in percentage return between my highly respected Magnavox, -93.8%, and his low-priced, depressed Texas Gulf Sulfur, +2700%, is a lesson I never forgot.

Gains Available from Low-Priced Stocks

The Texas Gulf Sulphur stock scenario is repeated every day. Low-priced and depressed stocks invariably account for the major stock gains. Last year, 1993, the average capital gains of the top 10 winners was 207%. The average price per share was $12.375. The Dow was up 13.72%. Just an aberration? Not really.

In 1992, the top 25 stocks on the New York Stock Exchange (NYSE) ranked in terms of capital appreciation had average net gains of 182%. The top 10 had average capital gains of 229%. The Dow was up 4.17%. For those who disdain the Dow, the S&P 500 was up 4.46%. The returns from either the Dow or the S&P were no big deal. Stock picking, though, can be very rewarding.

The intriguing aspect is that the price of the 1992 top 25 performing issues averaged $8.41 per share at the first of the year. The price of the top 10 performing issues averaged a little over $5 a share—$5.36—at the first of the year. The largest gains, the best performers, the big winners, came from the lower-priced stocks.

NYSE Top 50
12/31/91 to 12 /31/92

	Average Gain (%)	Average Price ($)
1 - 10	229.8	5.35
11 - 20	157.7	10.96
21 - 30	130.5	9.71
31 - 40	116.9	23.75
41 - 50	106.7	21.62

And these gains took place in a market environment that was largely lackluster.

The following table ranks the top 50 in terms of price.

1992 NYSE Percent Gains
Top 50 Performers

Price ($)	Number of Stocks	% of Total Number	Average Gain (%)
Under - 5.00	17	34	175.0
5 - 9.99	8	16	148.6
10 - 14.99	7	14	137.5
15 - 19.99	6	12	145.0
20 - 24.99	2	4	136.9
25 - 29.99	4	8	121.5
30 - 34.99	1	2	100.7
35 - 39.99	2	4	109.3
40 - 44.99	1	2	102.0
45 - 49.99	2	4	120.5

In the previous year, 1991, the major market indexes all showed gains better than 20%. By contrast, the top 25 winners showed gains of 391%. The average price was under 7.08 a share. The top 10 winners for 1991 showed gains of a 532%. The average price of the top 10 issues was under $5 a share—$4.20. A stronger market makes for greater performance of low-priced stocks.

Now contrast the performance of the 25 stocks showing the best capital gains with the performance of another select group of stocks, the 25 NYSE Most Actively Traded Issues.

	Price 12/31/91	Gain by %
Chrysler	11.750	172.3
Unisys	4.125	145.5
Citicorp	10.375	114.5
Chemical Bank	21.250	81.8
Ford Motor	57.625	52.4
Disney	114.500	50.2
AT&T	39.125	30.4
PepsiCo	33.875	22.5
American Express	20.500	21.3
Telefonos de Mexicos	46.750	19.8
General Motors	28.825	11.7
WalMart	58.875	8.7
Coca-Cola	80.250	4.4
AMD	17.500	3.6
GTE	34.625	0.0
Philip Morris	80.250	−3.9
Limited	28.500	−5.3
Boeing	47.750	−16.0
RJR Nabisco	10.750	19.8
Merck	166.291	−21.7
Bristol-Myers	88.250	−23.7
Glaxo Holdings	31.750	−25.2
Westinghouse	18.000	−25.7
IBM	89.000	−43.4
Syntex	48.250	−52.3
Average	47.552	20.1

During 1992, as a group, the average gain in this select group was 20%. The top 25 winners with average price under 10 beat the average gain of the NYSE Most Actively Traded Issues by 9-to-1.

Let's look more closely at that 20% gain. While the top 25 in terms of NYSE market activity showed gains "on average" of 20%, only three issues accounted for most of the gain, and these three issues were all low-priced stocks. Chrysler, Unisys, and Citicorp showed the best gains, 172%, 145%, and 114%, respectively. Chrysler, Unisys, and Citicorp were also three low-priced stocks, 11 3/4, 4 1/8, and 10 3/8. Without the benefit of these low-priced stocks, the gains from the 25 most actively traded issues drops to a mere 3%.

Let's look at another listing of 25 stocks, the 25 most widely held issues on the NYSE. At the end of 1992, this list showed a loss of 3.2%. The average price of the 25 largest capitalized stocks was just under $71 a share. Contrast this dismal performance with the gains available from the 25 best gainers where the average price was $8.41 and the performance differential is even greater. Who would ever want to trade in the large cap stocks?

The Dow Jones Industrial Average is based on 30 stocks. Through the years the lower-priced issues among the Dow have beaten the average of the 30 Dow stocks. Sometimes the low-priced stocks have really walloped the Dow.

Last year the ten lowest-priced Dow stocks showed an average gain of 19.4%, compared to the ten highest-priced Dow stocks with a gain of 9.9%.

In 1992, for instance, the total return of the ten lowest-priced Dow stocks was more than 30%, over three times the 7.95% total return for the Dow. The leader that year was Union Carbide, up more than 90%. At one point during the year, Union Carbide was selling at 10 3/4.

The year before, 1991, the total return of the ten lowest-priced Dow stocks was over 42%, compared to a Dow return of 24%. Goodyear was the big winner, up 183%. Goodyear sold as low as 16 3/4 during the year.

While the low-priced Dow stocks have produced some great winners, just buying the low-priced Dow stocks is not the answer. The lower-priced Dow stocks have beaten the Dow through the years, but some exceptions have occurred.

In 1990, when the Dow showed a slight total return loss of about 50 cents, the ten lowest-priced issues lost more than 20%. Many of the lower-priced issues had substantial declines, ranging over –40%. The lower-priced Dow stocks, regardless of yield, can result in a big loss in investors' portfolios if bought at the wrong time.

Although lower-priced stocks on the NYSE can deliver some big, big gains, some are among the largest losers. While the average price of the 25 largest losers on the NYSE was significantly higher than the average price of the 25 largest gainers, more losing stocks were priced at less than $10 per share than at more than $50 a share.

While low-priced stocks can deliver some very impressive gains, an investor must have more than just price to guide investment decisions. Technical analysis plays a role in making these investment decisions. While low-priced stocks can pay off big, it pays to be on the right side of the market.

No matter what perspective is taken, low-priced stocks are where the big winners will be found.

Why Low-Priced Stocks Perform Best

Numerous theories try to explain why low-priced stocks perform well. One says that low-priced stocks are more volatile, that is, low-priced stocks exhibit larger swings on a percentage basis. A one point move on a $5 stock is also obviously more significant than a one point move on a $50 stock. It is not surprising that a $5 stock tends to have twice the percentage price movement than a $50 stock.

Low-priced stocks' up-and-down or back-and-forth price swings are not the reason for investing in them. Low-priced stocks are good bets because of the potential for big gains, for finding winners that may double, or triple, or more. Low-priced stocks are capable of delivering some very high percentage performances. The pharmaceutical chemist always reminded me that he would rather own 1,000 shares of a $10 stock than 100 shares of a $100 stock.

Various theories try to account for the superior performance of one stock group versus another. Low-priced and depressed stocks generally fit into the "contrarian" theory of investing, or the "value" theory of investing, or the "overreaction" theory of investing, or the "neglected" theory of investing.

There is no shortage of theory. Hundreds of books, academic papers, and magazine articles have been written trying to prove or disprove this or that theory. During the initial research for this Chapter, a debate was going on about who should get credit for "inventing" contrarian investing in the first place.

No matter which theory is used, the basic reason why lower-priced stocks can deliver outstanding gains is because they can be bought cheaply. Buy low and sell high is a cliche; it is also the road to investment success.

The Battle for Investment Survival

A deluge of new investment books appears each year. Many are get-rich-quick schemes. Few have improved on the essence of successful investing expressed by Gerald M. Loeb in his 1935 classic, *The Battle for Investment Survival*.

In one chapter, "What to Buy—And When," Loeb states one cornerstone of investing: "It is important to stick to issues which in past times of bullish enthusiasm have had active markets and which can be expected to have active markets again. However, at the time of purchase they must be low-rated and unpopular, with their prices down and discouragement about their prospects quite general."

Loeb continues, "The objective is always buy that which the majority thinks is speculative and sell it when the majority believes that quality has reached investment grade. It is in this policy that both safety and profits exist." In a nutshell, buy cheap and sell dear!

The debate over what is cheap is always going on. Just because a stock appears cheap does not mean it should be purchased. A lot of cheap stocks tend to get cheaper. A $10 stock that declines to $1 is still a 90% loss.

Here again, Loeb's classic offers some advice. He states, "When all is said and done, it is the price of your stock that counts—or whether it is going up or down." Price and trend were Loeb's "traffic signals."

To Loeb determining a stock's theoretical value is not enough. Full consideration has to be given to what investors think it is worth. Loeb believed in an efficient market to the extent that a stock is worth exactly the price at which it is selling at any one point in time, no more, no less. Likewise, Loeb really doesn't think you could know what is "cheap" or what is "dear".

Instead, being able to appraise the desire and ability, or lack of ability, of investors to bid or offer stock, or the action of the market itself, in terms of actual price movement or trend, is the most important factor in "the battle for investment survival."

In short, technical analysis tells us what and when, and that is why low-priced and depressed stocks and technical analysis go hand in hand.

The Plight of the Herd

An investor may wonder: If Loeb's perceptions on the road to investment success are so wonderful, why isn't everybody rich? The answers are several but interrelated.

First, buying low-priced and depressed issues does pose substantial risk. Gains of 100% or more do not accrue to investors who follow the middle of the road. Superior gains come only to investors willing to take risks. Many investors are not willing to do so. The purpose of *Finding Winners* is to help individual investors size up and take those risks necessary to achieve superior gains.

Second, the nature of the stock market is changing, and individual investors have increasingly abdicated their investment responsibilities to Wall Street professionals, sometimes referred to as the "herd". The growth of corporate and other institutional investment plans has led to a demand for professional investment management. Many individual investors, too, have fled from their individual responsibilities and handed over their investments to Wall Street professionals who tend to be more risk-adverse than individual investors. And, simply put, Loeb's style of buying unpopular stocks is not the way Wall Street does business today.

At the start of the major bull market in 1946, stock trading and the individual investor were considered one and the same. As late as 1970, institutional trading was less than 25%. Today, institutional trading accounts for more than 80% of all trading.

The movement away from the individual investor toward the pros also shows up in the declining percentage of stock owned by individual households. At the start of the post-World War II bull market, individual holdings accounted for more than 90% of stock ownership, a scant 5% for institutions. By 1992, institutional ownership had increased 10-fold, and individual holdings were down nearly 50%.

The statistics show that the individual investor has been giving ground to Wall Street investment professionals. Isn't this a good idea? Isn't movement toward professional money management a rational tactic on the part of individual investors? Don't the best and the brightest of Ivy League–trained MBAs provide more expertise than the average guy? The answer is: not really.

When flying back from visiting customers in Florida in February 1993 I saw *USA Today*'s Money Manager Survey. *USA Today* surveyed 120 leading money manager's for their advice. Highly paid money managers should have a handle on where winners are to be found.

Their record was not so great. In the first survey, which was conducted in July 1992, the return from their stock picks would have resulted in a gain of about 1%. If an investor had just bought the S&P 500, the gain would have been 5%. Further results are even more disconcerting. Buying the top ten recommendations in the *USA Today* survey would have resulted in a loss of 15%. Buying the bottom recommendations would have brought a gain of 10%.

The next results should be interesting. The five favorites in the February 1993 survey were Philip Morris, Bristol-Myers Squibb, BankAmerica, Microsoft, and Federal National Mortgage. The only stocks selling under 20 in the Survey—Glaxo Holdings and Westinghouse—were ranked at the bottom.

What does this mean? Wall Street experts are polled, but instead of following the herd, investors do the opposite, buy their dogs and sell the experts' favorites? The inability of Wall Street experts to pick the winners in the *USA Today* poll is not the first embarrassment, nor will it be the last.

The Loser's Game

Some investors could dismiss the *USA Today* study as "unprofessional." One of the best discussions on the poor stock-picking prowess on Wall Street is in Charles D. Ellis's classic, *Investment Policy—How to Win the Loser's Game*.

In Chapter 1, Ellis documents the fact that Wall Street professionals consistently fail to perform as well as the market averages. Whether affiliated with mutual funds or independent investment advisors, professional investment advisers are not beating the market. The market is beating them.

Because most investors buy mutual funds for their professional management, the Ellis book should be given more than a cursory glance by the hundreds of thousands of investors pouring billions into mutual funds. There are nearly twice as many mutual funds as there are stocks listed on the NYSE, and Ellis implies that throwing a dart will provide better performance.

In addition, thousands of investors pay high commissions and fees in the current Wall Street fad, "wrap accounts." The brokerage house is paid to select the best investment managers for individual accounts. These investors should examine the bottom line to see if they are being sold a bill of goods.

The Ellis book concludes that most investors pay big bucks in what is basically a loser's game. It's not a loser's game for the broker or the investment manager, but for the investor. Every investor should read *Investment Policy*.

Beyond the Loser's Game

Why is professional money management a loser's game? Why can individual investors take the advantage? As suggested by Ellis, the reason is that the institutions have become the market. Because each participant is very good at what he or she does, no one investment manager can maintain an advantage for very long. Thus, trying to beat an increasingly efficient market is a loser's game.

And therein lies the ultimate advantage to the individual investor. Individual investors can use this reality of the investment process as it is practiced on Wall Street by looking beyond those stocks considered the realm of the professional money manager, by looking for opportunities outside the loop, beyond the herd. Opportunities that can be turned into profits. Many of these are in low-priced and depressed stocks.

How many stocks might be considered outside the loop? One direct measure might be represented by the number of issues which are followed by those "oracles" employed by the professional money managers, the analysts.

Zacks Investment Research of Chicago tracks analysts earnings estimates from 180 brokerage firms. The numbers are revealing. While the typical NYSE-listed stock is followed on average by 4.5 analysts, the majority of analysts follow a minority of stocks. For instance, just about 50% of all earnings estimates are for just 20% of the stocks. Just about 3/4 of all estimates are for 10% of the stocks.

Conversely, only a minority of analysts follow the majority of stocks. Nearly 50% of all stocks are only followed by fewer than 15% of the analysts. Over a quarter of all stocks are followed by less than 3% of the analysts.

If market efficiency is in any way related to the number of analysts following a stock, there is a large number of stocks listed on the New York Stock Exchange which may be considered "inefficiently" priced. For the individual investor willing to do some work in sorting out the "inefficiently" priced stocks and take some risk, the payoff can be substantial.

The Zacks data tracks well with other statistics that suggest that the majority of stocks are not covered very well compared to a select few. Following my hunch, Zacks further broke down the data between stocks selling over 20 and stocks selling under 20. The results are interesting (see Figure 1-1).

There were 585 stocks priced under 20. There were 3,289 earnings estimates for those issues. There were 963 stocks priced over 20. There were 11,722 earnings estimates. Stocks selling over 20 received over three times the coverage than stocks selling under 20.

Clearly, most stocks remain outside Wall Street's loop, with a majority of them apparently low-priced and depressed issues. Given Wall Street's relative mediocre stock picking ability, might the results suggest that some "silk purses" lie among what Wall Street considers a pile of "sows' ears?"

There are a number of reasons, of course, that most stocks are outside the "loop." By far the largest grouping that tends to be outside the loop is stocks that are out of favor. This follows Loeb's idea that the perceived prospects for the stock are thought to be so weak that it sells at low prices and is generally given poor ratings. While many speculative issues fall in this category, a fair number of "fallen" blue chips are in this classification as well.

Wall Street generally does not like issues whose earnings prospects are not bright. Wall Street tends to be driven by short-term earnings momentum, toward stocks that are reporting higher earnings, away from stocks that report one or two bad quarters.

In terms of analysts following stocks, a built-in bias works against the losers. Investors are programmed to buy "stories", and thus analysts paid by the brokerage houses are directed to concentrate on the issues doing well. The policy is a little self-serving, but it is the nature of Wall Street.

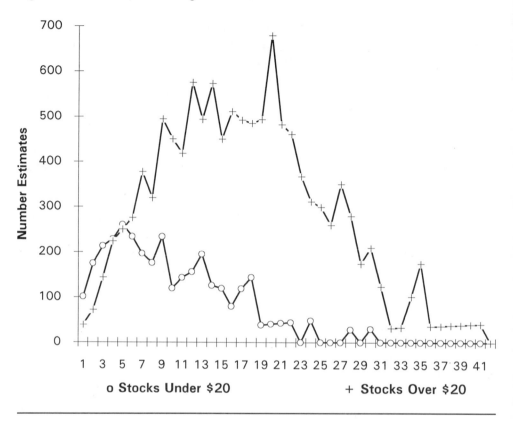

Figure 1 • 1   Zacks's Earnings Estimates

o Stocks Under $20   + Stocks Over $20

Source: Zacks Investment Research, Chicago, IL 8/6/93

This tendency to follow "stories" is related to the window-dressing efforts; mutual fund managers will dump the badly performing stocks so that their investors do not see them in the portfolio. Investment managers believe that you are known by the company you keep, and stocks that have taken a spill are brushed under the carpet.

The tendency of Wall Street to follow the "stories" and to dump the losers results in an overvaluation of stocks showing excellent growth or other bright prospects. It also results in an undervaluation of issues because of unsatisfactory developments of a temporary nature. This is what Benjamin Graham called the "fundamental law of the stock market" and is what gives the individual investor the advantage.

The Intelligent Investor

Benjamin Graham is best known for teaming up with David L. Dodd, Sidney Cottle, and Charles Tatham to produce the bible of security analysis. *Security Analysis* is must reading for aspiring Chartered Financial Analysts. *Security Analysis*, however, is a bit heavy for the average individual investor. Graham's *The Intelligent Investor*, first published in 1949, was written with the lay investor in mind.

Graham discusses a wealth of principles regarding a general approach to investing and security selection. Despite the many changes in the financial markets, these principles are very much applicable today.

In the chapter "Portfolio Policy for the Enterprising Investor: the Positive Side," Graham discusses some concepts that provide the basis for buying low-priced and depressed stocks.

In Graham's day, like today, stock market investors tended to buy growth stocks. The growth stock theory is enticing. By buying stock in companies that will do better than average for a period of years, an investor should be able to not only achieve substantial returns, but beat the market. Thus, the intelligent investor should concentrate on growth stocks.

The problem with this logic, in Graham's opinion, is twofold:

1. Stocks with good records and good prospects sell at correspondingly high prices.
2. Judgment regarding future growth prospects may prove wrong.

Graham concludes from studying actual investment returns that "no outstanding rewards came from diversified investment in growth companies as compared with that in common stocks generally."

Graham then coins his fundamental law of the stock market: If the market tends to overvalue glamour stocks, it can be expected to undervalue companies that are out of favor.

Graham's advice, similar to Loeb's a decade earlier, is to buy stocks whose prices have been drawn to "unduly" low levels. This can be partly due to either currently disappointing results, or protracted neglect, misconception, or unpopularity, or both. To Graham the market is "fond of making mountains out of molehills and exaggerating ordinary vicissitudes into major setbacks. Even a mere lack of interest or enthusiasm may impel a price decline to absurdly low levels."

In other words, the cornerstone of Graham's advice for individual investors looking "to obtain better than average investment results over the long pull" is to buy the out-of-favor issues.

For the individual stock picker, Graham's *The Intelligent Investor* is still among the best books ever written.

Winners versus Losers

A recent landmark study suggests that Graham's thesis, buying the out-of-favor issues, is still the way to beat Wall Street.

In "Does the Stock Market Overreact?", first published in *The Journal of Finance* in July 1985, and updated in 1987, Werner F.M. De Bondt and Richard Thaler explored the theory of whether investors overreacted in the market. They tested two hypotheses:

1. Extreme movements in stock prices will be followed by price movements in the opposite direction; and
2. The more extreme the initial price movement, the greater will be the subsequent adjustment.

After a weighty discussion of test methods befitting an academic journal, the conclusions got right to the point. De Bondt and Thaler found in studying monthly returns for NYSE-listed issues from 1926 through 1982 that a portfolio of prior losers outperformed prior winners by about 25%. The loser portfolio outperformed the market by 19.6%, and the winner portfolio underperformed the market by about 5%. The greater the prior loss, the greater the subsequent gain. Finally, most of the superior return occurred at the turn of the year. The latter result will be discussed in Chapter 4, "The January Effect." Buying the losers does provide better gains than buying the winners (see Figure 1-2). The authors further found that the portfolio of losers had a lower beta than the portfolio of winners. While beta, a measure of volatility, has lost some respect as a measure of risk, it is very interesting that the loser portfolios were less volatile than the winner portfolios. Riding with stocks that were "down and out" could be expected to be bumpier than investing in winners.

The study also examined the time element. As discussed earlier, Wall Street tends to be fixed on short-term results. Partly as a result of statistical consider-ations, but also in line with Benjamin Graham's contentions that the time required for an undervalued issue to correct itself is between 1 1/2 and 2 1/2 years, the authors tested the returns of the following 36 months. The results suggested that not only did the losers outperform the winners, but also the differential was most significant during the second and third years.

Figure 1 • 2   Winner Portfolios versus Loser Portfolios

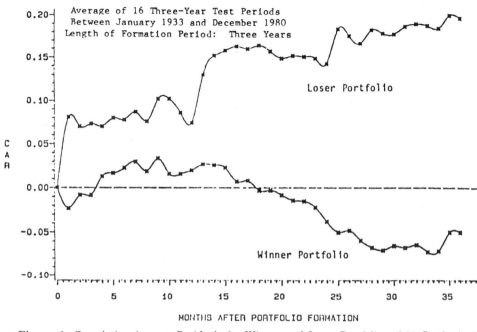

Figure 1. Cumulative Average Residuals for Winner and Loser Portfolios of 35 Stocks (1–36 months into the test period)

Source: The Journal of Finance, Vol XL, No. 3, July 1985. Used with permission.

To reap the benefit of buying underperforming stocks, some understanding of the process by which a stock moves from loser status to winner status is important. Another requirement is patience.

Ellis devoted Chapter 5 of his *Investment Policy to* time. He began with some Greek mythology: "Time is Archimedes's lever in investing." Archimedes said "Give me a lever long enough and I can move the earth." In investing, Ellis believes that lever is time.

The time element is crucial in investing. Individual investors, without any investment committee looking over their shoulders quarter by quarter, are in the enviable position of letting their positions work out. Not only can they invest in issues that are disdained by Wall Street, but also they have the time to wait for them to work out. Both of these tactics are strongly endorsed by De Bondt and Thaler as well. Low-priced and depressed stocks are indeed the province of the individual investor.

The Anatomy of a Stock Market Winner

A study done a few years ago by Marc Reinganum provided some interesting insights for finding winners. Reinganum reviewed the 222 firms whose stocks at least doubled in price during one year in the period from 1970 to 1983. His study, "The Anatomy of a Stock Market Winner," was published in the March-April 1988, issue of the *Financial Analysts Journal*. Reinganum set out to examine a range of variables. These included "smart money," such as insider activity; valuation measures, such as book value and P/E ratios; and "technicals," such as relative strength.

The momentum variables showed up well. Winners were characterized by accelerating quarterly earnings, and the stock showed a high and increasing relative strength prior to their advance. For those investors familiar with William O'Neil's stock rating system, these results are not surprising.

The median relative strength rank during the buy quarter was 93, with 212 of the 222 winners having a relative strength measure in excess of 70. Between the buy quarter and the preceding quarter, the median relative strength rank jumped from 81 to 93.

Also of technical merit was that over 80% of the firms were selling within 15% of their previous two-year high. The stocks, already showing a high and increasing in relative strength, were about to "break out," that is, move to new highs. In other words, the stocks were trending higher.

However, one of the most interesting factors was that the winners generally started their advances when the price of the stock was selling under book value. Among the 222 winners, 164 were selling for less than book value in the buy quarter. The median price/book value was 0.60. In the two quarters prior to the buy, 183 and 184 of the 222 winners were selling for less than book value. Of all the variables, a stock selling under book value was most important.

During the test period, 1970–1983, the Dow traded under book value during 1973, and then in each year from 1977 through 1982. At year-end 1983, however, at a time when the Dow was selling at a price/book value of more than 3.0, such winners based on book value could be expected to be harder to come by (see Figure 1-3).

Indeed, as summarized in a *Wall Street Journal* "Heard On The Street" of September 10, 1993, entitled "Book Value Is More Rarely Required Reading Now," proponents of book value are almost an endangered species.

Present-day winners, though, still arise from stocks generally selling under book value. The big winners, such as the Goodyears, the Union Carbides, the Chryslers, the Citicorps, all sold under book value when they began their advances.

Figure 1 • 3   Dow Jones Industrial Average/Book Value—1946 – 1992

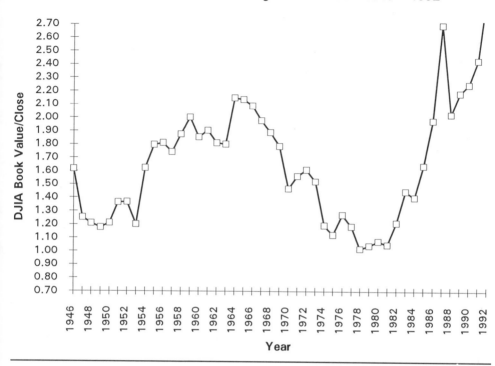

Wendy's, which will be used later to highlight the rules of technical analysis, started its advance when the stock was selling under book value.

While the trend in current financial analysis is to lessen the importance of book value, investors looking for winners are well served to keep book value at the top of their checklists. As "The Anatomy of a Stock Market Winner" implied, buy when the stock starts to go up.

The study also examined whether capitalization and share price had an effect on winners. Reinganum concluded that the "selected companies are clearly not in general low-priced stocks." However, capitalization was further broken down by number of shares and price. The mean price of the 222 winners when purchased was 26.25. One-quarter were selling for less than 18.25. Only 25% were selling higher than 34.82. The average selling price of NYSE issues during the same time period was 34.15. The better performance came from the lower-priced shares.

As noted earlier among the 25 NYSE Most Actively Traded Issues in 1992, just three low-priced stocks provided the biggest return. The "Anatomy" study did not evaluate whether the lower-priced stocks disproportionately accounted for any greater advance than the higher-priced stocks.

Further, as indicated by the results of the Reinganum study, the stocks had already advanced considerably before a buy was issued. Because the technicals generally lead the fundamentals at pivotal turning points, I will examine what the realm of technical analysis offers to enable earlier identification of the stock market winners, i.e., at lower prices.

Additional studies have been done on price. The interaction between the January Effect and price is so important that a whole section in Chapter 4 has been devoted to this topic.

What is Low-Priced and Depressed?

At some juncture an investor looking to buy low-priced and depressed stocks will require guidelines as to what is meant by low priced or what is depressed regarding price. Unfortunately, no easy measure is available. What is low priced and depressed is largely a matter of degree.

One of the most famous money managers of our day was able to set a rigid rule as to what he considered low priced. He had great success. In his book, *The Money Managers*, John Train begins his chapter on John Templeton, "To Everything There is a Season," with a story.

One day in 1939 Templeton phoned his broker with the order "I want you to buy me a hundred dollars' worth of every single stock on both major exchanges that is selling for no more than one dollar a share." At the end of the buying spree, Templeton had bought a "junkpile" of 104 companies in roughly $100 lots.

Many were obviously not suitable for aunts and orphans. Thirty-four of the companies were in bankruptcy. But, after holding the issues for about four years, Templeton saw his initial pot triple to $40,000, roughly four times his cost.

Templeton has come a long way since his 1939 buy order. He has refined his approach to stock selection and expanded it to a worldwide search. However, Templeton's method of searching for bargains, buying what is being "thrown away," looking for companies selling "for the smallest fraction of their true worth," first surfaced in those 1939 transactions among the lowest-priced listed issues.

Investors should not forget the importance of the holding period. Templeton waited for four years for the low-priced issues to advance before cashing out. Institutional investing tends to be very short-sighted. Time is the individual investor's best advantage.

The Risks

Spectacular gains can come from low-priced stocks. Some of the largest percentage losses come from low-priced stocks as well. Point gains or losses on low-priced stocks are magnified in either direction. While investors have to be careful about being too risk-adverse, as the gains from low priced and depressed stocks in large part are due to the fact that the perceived risk has been over-compensated for in the decline of the stock, some steps can be taken to control certain types of risk.

One way to lower our risk and improve the opportunities for finding depressed stocks that have big rebound potential is by confining the search to NYSE-listed issues.

The numbers alone suggest that opportunities will exist from time to time among NYSE-listed issues. The NYSE represents approximately 87% of the total capitalization of the U.S. equities markets. More than 2,600 issues are listed there.

Dealing with a listing on the NYSE lowers the potential financial risk to a degree. This book is not for the investor looking for "penny" stocks.

NYSE listing requirements include meeting listing standards as outlined in Table 1-1. Stocks listed on the NYSE also have to demonstrate staying power.

By confining the search among stocks listed on the NYSE some types of risks are lowered, and the investor can concentrate on low-priced and depressed stocks with the most potential.

Table 1 • 1   Minimum Quantitative Standards for Listing on the NYSE

Round-Lot Holders		*or*	**Total Shareholders**	2,200
(Number of holders of a			*and*	
unit of trading—generally			**Average Monthly Trading Volume**	100,000
100 shares)	2,000		(for most recent 6 months)	
Public Shares	1,100,000			
Market Value of Public Shares	$18,000,000			
Net Tangible Assets	$18,000,000			
Pre-tax Income		*or*	**Pre-tax Income**	
Most recent year	$2,500,000		Aggregate for last 3 years	$6,500,000
Two preceding years	$2,000,000		*together with*	
			Minimum in most recent year	$4,500,000
			(All 3 years must be profitable)	

For instance, before being listed, firms have to have a decent track record. They are seasoned to some extent, and investors don't have to worry as much about marginal operations, firms with illegitimate business interests, or promoter's stocks.

The NYSE is also an orderly, well-regulated market. The common perception that institutional dominance has made stock trading more volatile is incorrect. Except for the 1987 crash, trading is no more volatile today than it has ever been.

Because the idea behind technical analysis is to use the action of the market itself to make the analysis, a high degree of confidence in the "market" for each individual stock is essential. The risk of manipulation must be as minimal as possible.

Although other markets have made strides in liquidity, and the NYSE's own specialist system has a few faults, the relatively orderly markets on the NYSE are conducive to technical analysis.

The Rewards

Finding Winners examines low-priced and depressed issues in search of those with the potential to double and triple in price and earnings. The potential for a significant turnaround is in leverage, both earnings and price. Because the NYSE-listed issues include virtually all of the Fortune 500 companies, as well as many small- and middle-market corporations, they tend to have the attributes necessary for big gains. Those attributes are depressed prices and depressed earnings, with an important plus—the potential to return to a significant earnings basis, with an accompanying major advance in price.

Recent advances prominent among the large cap issues include Chrysler, up over 500%; Citicorp, up over 300%; and Goodyear, up over 600%. These percentage increases took place when the firms' stocks soared after depressed earnings rebounded sharply and then advanced.

Due to sheer size alone, a company like Chrysler, with several ten billions in sales, can post a huge advance in earnings and stock price, when results turn positive. The leverage potential from fallen blue chips can be enormous. The potential is all in the numbers.

Previous year's winners in the middle- and small-market capitalization corporations posted gains like BancFlorida Financial, up 357% as the S&Ls returned to profitability; Western Digital, up 228% as profits rebounded; and Salant, up 204% coming out of bankruptcy.

While these firms may not be household names, a couple of years ago Dave Thomas could not give away Wendy's stock at $4 a share. Investors took notice of Wendy's because the stock tripled from those lows—4 to 17 3/8, as you'll see in Chapter 2.

Availability of NYSE Low-Priced Stocks

Thoughtful investors may be asking, "OK, some outstanding capital gains have come from some NYSE issues, but I've always been told that the best market for low-priced stocks is over-the-counter." First, *Finding Winners* is not interested in the coveted small-caps. The small-firm stocks, often referred to as trading over-the-counter or on the NASDAQ, tend to be overvalued. Low-priced and depressed stocks may have small capitalization as a result of their low price. These stocks offer big rebound rewards. Second, more low-priced stock opportunities are on the NYSE than an investor could ever take full advantage of.

Consider NYSE-listed common stocks. Eliminate the closed-end mutual funds, the preferreds, and the warrants. At the beginning of 1993 there were about 1,780 such common stock listings. Of those, 44%, 782 issues, were under $20 a share. Note that 164 stocks were less than 5; 216 stocks were between 5 and 9 7/8; 206 stocks were between 10 and 14 7/8; and 196 stocks were between 15 and 19 7/8 (see Table 1-2).

NYSE statistics give a false impression. The 1992 average price per share was $35. The NYSE is associated with giants such as Exxon, General Motors, Philip Morris, IBM, and AT&T. The big block trades of 10,000 or more now account for approximately 50% of all trading volume. These statistics do not give you the impression that the NYSE is a market of low-priced stocks.

But consider this, even with the Dow beginning 1993 over 3300, high by all the standards, the prices of nearly half of all listed common stocks was under $20 a share. And those stocks are the domain of the individual investor.

Table 1 • 2   Universe of Low-Priced Stocks: NYSE Year Beginning 1993

		% of total
Total Number of NYSE Common Stocks	1780	—
Stocks under $20	782	43.9
Stocks under $5	164	9.2
Stocks between $5 and $9.875	216	12.1
Stocks between $10 and $14.875	206	11.6
Stocks between $15 and $19.875	196	11.0

Being listed on the NYSE does not guarantee any capital gains, by any measure, but it does lessen some types of risks, and, most importantly, very clearly affords the type of capital gains turnaround potential present in depressed issues.

Classification of Low-Priced Stocks

Another level of risk is determined by the different types of low-priced stocks, which can be ranked in terms of degree of decline and subsequent potential for advance. The three classes of low-priced stocks include:

1. Bruised Blue Chips
2. Depressed Blue Chips
3. Secondaries

When buying low-priced and depressed stocks, a preference should be given to what Graham called "the relatively unpopular large company." First, look for companies that currently may be out of favor, but possess the "resources in capital and brain power to carry them through adversity and back to a satisfactory earnings basis." And second, search out companies wherein "the market is likely to respond with reasonable speed to any improvement shown." Thus, the first line of stocks to be bought are fallen blue chips.

The Blue Chips

What is a blue chip? Why is a blue chip important when buying low-priced and depressed stocks?

Academics probably could hold a long discussion about the definition of a blue chip. One definition that aptly captures its essence is in *Webster's New World Dictionary*—as a "high-priced stock with good earnings and a stable price."

The blue-chip club is exclusive. Firms with low-priced and depressed stocks have to resign or at least take a leave of absence.

Blue chips tend to be well-established, widely known, and widely held, with a "presence" of history or tradition. A blue-chip is usually the primary player in its industry. It has name recognition.

Buying the blue chips is important because blue chips are the preference in the stock market. Name recognition is an important characteristic because the institutions control so much of the trading.

In spite of all the literature concerning the better performance of small cap stocks, most of the money continues to be pumped into blue chips. Most investors responsible for other peoples money prefer investment-grade blue chips to the small cap stocks because of the latter's greater volatility. The smart investors' first line of buys is the blue chips.

Bruised versus Depressed Blue Chips

Among blue chips a distinction between bruised blue chips and depressed blue chips can be made. Generally, a bruised blue chip is down substantially, either due to lower earnings, or in line with an overall market correction; however, it is not "depressed."

How far a stock must drop to become depressed is one of degree, but a blue chip can decline for all sorts of reasons, say over a period of a year or so, and become lower priced, without becoming depressed. Investment managers have just taken profits, or jumped on board an issue that looks better on the basis of momentum. A bruised blue chip will be down, but not out.

An issue that is truly depressed, however, has reached a point where the investment managers who have wanted to sell the stock have already sold. Few investment holdings are left. Buying interest is very low. A truly depressed stock will just languish.

Buying opportunities on bruised blue chips are more frequent and less risky than those of depressed blue chips. Bruised blue chips are, therefore, the first buying opportunity among low-priced stocks. I like to look at bruised blue chips as they enter the "red zone."

The Red Zone

In football the red zone is inside the 20-yard line. After a team crosses its opponent's 20-yard line, the team is expected to score. The 20 level is the price at which stocks become low priced. It is also the point under which investors have the potential to score.

The 20 level is of particular interest in bruised blue chips, the first-line, investment-grade issues, the issues considered A or A+, that are declining due to either a shrinking P/E ratio in line with the overall market, or a shrinkage of earnings. Normally, both factors are at work. A name issue, selling under 20, and down 40%, 50%, 60% or more, deserves a good look.

Every year selected bruised blue chip stocks move under 20. Sometimes a lot of them do. The last time investors were able to scoop up a broad selection of investment-quality issues under 20 a share was during the correction of 1990.

The stock market correction of 1990 was interesting because the major market indexes, the Dow Jones Industrial Average and the S&P 500, moved higher through most of 1990. The broader market, as measured by the advance-decline line, however, had peaked in the third quarter of 1989. The indexes would eventually come under a sharp sell-off during the third quarter, with the Dow falling from a high of 2999.75 on July 16 and July 17, skidding to an October 11 low of 2365.10, for a loss of 634.65 points or 21.1%.

Some of the stocks that fell to under 20 in 1990 included:

- American Express—fell to 17 1/2, both sales and earnings down, down 56% from 1989 high of 39.
- Dow Jones—fell to 18 1/8 on flat sales, lower earnings, in line with weak newspaper group, down 57% from a 1989 high of 42.
- General Dynamics—fell to 19 on lower sales, lower earnings, down 68% from a 1989 high of 60.
- Mellon Bank--fell to 17 5/8 in line with weak banking issues, down 55% from a 1989 high of 38.
- Merrill Lynch—fell to 16 1/8, in line with weak brokerage issues, down 55% from a 1989 high of 36.

These selected issues show that top-line names can stumble just like any stocks. All the stocks were under 20. All five stocks were down 50% or more. All had negative alphas, a widely used measure of a stock's performance relative to the S&P 500 over the previous five years.

- American Express   −1.06
- Dow Jones   −1.31
- General Dynamics   −2.04
- Mellon Bank   −1.76
- Merrill Lynch   −1.72

It is always worth taking a closer look as bruised blue chips enter the red zone.

During 1993 some name stocks dropped to 20 under. The drug stocks produced several: Alza, Baxter, Galaxo, Marion Merrell Dow, and Syntex. Borden, Jostens, K-Mart, and Safety-Kleen are other bruised blue chips that entered the red zone. In addition to falling under 20, these issues were all down over 50%. A top-rated DJIA stock, Woolworth, looked like it was getting ready to slip below 20. These stocks were not buys without some confirmation from technical analysis; however, they were worth following.

Depressed Blue Chips

Depressed blue chips are of widest interest to investors because they have the ingredients for the most substantial rebound. Some of the biggest names on the "best winners" listings—the Chryslers, Citicorps, Goodyears—were all depressed blue chips. They had the leverage potential to post strong rebounds. Depressed issues have the potential for 100%, 200%, 300% gains, or more.

Depressed stocks are also more risky. Stocks often become depressed not only because sales and earnings have declined but because the very existence of the firm may be in question. Instead of a 100% gain, a 100% loss can occur. The stock can end up in bankruptcy and delisted. Depressed stocks are high risk.

Some attributes of blue chips can give depressed blue chips a 9-lives-type quality. One phrase from my business school days is "critical mass," which is generally the resources it takes to be competitive in any given industry. A fallen blue chip may have lost its "club" status but still have the critical mass, in terms of assets, or distribution network, or manufacturing capability, or innovative capability, or market share, or financial clout, to return to the club.

Even Chrysler, long the most marginal of the automobile companies, represented at least a market share in an industry where new entry is extremely difficult. Chrysler also demonstrated that even a firm on the brink of financial ruin will be nursed back to financial health by bankers and debtors, because foreclosure is nearly always the least attractive option. The larger the vested interest by debtors in a company, the more accommodating lenders will be.

In today's competitive world, fortunes do change. Companies at the top of the list can easily slip up and fall. Conversely, firms at the bottom are usually taking aggressive steps to correct their competitive positions. They have as much motivation as needed, if not more, to do what it takes to climb back to the top. Depressed blue chips can be down for extended periods, but killing them off is a difficult thing to do. And, when the Penn Centrals of the market do rebound, the rewards can be extraordinary.

Typical Characteristics of Depressed Stocks

What are the guidelines for determining exactly what is depressed? The degree to which our leaders were down, by both extent and duration, is shown below.

	High	Low	Extent	Duration
Citicorp	35 1/2	8 1/2	76%	27 months
Chrysler	48	9 1/8	80%	36 months
Goodyear	76 1/8	12 7/8	83%	38 months

On average the three large cap issues that showed the best gains were down at least 75%, and were down nearly three years before they rebounded.

Depressed stocks typically sell for less than book value. Book value for truly depressed stocks will generally be declining, and at the bottom, the stock may be selling above book value.

Citicorp, at the lows, was 65% less than its book value a year earlier of 24.34. Chrysler at its lows was 71% less than its year-earlier book value of 32.42. Goodyear, at the lows was 65% less than its year-earlier book of 37.09.

While Citicorp, Chrysler, and Goodyear are just three examples, they do present the degree to which stocks are depressed, in terms of time, points, and book value.

The Dow Jones Transportation Average has performed exceedingly well, up from an October 17, 1990 low of 821.93, soaring into record high ground of nearly 1700 by early 1993. What accounted for the rise was not the airlines, as most investors would think, or trucking issues, or the railroads. The advance in the Transportation Average was largely keyed by rebounds in American President Companies, a container transportation firm up 500%, and XTRA, a firm in transportation equipment leasing, up more than 700%.

	High	Low	Extent	Duration
American President Cos.	51	10 3/8	79%	37 months
XTRA	44 1/4	13	70%	24 months

As the table above shows, both issues had declined more than 70% for at least two years.

Current Scenario

For the most part the stock market recently has not afforded a background for a wide number of depressed issues on a broad scale. For issues to be depressed, earnings have to be down sharply, and the outlook for earnings has been favorable.

The buying opportunities in depressed blue chips were certainly present in 1974, 1977, 1981, 1984, and 1990. Those were years when the earnings for the Dow Jones Industrial Average were declining.

At midyear 1993, only a handful of Dow stocks showed declines of much significance; the average one-year decline was 12%. The average decline during the past several years moves into the mid-30s percentage range. Some Dow stocks are depressed—Westinghouse is down over 60%—but a broad market of depressed stocks has not existed. Even in such a market, however, the investor can find opportunities among depressed issues.

Periodically the *Wall Street Journal*, among other sources, publishes group statistics. While at the midyear 1993, the DJ Equity Market Index was up 3.52% for the prior six months, some of the groups were showing declines of 10% or more (see Table 1-3).

Just because a stock group is showing a decline does not mean there are depressed issues in the group. However, the groups performing worse than the market over any extended period of time generally do afford a host of issues which are down sharply, if not depressed.

For example, while industry leader WMX (formerly Waste Management) was not depressed at 25, this former darling of the institutional money managers was down 50% from year earlier highs and looked as it was moving still lower. When the leaders like Waste Management hit the skids, other industry-related issues will be lower. Browning-Ferris, down over 55%; Safety-Kleen, down over 65%; Rollins Environmental, down from 15 to 5; Chemical Waste Management, down from 26 to 7; Western Waste Industries, 23 to 10; International Technology, 11 to 4; and MidAmerica Waste, 27 to 8. There are going to be some great potential buys in the pollutional control group for investors looking for low-priced and depressed stocks.

Table 1 • 3   Groups in Decline on the DJ Equity Market Index

Groups		Selected Stocks	
Advanced Med Devices	−26.23%	Acuson	−72%
Advertising	−11.46	Saatchi & Saatchi	−97
Biotechnology	−32.12	Synergen	−89
Clothing/Fabrics	−15.97	Hartmax	−91
Containers & Packaging	−11.44	Stone Container	−81
Footwear	−25.75	U.S. Shoe	−73
Food	−11.36	Chiquita Brands	−80
Industrial Technology	−10.20	General Physics	−78
Medical Supplies	−12.42	U.S. Surgical	−81
Pharmaceuticals	−12.20	Syntex	−68
Pollution Control	−14.41	Laidlaw	−75
Retailers/Apparel	−11.55	House of Fabrics	−78
Tobacco	−32.86	RJR Nabisco	−61
Trucking	−15.79	Consolidated Freightways	−68

Secondaries

Bruised and depressed blue chips represent some well-known household names. The better-performing issues that are not so well known I call "secondaries."

The secondaries are not blue-sky speculations. They are listed on the NYSE. They differ from seasoned blue chips by having smaller levels of sales, profits, assets, and capitalizations. In all likelihood, they are far from being considered among the leaders in their particular industry. No convenient cut-off statistic can be used to differentiate the secondaries. They come in all shapes and sizes.

The only definitive statement to be made regarding the secondaries is that in an era when institutional investors favor the "brand names," such as the Mercks, the Coca-Colas, the Wal-Marts, which tend to dominate the top of *Fortune's* annual Most Admired Survey, the secondary issues tend to offer, individually, and as a group, the most frequent instances of undervaluation and thus the potential for capital gains.

Individually, for example, the NYSE's best performers for the first half of 1993, showing gains ranging from 114% to 412%—Allied Products, National Standard, Western Company of North America, Callaway Golf, Weirton Steel, General Datacomm, Oak Industries, Wheeling Pittsburgh, Tejas Gas, and Lifetime Corp.—were not exactly household names. These issues were secondaries.

As a group, the stocks that tend to comprise the Standard & Poor Low-Priced Stock Index are secondaries. Over the past 20 years, these issues have outperformed the Standard & Poor's 500 by nearly 2-to-1. There is money to be made in secondaries (see Figure 1-4).

The gains in these issues are likely to be less sustained than blue-chip gains. Depressed blue-chips have the capacity for major advances. The secondaries, on the other hand, are likely to be more cyclical and seasonal.

Depressed blue chips should be held until they move into investment-grade status. The same cannot be said for the secondaries. With secondaries, the technical analysis rules regarding when to sell will be more appropriate, because gains in secondaries can be particularly fleeting.

With those qualifications in mind, however, it always pays to check out the daily listing of low-priced stocks showing some volume and price appreciation, especially late in the year. Catching a ride on an uptrending secondary is the best way to double your money.

Figure 1 • 4   S&P Low-Priced Stock Index versus S&P 500

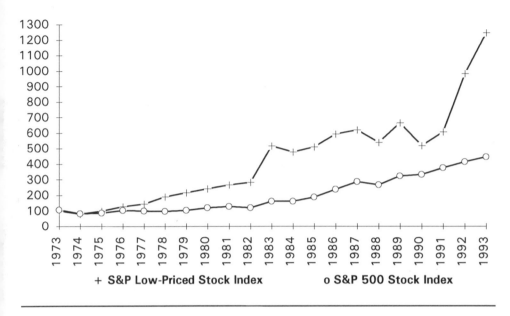

+ **S&P Low-Priced Stock Index**   o **S&P 500 Stock Index**

Distress and Opportunity

". . . one person's distress is another's opportunity," says Peter Lynch in *Beating the Street*. Nine out of ten investors have heard of Peter Lynch. And nine out of ten investors think of Magellan as a growth fund. But Lynch scored big not by buying Wall Street's favorites, but by buying stock dirt cheap.

Lynch's quote comes out of the chapter, "Nukes In Distress." In it he reviewed the opportunities in the fallen electric utilities, such as General Public Utilities, Public Service of New Hampshire, Long Island Lighting, Gulf States Utilities, and Middle South Utilities.

Each of these utilities had had problems with nuclear plants, most often with construction financing. In every example the wholesale selling panic of shareholders afforded outstanding capital gains opportunities for investors willing to buy.

Several times in his book, Lynch states that most considered his Magellan fund to be a growth mutual fund. In many periods of his stewardship, the stocks found in Magellan were anything but growth stocks.

While Lynch describes his stock-picking method as eclectic, with no pat formula, he states that "bargains are the Holy Grail of the true stockpicker."

Readers will run across "bargain" quite a bit, as well as other descriptive words, such as "turnaround," "depressed," "comeback," "beaten down," "off beat," "disparaged," "on the rebound," "secondaries," "cyclicals," the "bargain bin," and investing in stocks "still on the downswing" or investing where others "fear to tread." Out-of-favor stocks spelled opportunity to Lynch.

The premise of the Lynch book is that individual investors who do their homework can beat the professional money managers. Basic homework to Lynch is being able to correctly recognize whether a company's fundamentals are improving, and where a correct tally of the underlying finances is essential.

Beating The Street shows how Lynch evaluated stocks. The basic theme is that the stocks have to be undervalued, and that stocks cannot be undervalued if the majority of Wall Street analysts are already warmed up to their prospects. And if an individual investor is to beat the pros, a willingness to invest against the crowd is a must.

Chrysler is a case study in *Finding Winners*. It is referred to frequently in Lynch's book as being one of the most important stocks accounting for the success of Magellan. While a low price per se is not a reason for Lynch to invest in a stock, Chrysler is discussed when it was selling at 2 per share in the spring of 1982. Lynch did not buy Chrysler when it was acceptable to the majority of Wall Street analysts and its financial survival was assured. He bought Chrysler as a turnaround opportunity when it was a very low-priced stock; he scored big.

The same principles are found throughout the book. Investors who only look to invest in the most widely followed and tranquil stocks on Wall Street are bound to do about as poorly as most money managers. Investors willing to invest in "off the street" stocks, which are often turnaround issues, stand a good chance of beating the street.

Conclusion

This Chapter has presented the opportunities afforded by low-priced stocks, suggesting where to look for them, the potential gains, etc. The most important question, when to buy, remains. Gains from low-priced and depressed stocks can be tremendous, if the stocks are caught on the uptrend. That is where technical analysis, the subject of Chapter 2, comes into play.

· 2 ·

Why Technical Analysis?

Many readers will be reluctant to move into a chapter on technical analysis. Most investors tend to steer clear of anything remotely identified with technical analysis, even though it is one of the oldest methods for the analysis of stock prices. Its basic principles are generally attributable to the writings of Charles H. Dow on the general theory of stock trends more than 90 years ago.

Just the name alone, technical analysis, sounds imposing. Many investors think of technical analysis as something akin to the applied sciences. They think that a high score on the math portion of the SATs is a prerequisite to understanding "technical analysis."

Much of the current emphasis in technical analysis presents a fairly complicated challenge even for those with a mathematical bent. The current literature among technical analysis practitioners is not concerned with individual security selection. It deals with more exotic topics, such as oscillators and stochastics, fibonacci numbers, and cardinal squares. Summation indexes do not sound too forbidding, but neural networks sound a bit heavy. These systems all have their time and place in technical analysis, but are not exactly user-friendly to the average stock buyer.

Further adding to investors' uneasiness is the association of technical analysis with trading systems. Technical analysis in recent years has largely evolved as one type of trading system or another. Coupled with the number-crunching abilities of the computer, and spurred on by innovations in the security markets like options and futures, the connotation of technical analysis and trading systems is even stronger.

Much of what is known as technical analysis today is not very practical to the needs and goals of individual investors. Most of them get turned off by modern-day technical analysis.

I am not writing for the "in-and-out" trader. Most investors want to buy a stock low and perhaps sell it in a year or two, if not longer, at double or triple what was paid for it. The majority of individual investors are still trying to pick winners. *Finding Winners* employs technical analysis not as an elaborate trading system, but as a method of improving the chances of buying the right stocks at the right time. The objective of technical analysis as developed in the following pages is simply to lessen the risks of buying and, at the same time, improve the odds of finding winners.

Technical Analysis Defined

Technical analysis is the study of price movement. Technical analysis is an effort to determine whether a stock is being accumulated or distributed, whether a stock, on balance, is being bought or sold, whether a stock is in an uptrend or a downtrend, whether a stock is bullish or bearish, whether the stock is acting well or not acting well, in order to make inferences regarding likely future price patterns.

Technical analysis is a method of measuring the relative supply/demand factors in order to predict the future course of prices. Some systems have become fairly elaborate and a bit pedantic. The underlying process of price movement is not as technical as most investors believe. The reason is because price in the final analysis reflects the psychology of the markets, and psychology is a most inexact science.

Stocks are bought or sold for a myriad of reasons. Fundamental analysis is the prevailing school of thought on and off Wall Street. Investors weigh "bottom-up" factors, such as income statements and balance sheets, or "top-down" factors, such as money supply and GDP outlook, to determine whether to buy or sell a particular stock. The "firm-foundation" theory of stock prices, as Burton G. Malkiel calls fundamental analysis in his highly readable and perceptive book, *A Random Walk Down Wall Street*, is the prevailing method of security analysis today.

In the long run stock prices do reflect fundamental value, but a stock will rarely be priced at intrinsic value. Instead, a stock will be trading either above or below the line of value, as expectations and perceptions, greed and fear, and confidence and anxiety come into play. The psychology of the investor is by far the most important factor in price.

In theory, stocks are supposed to be efficiently priced, based on concepts such as capital asset pricing mechanism. In reality, psychology, more than balance sheets and income statements, is the driving force behind stock prices. The crash of 1987, with stocks falling more than 500 points—22%—on a single day, should settle the relative roles that efficient market pricing and the psychology of prices play.

The 1987 crash further dramatically highlights the fact that technical analysis reflects how investors themselves react to changes in stock prices. The key to technical analysis is understanding that investors do react to stock price changes. What a stock did previous to, and leading up to, the current price will influence how investors will react at any one moment in time.

Fundamental analysis provides investors with an indication of value; technical analysis is simply what investors actually think a stock is worth. Only technical analysis can provide guidelines as the stock bobs and weaves around its line of value, helping investors to act.

At the extremes, such as in the arena of low-priced and depressed stocks, there is very little agreement even as to value. In depressed stocks, the appraisal of the fundamentals themselves often becomes helter-skelter. Fundamental analysis is probably least useful appraising the type of stocks that offer the best potential for gain. Technical analysis alone will provide the few available clues.

With all the vast increases in computer power, no one has ever come close to being able to model all the factors—fundamental, psychological, or otherwise—that enter into the decision to buy or sell. All the investor knows is that a certain number of shares were traded at a specific price and at a specific time. The investor can only speculate about the reasons; however, the end results can be measured.

Price and Volume: Tools of the Trade

Price and volume are the basic tools of technical analysis. Indeed, technical analysis might seem less threatening and more useful if it were called "transactions analysis." It is simply keeping track of the buying and selling decisions in the stock market. A transaction for so many shares is made at a specific price. That is the basic input to technical analysis.

Taken alone, one buy/sell decision does not mean a lot. But, can any conclusions be made about a series of transactions? Can whether a stock is being accumulated or distributed be detected? Can observations be made about whether the buyers or the sellers have more conviction? Can inferences be made about whether the demand for any particular stock is greater than the supply?

Weighing the demand/supply equation is where technical analysis can benefit the program of the everyday investor. While not infallible by any means, technical analysis can provide clues regarding the outlook for stocks.

Chart Basics

If investors were following just a couple of stocks, they could keep price activity in their heads or on some ledger sheets. They could remember that so many shares were traded at this or that price. Many old-line investors were able to astutely judge the underlying demand for a stock just by "reading the tape." Gerald Loeb's classic, *The Battle for Investment Survival*, provides some vivid examples on tape reading.

Charts serve the same purpose. The chart is a graphic presentation of the buy/sell transactions during some specified time period. Charts are a matter of convenience.

Some investors are turned off by the seemingly complexity of charts. They may look like a version of the Rorschach personality test, which is based on interpreting inkblots. Successful chart reading is not that far removed from the Rorschach test. Proper interpretation is in the eyes of the beholder. Technical analysis is about as far removed from a mechanical science as you can get.

The basic data on the chart are the high, low, and close for a stock, plus volume. The time period can be by minute, by hour, by day, by week, by month, by year. Each time period serves a different purpose.

The graphs presented in *Finding Winners* are daily charts; day-to-day trading activity is reported covering a period of time. Daily charts highlight the lesser trends of the market; the investor may be missing the big picture. All trends start with daily action, however, and the investor should buy as close to the start of a trend as possible. As will later be shown, the day-to-day and week-by-week patterns can be extremely helpful in buying low-priced and depressed stocks.

The long-term charts, covering periods of from several up to ten or more years, provide perspective as to the major trends of the market, help the investor understand how trends form within trends, give clues about major support areas, and give a visual overview of when a stock is truly depressed.

Charts in themselves can often appear unfriendly. Many charts have all sorts of additional bits of information. But the basic data used here is the high, low, close, and volume.

Stock Trends

The notion that stocks have trends is not new. Charles Dow, a cofounder of Dow Jones & Company and the first editor of the *Wall Street Journal* and later *Barron's*, devised the first stock market indexes and began to write about the nature of stock trends.

Anyone who has ever owned a stock has been aware that at times stocks have trended higher and at times stocks have trended lower. Investors may have asked themselves why a stock trends this way or that way for some period and then reverses in the other direction.

A trend can take on any shape and form. It will have direction: up, down, or flat. A trend will have duration: short, intermediate, or long. A trend will have a slope: flat or steep, straight or curved. All trends reflect some characteristic of the zigzag or wave, with the zig reflecting a stock moving higher, and the zag, the ensuing decline.

When takeovers and arbitrage were prevalent prior to the 1987 crash, some stocks traveled from one price to another without any zigzag at all. But 99% of the time in an auction market, a stock price trend reflects alternative forces of demand and supply. Buyers may temporarily have the upper hand by bidding the issue higher, but then their buying power begins to subside.

The higher price attracts some sellers, perhaps short sellers as well, and at a point, equilibrium is reached between demand and supply. A renewed burst of buying could send the issue higher, but in the majority of cases, the stock drifts lower as the stock is marked down until some fresh demand is found for the stock.

This goes on until a new set of buyers, or at least renewed convictions on the part of buyers drives the issue higher; buying then ebbs and selling picks up, and then the stock falls "under its own weight" in the ensuing decline.

These zigzag or self-correcting trends are all normal trend development. Some trends are not very useful at all, but most take on the typical zigzag or staircase pattern. Strung together, they reflect a straight trend line.

For example, from January 1991 to January 1992 Home Depot was unfolding in a nearly perfect straight trend line (see Figure 2-1). During the same time period, so was Halliburton but in the opposite direction (see Figure 2-2).

Defining The Trend

Robert Rhea in his *The Dow Theory* listed the basis for trend classification techniques: successive rallies penetrating preceding high points, with ensuing declines terminating above preceding low points, offer a bullish indication. Support is greater than resistance.

Conversely, failure of the rallies to penetrate previous high points, with the ensuing decline carrying below former low points, is bearish. The action of the rallies and declines on the Home Depot and Halliburton charts define the trends.

Knowing that stocks move in trends is one thing. Being able to take advantage of trends is another matter. The objective of the investor is to detect

Figure 2 • 1   Home Depot: Model Zigzag—Bullish Trend

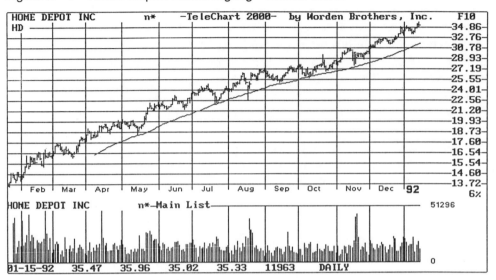

Chart courtesy of TeleChart 2000™ by Worden Brothers, Inc. Used with permission.

Figure 2 • 2   Halliburton: Model Zigzag—Bearish Trend

Chart courtesy of TeleChart 2000™ by Worden Brothers, Inc. Used with permission.

the beginning of a trend early enough, and to detect the end of a trend early enough, to make practical buy and sell decisions.

Throughout this and the other chapters, the various facets of trend will be discussed. Some working knowledge of trends is useful for all investors, but particularly for those investing in low-priced and depressed stocks because technical analysis is about the only analysis investors in those situations can count on.

Dow's Three Movements

Dow classified the trends of the market as:

- The primary or major trend, known as bull and bear markets lasting several years or more;
- The intermediate or secondary trend lasting a period of months; and
- The minor or day-to-day to week-to-week trend.

All three trends operate concurrently, although not always in unison.

As with the overall market, individual stocks move in trends that can be classified as major, intermediate, or minor. An investor must understand the approximate definition of these trends to know where a stock stands within its trend because the three different trends afford three separate buying and selling opportunities and levels of risk.

For example, Wendy's International (Figure 2-3) shows the primary trend as being bullish since the stock bottomed out at 3 7/8 in February 1990.

Wendy's primary trend, in turn, has been made up of a series of intermediate advances/declines.

Each intermediate advance is in turn made up of a series of minor advance/decline sequences. It is not unusual for an intermediate advance to be made up of three minor advances.

Investors are most interested in identifying the turning or reversal points in depressed stocks, such as when the major or primary trend *may be* turning from bearish to bullish. Keying in on the turning points in the major trend is what produces the high-percentage capital gains.

The words *may be* are emphasized to indicate that the major trend may be turning from bearish to bullish. While the major trend is the most important trend, it is the last to be recognized. When the major trend is turning from bullish or from bearish few Wall Street analysts proclaim "the trend is turning," although, after the fact, you hear a plethora of claims to have "called" the turn.

Figure 2 • 3 Wendy's International: Trends Within Trends

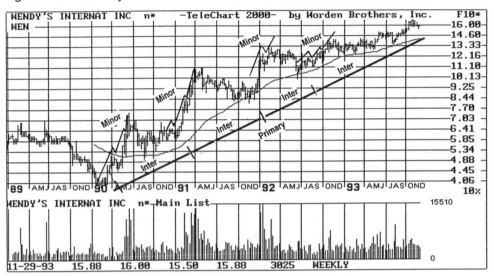

Chart courtesy of TeleChart 2000™ by Worden Brothers, Inc. Used with permission.

What investors can do is piece together bits of information via technical analysis to make an educated guess as to the likely trend. First analyze the minor trend. Then analyze the intermediate trend. If the lesser trends, that is, the minor and the intermediate, are correctly analyzed, investors can be in a stock long before the primary "up" trend is recognized.

Continuing with Wendy's International (see Figure 2-4), the only information at first is a bullish minor trend (A).

After a stock has had two minor zigzags, the intermediate trend can be classified as positive (AA). After a stock has put together back-to-back intermediate advances (AA-BB), the major trend may be classified as bullish.

Buying at the time the major trend is obviously bullish is buying late, often too late. Wall Street will be turning bullish on the stock at that time, and with increased sponsorship, there certainly will be further significant gains.

The best gains are achieved when the trends are just beginning to unfold, when the stock rises up from a depressed, oversold status. The objective is to buy when the minor trend is turning bullish, and certainly no later than when the intermediate trend is turning bullish. Lucky investors will be buying into a bullish primary trend as well.

Figure 2 • 4   Wendy's International: September 1989 – August 1990

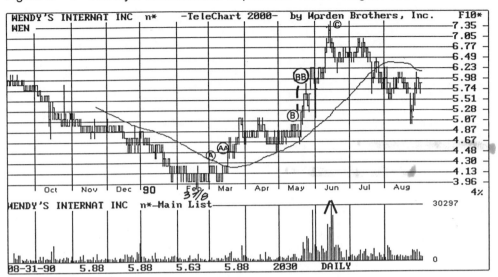

Chart courtesy of TeleChart 2000™ by Worden Brothers, Inc. Used with permission.

Minor Trend: Deceptive

Because any price movement begins with the minor trend, the minor trend is obviously important. It is more often than not the most deceptive as well.

The minor trend tends to receive the most publicity. Investors pick up an issue of the *Wall Street Journal* or *Investor's Business Daily,* and what is discussed?—what happened yesterday—the minor trend, and a guess on what might happen tomorrow—the minor trend.

The result is a tendency of most investors to attribute far too much significance to the minor trend and to get in right at the top. Only in the context of the larger trends does the minor trend take on meaning.

Referring back to Figure 2-4, consider the action of June 14 (C), when Wendy's volume surged with the stock moving above 7. Average daily volume had been running less than 500,000 shares daily, and Wendy's made news by being among the best performers of the day on very high volume.

By the time Wendy's appeared most bullish, and was receiving the more-favorable comments in the media, the stock had already doubled. Not unexpectedly, the high volume signaled the end of the intermediate advance.

By contrast, no mention was made of Wendy's on March 19 (AA), as the issue put together its first minor advance series in more than 6 months. On May 21 (BB), no mention was made as the issue, on its minor advance, signaled that an important intermediate trend was underway in decisively breaking out above 5.

The minor trend can be very, very important, when related to the larger trends, but also very deceptive when taken alone.

The Intermediate Trend

The intermediate trend is the least-talked-about trend. For all practical purposes, however, it is the most important. Investors can only buy once at the start of the major trend, and buying on the minor trend can be very deceptive. Investors have some potentially very rewarding buying opportunities based on the intermediate trend time and time again, as nearly all stocks such as shown in Figure 2-3 go through repetitive intermediate advance/decline sequences.

Sometimes the classification of the trends fits into a neat formula, sometimes it does not. For example, in Figure 2-4, is the rally from February 21 to March 28 a minor rally or an intermediate rally? Is the move from February 21 to June 14 one intermediate trend, or two?

Correct classification of the trend is obviously important, but trends do not always unfold as if they are made from a single cookie-cutter. But the more important consideration is that investors have some expectations as to trend development and to be ready to act for instance when, after an extensive decline, an important rally is underway.

Taking action in anticipation of likely trend development is more important than waiting for classification. Trend classification is not all investors have to rely upon. The most important factors in determining trend patterns will be influenced by the stock's position relative to support and resistance levels.

Support and Resistance

Support and resistance are key concepts throughout this book. Support and resistance are the basic building blocks, the foundation, of technical analysis. Support and resistance tell the investor how a trend develops, help define the trend, tell the investor when the trend changes.

Support and resistance tell the investor how far and how fast a stock might advance or fall. Support and resistance will indicate when to buy, when to sell, or at least when not to buy. After the basics of support and resistance are understood, technical analysis will become very common sense and practical.

Support can generally be equated with demand, resistance with supply. Support can be equated with accumulation, where enough buying develops to start an uptrend in an issue or halt a decline. Resistance can be equated with distribution, where enough supply comes on the market to either stop an advance or to precipitate a decline.

Support and resistance can be considered in two ways. The first way is considering where support and resistance actually materialize, support to either stop a decline in a stock and/or to spark an uptrend, resistance to either stop an advance in a stock and/or to precipitate a decline.

Second, the concept of support and resistance can be carried a step further to where support and resistance can be *expected* to materialize. Once investors can grasp the notion that stocks move between *existing* levels of support or resistance, they will have taken an important step in making technical analysis understandable.

Technical analysis in large part is how investors are reacting to changes in stock price. Support and resistance levels tell the investor where a larger number of investors with a vested interest in a stock are to be found and how they are likely to react.

Have you ever been a "sold-out bull?" You bought a stock at 40, sold at 50, only to see it rise to 60. You felt pretty good at first, but you sold too soon. You were right, but you are now a sold-out bull. Selling too soon is psychologically a worse mistake than buying a stock and seeing it drop. Would you be tempted to buy back in if the stock drifts back to 50? Is 50 not support?

Or, say you bought a stock at 50, only to see it fall to 40. Would you be tempted to cut your losses short as the stock rebounds back to 50? Is 50 not resistance?

Some other groups of investors determine support and resistance. In depressed and low-priced stocks short-sellers are often very active. If a professional investor sold short at 20 and then saw the stock rise to 25, don't you think they might be tempted to "cover" if the stock reacts back to 20?

Or, if the short-sellers sold at 20, saw the stock decline to 15, took profits, and then saw the stock rebound back to 20, might they be tempted to short once again?

Support and resistance levels simply reflect how market participants react to changes in stock price in everyday market activity.

Volume determines which price levels will be important. Support and resistance levels are associated with price, but volume is the key. Which price levels will be significant is determined by concentration of share activity and turnover.

Previous highs and lows, or reversal points, are typically associated with increased levels of trading. Thus, support and resistance levels are identified with prior highs and lows.

Most investors tend to associate support with previous lows and resistance with previous highs. To a degree, previous lows can offer support and previous highs can offer resistance. However, once a stock has moved higher, a more significant support level can be expected to form at a previous high, and once a stock has declined, a more significant resistance level can be expected to form at a previous low. These represent the "edges" of price trading activity.

Support and resistance help define the zigzag nature of trends. Declines tend to stop at support. Advances tend to stop at resistance.

Support and resistance help define trendlines. An up trendline reflects support areas. A down trendline reflects where the rallies stop at resistance.

Support and resistance levels are the most important concepts in technical analysis because they help tell investors when to buy and sell. Investors buy at support and sell at resistance.

Support and resistance have some additional characteristics.

First, support and resistance levels tend to repeat. While time will lessen the significance of support and resistance levels, price levels associated with heavy trading may come into play repeatedly.

For instance, in Figure 2-5 Wendy's bottomed out in February 1990 at 3 7/8. The stock's low following the 1987 crash was 4 1/8. The stock's low at the bottom of the 1981–82 bear market was 3 3/4. (See Table 2-1.) Some interest in Wendy's has repeatedly stepped in to support the stock around 4; 4 is a major support.

Second, support and resistance levels also trade places. Support and resistance levels are just areas of large concentration, or a large vested interest. Whether they act as support or resistance depends on the relative position of the stock prices. A support level, after a stock has declined below it, now becomes a resistance level on any rebound rally. A resistance level, after a stock has moved higher, becomes a support level on any subsequent decline.

When Wendy's advanced smartly from the low of 3 7/8 to 5 1/8 in late March 1990, resistance appeared at 5.

The resistance at 5 reflected the October through December trading range of the previous year. Take a close look at Figure 2.5. During October, 5 initially was support. In November the stock declined, and 5 thus became a resistance. Then, during the March rally, that same level of trading at 5 was resistance once again. Following the March high of 5 1/8 the stock declined to a support level around 4 1/2, which also had some prior history. During mid-December, 4 1/2

Table 2 • 1   Wendy's International High-Low Price: 1981 – 1993

	Price	
Year	High	Low
1982	7.500	**3.750**
1983	10.000	5.875
1984	12.250	7.875
1985	15.250	9.875
1986	17.750	10.000
1987	13.250	**4.125**
1988	8.000	5.125
1989	7.000	4.500
1990	7.500	3.875
1991	11.000	5.875
1992	14.250	9.375
1993	17.375	12.625

Figure 2 • 5   Wendy's International: September 1989 – August 1990

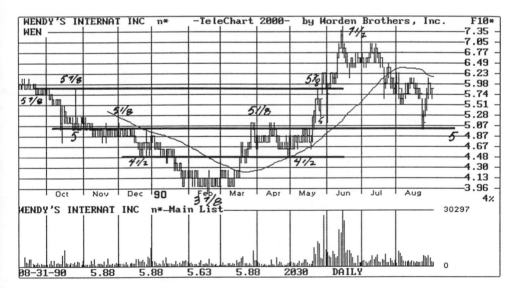

Chart courtesy of TeleChart 2000™ by Worden Brothers, Inc. Used with permission.

acted as support. During the rise in March, 4 1/2 provided resistance. During the decline in April, 4 1/2 was once again support.

Charts oftentimes take on an air of symmetry. The repeating concentrations of trading, providing either support or resistance, account for the symmetry.

Wendy's subsequently rose to 5 7/8 in late May, where the advance briefly stalled. The stock stalled because it moved into the resistance as represented by the trading range of the prior July – September 1989, whose low was 5 7/8.

Day-to-day movement can be deceptive, but look at the decline of May 28. The decline stopped right at support at 5 as represented by the previous high.

The advance resumed in June, with volume skyrocketing on June 14 as the stock moved through 7. On June 15 the stock hit resistance at 7 1/2 and then reversed.

Following the reversal at 7 1/2 the stock declined sharply into August.

Where did the stock find support? At 5.

For a different outlook refer to Figure 2-6 showing the primary trend being made up of a series of intermediate advances/declines. Look at how the declines tend to find support right around previous intermediate highs.

Support and resistance levels are what give trends their zigzag characteristics, whether minor, intermediate, or major.

Trendline Analysis

Nearly all investors are familiar with trendlines. Up trendlines are drawn connecting the lows. Down trendlines are drawn connecting the highs.

However, support and resistance influence how and where trendlines are drawn. The lows used in up trendlines represent support levels. The highs used in down trendlines represent resistance. Trendlines form at support and resistance levels.

Trendlines can be useful in analysis, but they have to be taken in the right context.

Trendlines have three levels of significance: major, intermediate, and minor.

Wendy's major trend is bullish, as is its major trendline. The Wendy's chart (see Figure 2-7) shows the advancing intermediate trend during the first quarter of 1991. The intermediate trend, in turn, is made up of three minor rallies.

A break in a trendline signals a change in trend. A break in the trendline may be just a hesitation or consolidation, or a reversal. A reversal, however, requires a break in support.

Minor trend reversals happen all the time. A break in minor support may lead to a reversal in the intermediate trend, and a break in intermediate support

Figure 2 • 6   Wendy's International: Trend Development

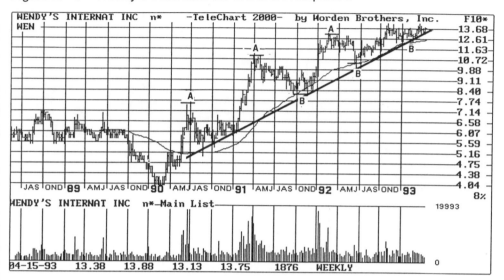

may lead to a reversal in the major trend. Trendline analysis can provide some important guidance, but support levels are still the traffic signals.

Support Failure

During the first-quarter 1991 intermediate advance Wendy's had three minor reversals. Stocks post minor reversals all the time. A more important intermediate development occurred during April.

One early indication of a change of trend is that a stock fails to do what is expected (see Figure 2-7). In the rally of early April, the inability of Wendy's to move above its previous high of 11 was not bullish. Instead, the issue declined back to prior support at 10.

At 10 Wendy's could have just moved sideways. Many intermediate consolidations or corrections are marked by a sideways hesitation. However, when prior support at 10 was broken, it indicated that the intermediate trend had turned bearish.

Note the rally to 10 1/8 of the week of May 24. What had been support—10—was now acting as resistance. Wendy's rally was stopped at 10, and the stock proceeded to move lower.

Figure 2 • 7   Wendy's International: December 1990 – June 1991

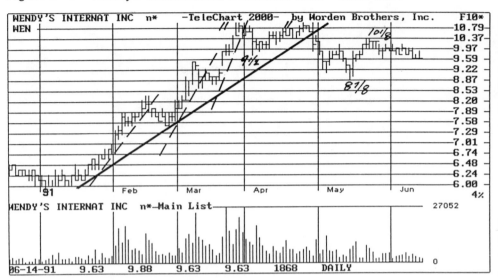

Chart courtesy of TeleChart 2000™ by Worden Brothers, Inc. Used with permission.

Figure 2 • 8   Wendy's International: February 1984 – April 1992

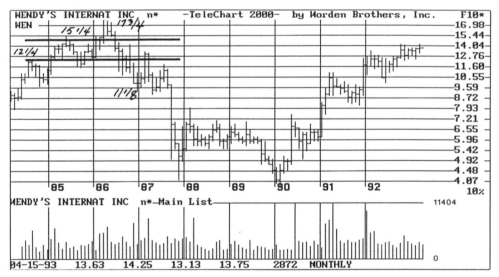

Chart courtesy of TeleChart 2000™ by Worden Brothers, Inc. Used with permission.

Wendy's last major bearish change of trend was in 1986 (see Figure 2-8 above).

From 1982 through 1986 Wendy's had a perfect stair-step trend, and a straight trendline. At each intermediate decline, the stock stopped falling at the prior intermediate support, as indicated by the prior intermediate high.

The prior intermediate high during 1985 was 15 1/4. When Wendy's broke that high during July 1986, it had bearish implications. The stock fell all the way to the prior level of intermediate support at 12. When, after a rally attempt, the stock fell through support at 12, the major trend for Wendy's was clearly bearish.

Wendy's change of intermediate trend in April 1991 was nearly a carbon copy of Wendy's major trend change in July 1986. The trends were different, but the same principles of support failure were working.

Momentum Analysis

Momentum reflects the ebb and flow of buying and selling pressures. Momentum can be fast or slow, increasing or decreasing, or not reflecting any price movement at all.

Momentum can be thought of as representing the three phases of a stock price cycle, as stock moves through the accumulation phase, to the markup phase, to the distribution phase, to the markdown phase, then back to the accumulation phase.

These various momentum elements of technical analysis can be used to measure degrees of momentum in order to buy more intelligently. A bullish indicator is given when the relatively steep markdown leads momentum and gradually gives way to a *flattening out* in stock prices and then begins an upturn. Many low-priced stocks assume a *saucer* pattern.

In buying, speculative positions are first taken when the downward momentum runs its course.

Several patterns can indicate the first sign of a break in downward momentum and the formation of a significant bottom.

One case occurs when a stock, after moving to a new low, fails to follow through by dropping as expected. This may sound bizarre, as if it represents a failure in technical analysis, but it's really technical analysis working as it is supposed to work.

In a typical zigzag downtrend, a stock will tend to move in a channel, falling to new lows by X number of points, rallying up to resistance, then falling to further new lows. The upper line of the channel is formed by resistance, the lower line by support.

When the stock fails to decline as far as has been the pattern to date, a loss of downward momentum is indicated. A decline is expected to move to the lower line of the channel, but some combination of a slowdown in selling or a step-up in buying keeps the issue from falling as far as it should based on its current trend channel.

The importance of failing to fall far enough is in the subsequent development of resistance. One of the requirements for effective resistance is that a stock must drop a sufficient distance under a previous low; otherwise, a resistance level is not activated. The first loss of downward momentum is when the stock fails to decline far enough to create resistance.

In the Wendy's chart (Figure 2-9), the channel had been pretty well confining the stock price through the second and third quarters of 1991. The rally in October carried the stock right back to the top of the declining channel, to 9 7/8, just as it should have.

If the downtrend had still been in effect, the stock would have fallen to below 8 on the next decline. The stock did fall to a new low, but the failure of the stock to follow through and fall decisively to new lows broke the downward momentum. Then the start of an upward minor zigzag pattern instead was undeniably bullish.

Figure 2 • 9   Wendy's International: March 1991 – February 1992

Chart courtesy of TeleChart 2000™ by Worden Brothers, Inc. Used with permission.

The downward momentum had been broken, and the stock began to drag sideways. However, there was no indication that the stock was ready to move higher. An issue may just move sideways for a month or so, and then move lower. The stock still must breakout to the upside.

Identifying Intermediate Support Levels

The reason why the downward momentum had been broken is not random. The stock, as shown in the Wendy's chart, had declined to intermediate support at 8 in mid-November.

Buying at intermediate support is one of the most important of the buying opportunities. Buying at major support occurs only once every few years, if then. Buying on minor support can be profitable if done early. Buying on intermediate support, however, is a frequent and most rewarding opportunity. The prior intermediate top in Wendy's was 7 1/2 on June 15, 1990 as shown in Figure 2-5.

Prior highs determine support, and when Wendy's rose above 7 1/2 in its advance to 11 in April 1991, those former highs at 7 1/2 became support. The most important key in buying during an intermediate decline is to expect the stock to bottom out at expected support.

Sometimes a stock will decline nearly exactly to theoretical support, like Wendy's did on August 24, 1990, when the stock found support at 5 (see Figure 2-5), but sometimes a stock will fall a little under support, sometimes stop a little short of support.

Technical analysis is far from exact. Nonetheless, support levels dictate how trends form, and are the most useful tool of technical analysis as indicating where and when to buy. Investors have heard the expression to "buy on declines." Now you know how to do it—buy on declines to support.

The next intermediate correction in Wendy's was during the early part of 1992 following a high of 13 3/8 on February 18 (Figure 2-10). At first the stock appeared as if the correction would move sideways, at support at just under 12, reflecting the high volume of trading between 11 and 12 in early January. But when support at 12 broke in June, the stock fell quickly.

Support for the stock formed at 10 1/2 to 11, which coincided with the previous intermediate high at 11. Refer to Figure 2-9 and look at the highs of the previous advance. In March and April 1991, 11 was resistance. In June 1992, 11 was acting as support.

Look at Figure 2-10 and think about 12: 12 was resistance in January 1992, support during the next 4 months, and resistance in July and August. When the

Figure 2 • 10   Wendy's International: November 1991 – October 1992

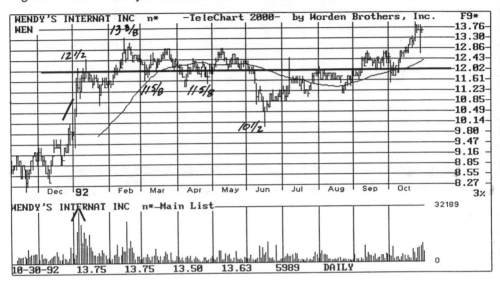

Chart courtesy of TeleChart 2000™ by Worden Brothers, Inc. Used with permission.

stock during early September 1992 once again rose above 12, 12 again became support.

After the subsequent advance to 14 1/4 in November, Wendy's moved into an intermediate decline. Where did the stock find support? At 12 (Figure 2-11).

These corrections are only intermediate in nature, but the declines afford many of the same principles that buyers of low-priced and depressed issues should look for at major lows as well as intermediate lows.

While catching a stock rising off its major low is ideal, buying opportunities at the start of a major advance are obviously less frequent than buying as one intermediate decline has run its course and another intermediate advance is underway. A major advance has only one beginning. However, there are likely to be recurring beginnings of intermediate advances.

Consider the situation from another perspective. Investors really will not know when a major advance is underway until sufficient time and duration have passed. What can be deciphered much closer to the lows is that an intermediate trend is underway. If an investor can correctly tab the beginning of intermediate advances, the investor will catch all the major advances anyway.

Figure 2 • 11   Wendy's International: September 1992 – August 1993

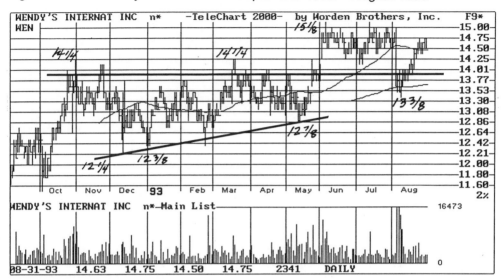

Moving Average Analysis

Moving averages have long been part of technical analysis. They are akin to the trendlines, the theory being that moving average eliminates the short-term volatility of the market, allowing the investor to focus on the more significant trends of the market.

Moving averages are also like support and resistance. By definition, a moving average represents a certain number of trading days, and for that reason, the degree to which they work depends on how well they represent support and resistance levels.

Because moving averages do not incorporate volume, they often do not provide all the analysis necessary to pinpoint precise support and resistance levels. However, as indicated in the last example, moving averages were useful in helping investors identify potentially profitable support levels, i.e., at 12.

Whether the investor chooses to use just moving averages, or prefers to get at the underlying facts by ferreting out support levels, the important point is that when a stock has declined to the area of important intermediate support, and is beginning to flatten out, or perhaps trend higher, even on only a minor trend basis, it is time to buy. It is not necessary to wait for a breakout and the knee-jerk Wall Street buy recommendation.

Breakout Analysis

Breakouts are often not easy to classify as they are occurring. In practice, breakout points are sometimes only identifiable by hindsight. More often than not, the breakout is a process.

Following the lows of 8 1/8, Wendy's had effected a nice bullish minor pattern of zigzags and had broken out of a symmetrical triangle. At 9 5/8 the stock then declined because it ran up against both the down trendline and resistance at the previous minor high in mid-October (see Figure 2-12). The stock backed off to 8 7/8.

On December 30, Wendy's rose to 10, thereby moving above both the down trendline and the previous high of 9 7/8 of October 23. Volume increased nicely despite the low-volume holiday trading season. Wendy's had broken out.

The stock "stutter stepped" for a couple of days, providing investors with an excellent chance to buy on the typical dull reaction under 10 following the breakout. Wendy's "clear-cut" breakout occurred the following week, it rose sharply from 10 to 12, rising past previous intermediate highs of 11, in a week.

The breakout from the following correction, during the summer of 1992, was also a process (see Figure 2-12). After bouncing off support at 10 1/2, there was not one dramatic breakout but a series of breakouts, each becoming more decisive.

Figure 2 • 12   Wendy's International: March 1991 – February 1992

Chart courtesy of TeleChart 2000TM by Worden Brothers, Inc. Use with permission.

By the time the "clear-cut" breakout occurred as the stock rose above the previous highs around 13, the move was just about over. The difficulty in judging breakouts, and the following quick mark-up move, underscores the importance of buying earlier at intermediate support.

Volume Analysis

I've always read that volume is good for stocks, that "as goes volume, so goes the trend." Regarding volume, Robert Rhea (*The Dow Theory*) stated that "a market which has been overbought becomes dull on rallies and develops activity on declines; conversely, when a market is oversold, the tendency is to become dull on declines and active on rallies."

The correct analysis of volume and price depends on the context. Volume can occur at several points, but the two most important times are (1) when the stock is breaking out, and (2) when the move is coming to an end.

Volume is one of the most important tools of technical analysis because it helps define the significance of any price level. However, volume tends to follow the trend.

Have you ever noticed a stock jump a few points, and then come the recommendations to buy? The same with volume. The stock rises to new highs and then volume expands. That is why buying on the breakout can be risky; especially the *clear-cut* breakouts. Often it's better to wait for the inevitable correction with volume shrinking.

Unfortunately, most investors tend to notice the volume at the end of the move. The stock has already been moving up nicely, and the exciting price action and high volume literally hooks them in. Most of the time investors who buy into the high volume moves will be buying at the top at the end of a minor move, or possibly worse—the intermediate move, or the worst time—right at the end of a major trend.

So, the next time volume catches your eye, be sure it is where it is bullish —on the breakout—like Wendy's on December 30, as the stock rose to 10 1/4, or even in the move to 10 1/2 the following week, and not after the stock has already advanced to new highs like in the following mid-January or mid-February, when the volume indicated that the bulk of the move was over.

Area Patterns

Many investors are familiar with the branch of technical analysis known as area patterns, at least to the extent that they have heard some of the names. The names are catchy:

- Head and shoulders, which may be top or bottom;
- Triangles, which in turn may be ascending, descending, inverted, right angle, or symmetrical;
- Rectangles;
- Diamonds;
- Wedges, both rising and falling;
- Flags and pennants;
- Scallops and saucers;
- Gaps, which in turn may be area, breakaway, common, or runaway;
- Bottoms of all types, spike, double, or triple, rounding, multiple, and even dormant.

Some interesting patterns do repeatedly occur in stock prices. The various area patterns, while uniquely interesting, still only serve the basic purpose of being able to provide an analysis of supply and demand, and support and resistance. Sometimes investors get so wrapped up looking for the ideal patterns, that they miss the larger picture. Ideal patterns generally only appear in theory.

Area patterns represent a level of equilibrium, where stocks are either hesitating, finding more support in order to move higher, or where a reversal in trend is underway, as support is fading. Area patterns are not so important as to have every price point encompassed by a ruler or a mathematical model. They are useful only in representing potential changes in the demand/supply balance.

During late 1992 and through nearly three quarters of 1993 (Figure 2-11), Wendy's was "consolidating" its gains of the previous advance to 14. On very heavy volume, the stock traded as high as 14 1/4 on November 2. Smart investors know to be somewhat skeptical of high-volume "flash in the pan moves" that occur after a stock has been advancing for more than four months.

The stock declined to 13, and then tried 14 again. The failure this time signaled the end of Wendy's intermediate advance. After the stock fell below support at 13, it fell sharply to the next level of support at 12.

The point of resistance for Wendy's several additional times was 14, and 14 would form the top line of an ascending triangle.

The ascending bottom line of the triangle reflected buyers a little more anxious to buy the stock. Earnings were rising nicely at Wendy's, and so was the stock price, a perfect fit for most of the momentum models that dominate Wall Street these days.

Many ascending triangles are continuation patterns, and Wendy's was no exception. On June 4 Wendy's broke out to the upside, rising above 14, on very heavy volume. Previously resistance, 14 was now support.

Wendy's initial move carried the stock to 15 1/8. The issue declined in the following weeks to support at 14 1/8, where buying could have been done.

News always has its impact on stock prices, and on August 5 Wendy's announced that earnings for the 2nd quarter were $0.26 versus $0.22 a year earlier. Institutions reacted by dumping the stock. While the panic carried the stock below 14, the stock quickly regathered at 14 and moved back up to new highs (see Figure 2-12). Support worked like it should.

Patterns could be discussed endlessly. The basic patterns have many variations. Patterns in and of themselves, however, are not important.

What is most important is that patterns, representing the forces of support and resistance, do often develop at important consolidation or reversal points. What is important for investors is to realize is that a period of equilibrium is being formed and to be alert to what trend traits the stock subsequently assumes.

The various principles of technical analysis reviewed with Wendy's are applicable to the majority of stocks, high-priced, low-priced, investment-grade, speculative-grade, etc. Investors should pick up a copy of Edwards and Magee, *Technical Analysis of Stock Trends*, 5th edition, (John Magee, Springfield, MA), if they want to read further on the subject. The next Chapter studies how low-priced and depressed stocks bottom out and how to find winners.

· 3 ·

Finding Winners

One of the most exciting phases of any stock's cycle is the markdown phase, when stocks have moved away from an orderly distribution to aggressive markdown, where bids are pulled, when sellers begin to sell at any price—in other words, when stocks are falling under their own weight. While the panic period of plunging prices is not a very pleasant experience for those holding a stock, and not necessarily a time to take a position, investors interested in low-priced and depressed stocks should begin to size up the issues among their growing inventory for potential buys.

Pivotal Point: The Swing from Distribution to Accumulation

In any sharp intermediate decline the precipitous selling characteristics of the markdown phase will give way to a more gradual and orderly decline. The panic conditions will gradually develop into a more distressed type of selling.

The sharp momentum will ebb, because all those who were anxious to sell have sold. As some interested parties, such as buyers of depressed and low-priced stocks, begin to take interest, the steep decline levels off and gives way to some degree of buoyancy.

The pivot or bottoming-out process can take a variety of forms. The stock may just move sideways, bouncing off or testing the lows. So-called double, triple, and multiple bottoms are just different variations of the test of the lows. Many bank stocks in 1990 reflected the sideways pattern of Chase Manhattan, with the stock bouncing off the 10 level for several months (see Figure 3-1).

During the subsequent test of the lows, which may occur for months if not for a year or so from the initial lows, a stock can either stop above, even with, or trade below the earlier lows.

What is important is that on the subsequent tests, volume becomes dull and the stock does not decisively break to new lows. A stock that moves to new lows

Figure 3 • 1   Chase Manhattan Corp. (CMB): Test of the Lows

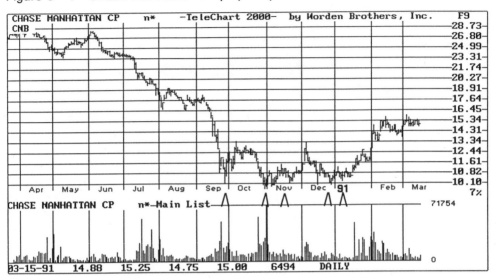

Chart courtesy of TeleChart 2000™ by Worden Brothers, Inc. Used with permission.

Figure 3 • 2   Mellon Bank Corp. (MEL): Test of the Lows

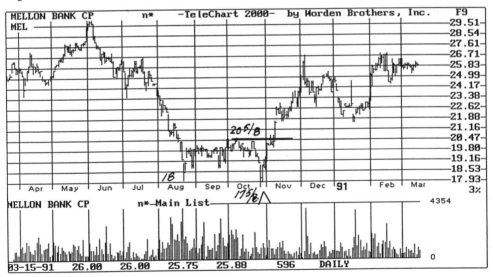

Chart courtesy of TeleChart 2000™ by Worden Brothers, Inc. Used with permission.

Figure 3 • 3   Santa Fe Pacific Corp. (SFX): Test of the Lows

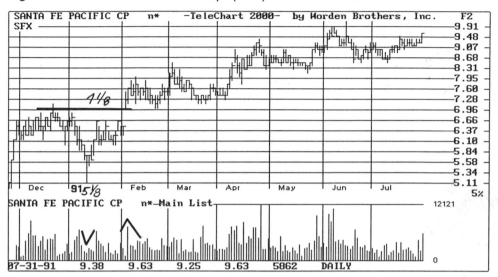

Chart courtesy of TeleChart 2000™ by Worden Brothers, Inc. Used with permission.

on low volume, then pops right back up into the previous trading range, is moderately bullish. That does not mean that a successful test of the lows has occurred. A success occurs when, after the decline, the stock rises on increasing volume and moves above the highs registered between the lows. On November 9, 1990, when Mellon Bank broke above the October 9 high of 20 5/8, it was a successful test of the lows and bullish (see Figure 3-2 above).

Another stock, Santa Fe Pacific (see Figure 3-3 above) had a double bottom where the second bottom was a new low. Volume, however, was also very low. No high-volume follow-through to the lows occurred. Note the gap on the successful "testing" of the lows as the stock rose above 7.

Maytag bounced along its lows for two months before moving higher. Note in Figure 3-4 that a few days after the stock registered a successful test of the lows in rising above 12 1/8, the stock reacted lower for a couple of days on news of a dividend decrease. Whether or not buying at the time of a dividend cut is a smart tactic depends on whether the trend is up or down.

Black & Decker's double bottom took 16 weeks. At the lows the stock was selling under book value. Note the increase in volume as the price broke out in January (see Figure 3-5).

Figure 3 • 4 Maytag Corp. (MYG): Test of the Lows

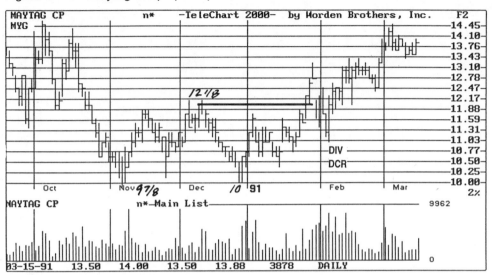

Chart courtesy of TeleChart 2000™ by Worden Brothers. Used with permission.

Figure 3 • 5 Black & Decker Corp. (BDK)

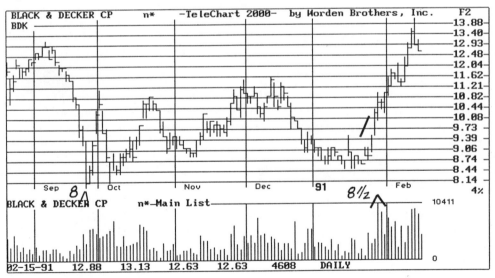

Chart courtesy of TeleChart 2000™ by Worden Brothers, Inc. Used with permission.

Figure 3 • 6   Pier 1 Imports Inc. (PIR)

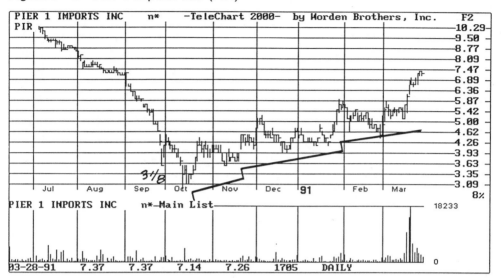

Chart courtesy of TeleChart 2000™ by Worden Brothers, Inc. Used with permission.

After hitting a low of 3 1/8 Pier 1 started to trend higher, slowly, gradually. In Figure 3-6, compare the typical stair-step pattern during the uptrend with the lack of any minor advance/decline sequence prior to the lows. After an extensive decline, buy when you see some development along the lines of a zigzag.

Other stocks may have different slopes to their advance. Often in low-priced and depressed stocks the bottoming patterns are round or bowl- or saucer-shaped (see Figure 3-7). Some sharp minor advances may appear, but the overall pattern is one of rounding.

Volume often closely tracks prices. Volume is high as the prices drop sharply, begins to ebb as the selling pressures subside, then gradually builds as the stock begins to slowly trend higher. Only at the end of the move, when the saucer has turned into nearly a vertical move, will volume increase dramatically.

No one set formula or model can describe the bottoming-out process. Each issue has its own particular demand and supply factors.

Generally, though, stocks that are just down with the market will rise and fall with the market. When a market correction runs its course, stocks will rise right along. Truly depressed stocks will find the bottom sticky. Some of these issues are down 40%, 50%, 60% or more. The bottoming process for the stock

Figure 3 • 7 Georgia Gulf Corp. (GGC): Saucer-shaped Formation

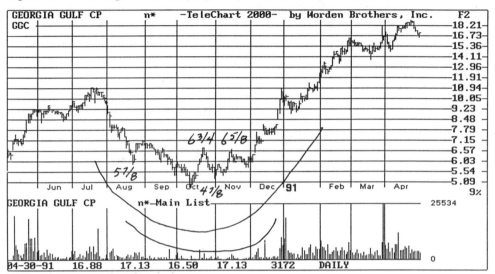

Chart courtesy of TeleChart 2000™ by Worden Brothers, Inc. Used with permission.

Figure 3 • 8 Goodyear Tire & Rubber (GT)

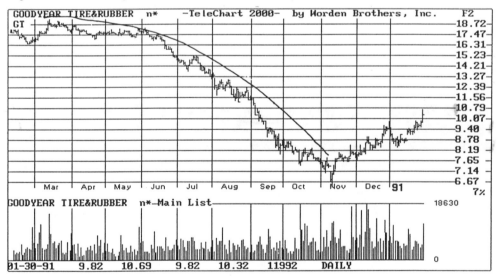

Chart courtesy of TeleChart 2000™ by Worden Brothers, Inc. Used with permission.

usually takes time. Figure 3-8 shows how extensive a decline Goodyear, a fallen blue chip, showed.

Investors should now have a clearer picture of what a depressed stock looks like. Of course, it takes buying to push it back up, but in most cases a truly depressed stock has a financial problem. Because most of Wall Street is driven by fundamentals, buying interest remains low.

Many fundamental investors are momentum investors, and because most depressed issues are totally lacking any relative strength at their lows, momentum investors will be kept at bay.

While a large number of investors will not be anxious to buy the stock, there always are some investors willing to step in, such as value investors, long-term investors, insiders, investors averaging down, speculators, etc.

As the ready supply of sellers dwindles and a growing number of bottom-fishers begins to exert to support, some semblance of a bullish uptrend begins to take shape in the stock.

The overall guideline for buying low-priced and depressed stocks is primarily based on the concept of shifting momentum. A gradual decline in selling pressure gradually shifts to a step-up in demand.

This does not mean that a major bottom has been seen. Any rally attempt may turn out to be just that, a rally attempt. The major trend of the market may still be bearish, with a further decline ahead. The future price pattern is pure conjecture.

While not an indication that the stock has reached a major bottom, the typical bottoming-out pattern of low-priced stocks offers a variety of clues to enable investors to act. That's what's important. Technical analysis allows us to anticipate, and then act.

As will be discussed in the Chapter 4, "The January Effect," depressed stocks sometimes do not wait for long. A severely depressed stock can be wound tighter than a drum. After tax-selling has run its course, a stock may be ready to go, no matter how extensive a base has been built.

Stocks have a drawn-out base more often than not. Investors have to be aware of general market conditions and anomalies such as the January Effect so that they are not caught short waiting for a textbook pattern to develop.

After a breakout occurs, an investor must be ready to move. After a depressed stock begins to build some momentum in rising from a bottom, the stock can spring back rather quickly, in dollar amounts, and most importantly, on a percentage basis (see Figure 3-9).

An investor must be ready with a price limit or buy point.

Figure 3 • 9   Valhi Inc. (VHI)

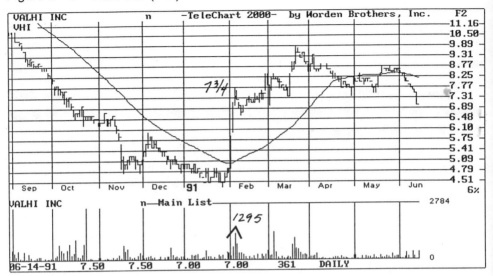

Chart courtesy of TeleChart 2000™ by Worden Brothers, Inc. Used with permission.

The Pivot Point: The Reversal

The bottom line of making money in stocks is to be on the right side of the trend. The point of maximum profits is close to the start of a favorable trend and not staying too long after the trend has turned unfavorable. The reversal in many ways is the most important aspect of technical analysis.

A reversal is more of a process, not a single event. It starts with a change of trend, with the stock breaking the previous downside trend activity and then perhaps starting to zigzag higher.

These early trend movements do not necessarily fit into the popular notion of breakouts with demand overpowering resistance, but they are true to form in the sense that they have broken through some resistance pattern by moving out of the downward zigzag cycle, and then by starting an upward zigzag cycle. Each is an important technical development for buyers of depressed stocks.

The early trend action is not as explosive as breakouts that occur later in the trend. With depressed stocks, there is just not much resistance around the lows, and the move higher is more often than not a relatively lazy uptrend, with modest breakouts. The modest breakouts that take place at the lows are among the most important of the developments. They are the seeds of a bull trend.

Investors will not know whether the lower intensity breakouts are the start of a profitable intermediate trend, much less a major trend, for some time. That is not as important as being able to buy right, i.e., to buy as close as possible at the start of a developing bullish trend.

When To Buy

An investor can buy a depressed stock at several points:

1. The stock breaks through and above the downtrend;
2. Confirmation of the buying trend–bullish minor zigzag wave;
3. Decline carries the stock to support;
4. Decline carries the stock to intermediate support;
5. Area patterns;
6. The countermove;
7. The breakout.

1. Break Through and Above Downtrend

The first point involves a break in the trendline. One of the most reliable patterns is when the stock breaks the downward momentum by breaking through and above the downtrend. The downward momentum is broken after a very extensive decline, with a well-defined declining downtrend and with the stock deeply oversold.

Many downtrends are not well defined, or tight, with periodic selling panics and sharp rallies raising havoc on the ideal straight-line trend and channel patterns. However, many low-priced and depressed stocks, and especially in their later stages of distressed selling, invariably follow a well-defined downtrend.

A rally of only a few days that may appear to just be a minor rebound, but succeeds in breaking the downtrend, is a significant change in the technical picture of a stock. The more well-defined the downtrend, or the longer it lasts, and the more oversold the stock, the more important the change in trend.

As an example, the Pittston Company had been generally declining for several years. Each year from 1989 to 1991 the stock traded in the 21–22 area. The overall direction was down.

Figure 3-10 shows the intermediate decline from the high of 16 5/8 on June 9, 1992, to the lows of 11 3/8 of October 16.

The first part of the decline was characterized by some rallies, but toward the end of the decline, the downtrend became tighter and tighter. The stock was becoming more and more oversold.

Figure 3 • 10 Pittston Co. (PCO): Break Through and Above Downtrend

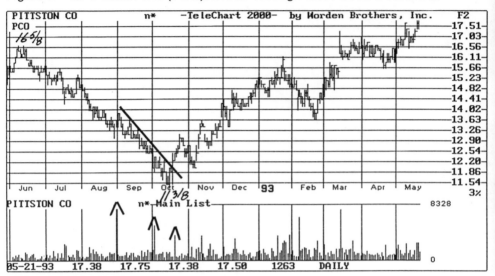

Chart courtesy of TeleChart 2000™ by Worden Brothers, Inc. Used with permission.

The low in the stock was on October 16, when it declined to 11 3/8. Volume for the day was one of the lowest of the year. Normally volume expands on a day that a stock drops to new lows. Instead, the stock reversed and closed at 12, the high of the day, and at the trendline. The stock declined 1/8 of a point on the following day, October 19, 1992, with volume very light once again.

On October 20, the stock traded lower again, trading at 11 1/2. Instead of moving lower, however, the issue reversed and closed sharply higher at 12 1/2, with volume picking up sharply as well.

Volume follows the trend. In rising to 12 1/2, Pittston broke the downtrend and a nice rally was underway.

With regards to volume, investors might note the previous high-volume days. On October 2 volume soared to more than 500,000 shares, with the stock dropping sharply. On August 31, the stock had set a new low of 13 on volume of more than 800,000.

A rally on September 2 broke a downtrend. It was not especially bullish. Volume was pathetic on the move higher. The rally of October 20, however, was on volume four times the daily average.

Breaking of the down trendline is not a sign that the bottom has been seen. A reversal of the trend has not occurred. By moving to the right, the stock has in-

Figure 3 • 11   Canadian Pacific Ltd. (CP): Break Through and Above Downtrend

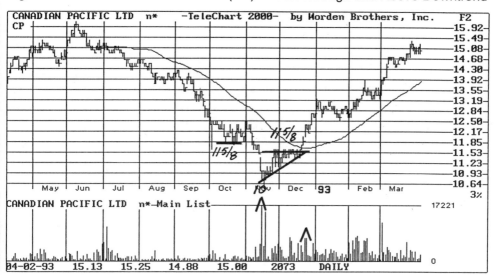

dicated a change of trend. It might just be a momentary pause, a sideways hesitation, with a further decline ahead.

Buying on the trendline break is speculative, but it is a timely place to speculate, because the predominant bottoming pattern in low-priced and depressed stocks follows the breaking of such a trendline.

Canadian Pacific (see Figure 3-11 above) had been falling from its June 10, 1992 highs fairly orderly, but when previous support at 13 was taken out, the stock began to decline more quickly. From late September through early November, the stock had a series of minipanics. The selling climax in the week ending November 13 was on very heavy volume. Somebody thought Canadian Pacific was worth $10 a share.

Selling climaxes are often the end of extensive declines. That was the case at Canadian Pacific. At first Canadian Pacific rebounded in late November to about 11 1/2 – 11 5/8, just at the edge of resistance as indicated by the five-week trading area ending October 30 and identified by the low of 11 5/8. Support and resistance is not supposed to be that exact, but sometimes it works out that way.

Note the interesting interplay during late November and early December. Resistance was at 11 5/8, but the area pattern resembled an ascending triangle. The top line was defined at 11 5/8, but the bottom line was gradually rising.

Figure 3 • 12   Bally Mfg. Corp. (BLY): Break Through and Above Downtrend

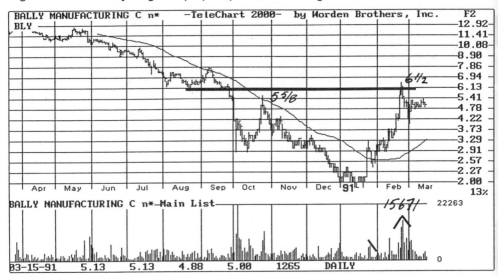

Chart courtesy of TeleChart 2000™ by Worden Brothers, Inc. Used with permission.

On December 22 and 23, Canadian Pacific broke out of the triangle pattern, moving through its 50-day moving average in the process. The bulls were in charge.

Sometimes with deeply oversold stocks, the breaking of a down trendline will lead to a sharply rising stock.

When Bally (see Figure 3-12 above) rose through its 50-day moving average on January 24, the breakout was the first in nearly nine months. The stock had flirted before with the 50-day moving average during the preceding months, but never had decisively broken through.

Following the breakout move, the issue retreated in the customary dull reaction for a few days, then started to trend slowly higher. Investors had plenty of time to buy Bally. When volume soared on February 25, as the stock moved into resistance at 6, the move was over for the time being.

2. Confirmation of the Buying Trend

A second buying opportunity is the confirmation of the minor trend. The most prevalent pattern is a bullish minor zigzag trend. With all the exotic patterns and names found in technical analysis, the simplest formation is the minor trend zigzag. It most often is the start of a major uptrend in the stock.

Figure 3 • 13   Varity Corp. (VAT): Confirmation of the Buying Trend

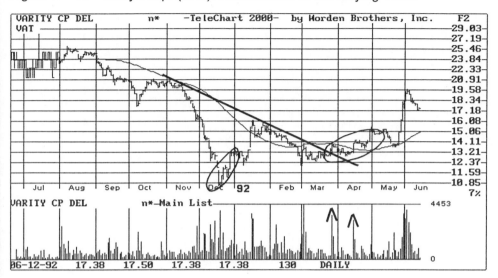

Varity's low was 10 1/2 on December 19, the day after the highest volume move in Varity for the prior six months. The start of the turnaround for Varity was just a minor, bullish zigzag pattern, as the stock moved upward and to the right (see Figure 3-13 above).

Note how the stock moved up sharply through the 50-day moving average during January but then promptly reversed. The stock was still working within a declining trendline. Not until the issue quietly moved out through that trendline in early March would Varity be free to move ahead.

Once free of that trendline, a beautiful series of minor advances/declines in April and May afforded investors excellent buying opportunities.

Most stocks in the depressed class will not begin trending up in earnest from the initial series of zigzags. Instead, the stock will encounter resistance. Tests of the lows will take place. Not until the resistance is taken out will the stock begin to trend higher.

Advanced Micro Devices (see Figure 3-14) was in a tailspin during late 1990. The stock bottomed at 3 5/8 in mid October, rallied briefly, and again began to decline into early November. However, the stock held above its earlier lows for more than a month.

Figure 3 • 14   Advanced Micro Devices (AMD): Minor Bullish Zigzag

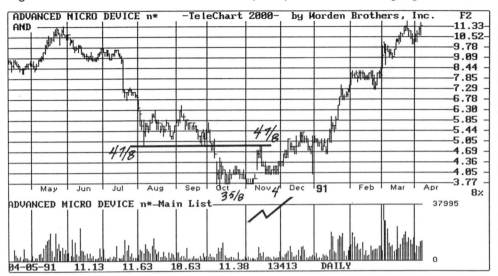

AMD advanced sharply on November 12 but quickly ran into overhead resistance at 5. The low defining the resistance, 4 7/8 of early August, turned out to be the exact high of the rally. The more extensive the decline, the more likely the issue will decline to the lows for a test of the lows. With AMD the stock declined to 4 in late November. Nonetheless, the overall pattern by early November was one of a bullish zigzag.

While AMD was trending higher from the absolute lows of October 4, the markup trend did not start until AMD was able to push through resistance at around 5. Trendlines for that reason are not drawn from the absolute lows, but the low preceding the stock's markup phase.

Investors may be disappointed to learn that a simple minor zigzag pattern is one of the most important technical formations. Technical analysis does not sound very analytical if all we are looking for is a minor bullish zigzag. Probably more than a few skeptical investors are thinking: "There has to be more to technical analysis than that."

Any bottom forms with a change of trend, and a change of trend first involves a bearish zigzag giving way to a bullish zigzag. When taken by themselves, these zigzags mean nothing. But when several months of consistently bearish zigzags give way to a bullish minor zigzag trend, the change is significant.

3. Decline Carries Stock to Major Support

The third guideline utilizes support theory to give us some direction as to when to buy. Some stocks have significant declines that find support at previous areas of major support. Major support levels in depressed, low-priced stocks may be shattered, but many low-priced, out-of-favor issues find support at previous support areas. One such issue was Occidental Petroleum(OXY) (see Figure 3-15A).

During the last part of 1990, Occidental Petroleum had a precipitous decline, falling nearly 50% from its highs of around 30. As with many low-priced stocks, the selling momentum of the sharp decline began to lose steam, and during the first four months, the issue found support in the mid- to upper-teens. The low was 16 1/2 on January 4, 1991, a few weeks before the company cut its dividend; 16 1/2 would be the low of the year.

In the last half of 1992 (see Figure 3-15B) Occidental was again declining. Because previous support levels tend to repeat, investors could begin to take an interest in Occidental as the stock moved toward the mid-teens once again in the October 1992 semi-panic sell-off.

As a stock approaches support, and a very high-volume, selling climax day develops, speculative positions can be taken. The 1991 low for OXY was 16 1/2.

Figure 3 • 15A   Occidental Petroleum (OXY): Major Support

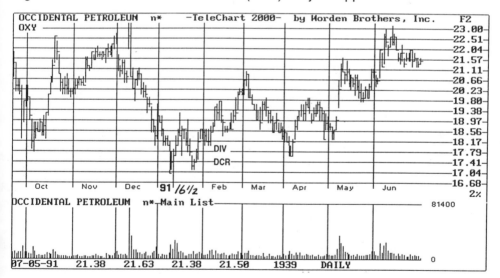

Chart courtesy of TeleChart 2000™ by Worden Brothers, Inc. Used with permission.

Figure 3 • 15B Occidental Petroleum (OXY): Major Support

Chart courtesy of TeleChart 2000™ by Worden Brothers, Inc. Used with permission.

On October 23, 1992 Occidental dropped to 15 3/4 on extraordinary high volume, the highest for months. The stock immediately reversed and rebounded to around 17. Important support had again entered the stock in the mid-teens, right where it could have been expected. In the first two weeks of November, volume receded as the stock sagged. The dull reaction was a buying opportunity. The stock had rallied at support, and the following decline was accompanied by low volume. The stock could have moved below 15 3/4, and investors could have closed out their positions. Instead, a bullish zigzag was evident by November 20; clearly a new intermediate trend was underway.

Philips NV (see Figure 3-16A) during 1990 was dropping for many of the same reasons it would later be dropping during 1992, lower earnings. In November 1990 the stock bottomed out at 11, dropping more than 50% from its highs.

The stock had a very robust breakout in rising to 13 1/8 on November 22, 1991 breaking the long downturn and the 50-day moving average as well. The 50-day moving average works best when it "hugs" the decline.

Following the breakout, the stock sagged for several weeks for a "test" of the lows, then started trending upward. A new trend high in late January 1991 was a successful completion of the "test" of the lows.

Figure 3 • 16A   Philips NV NY Shares (PHG): Major Support

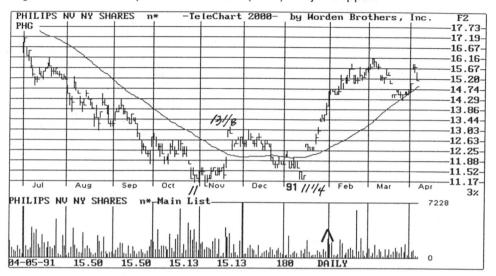

Two years later Philips (see Figure 3-16B) was again undergoing a significant correction. Because the issue was moving into an area where major support had developed before, Philips merited watching closely for support. Volume on the selling panic low of 9 5/8 in November 1992 was the highest in months.

On the initial advance off the lows, Philips stayed within the declining trendline, and the stock was turned back at 12. However, after spending some time trading just under 11 a share, the stock advanced past 12. The trend was bullish. Resistance at the 13 3/8 – 13 5/8 level was strong, and Philips retreated toward 11. On the next move to new highs past 13 1/2, the stock gaped.

4. Decline Carries Stock to Intermediate Support

Stocks return to intermediate support more often than most investors think. Figure 3-17A shows the activity of Computer Associates following its panic break of July 1990. Before the selling had run its course, the stock had declined down to 4 3/8 on September 24. Note the ascending triangle at the lows, with resistance at 6 defining the horizontal top line. Area patterns at the exact lows are not common.

Figure 3 • 16B   Philips NV NY Shares (PHG): Major Support

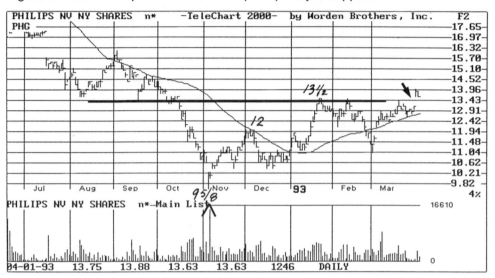

Chart courtesy of TeleChart 2000™ by Worden Brothers, Inc. Used with permission.

Figure 3 • 17A   Computer Assoc. Int'l. Inc. (CA): Intermediate Support

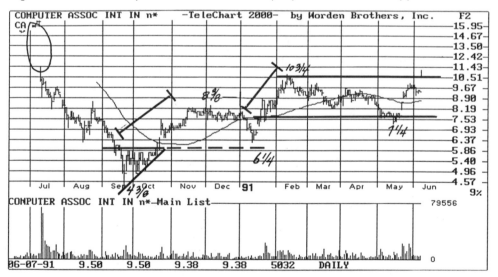

Chart courtesy of TeleChart 2000™ by Worden Brothers, Inc. Used with permission.

The first intermediate advance was from 4 3/8 to the high of 8 3/8 of December 7. The subsequent intermediate decline stopped at 6 1/4, right above support as defined by the ascending triangle top at 6 of late September.

The next intermediate rally carried the stock to 10 3/4. Support was indicated by the previous December 7 highs of 8 3/8. The intermediate decline stopped at 7 1/4. The previous high is the edge of the resistance level. Most of the trading at the previous high was just under 8. Most of the support during the next intermediate reaction was also just under 8.

The next chart (Figure 3-17B) shows the stock moving sharply higher in early 1992, to 17. Two gaps occurred during the move. The first chart (see Figure 3-17A) shows a large gap between 10 and 16 during the sell panic of July 12, 1990. The lack of trading, and hence, potential resistance between 10 and 16 on the way down created the potential for gaps on the way back up. Considering the importance of resistance, should an investor have bought as the stock churned at 16 after the January rise?

As indicated on the first chart, intermediate support was indicated by the February high of 10 3/4. The next intermediate decline stopped at 10 7/8.

On declines a stock may be bought at intermediate support. Sometimes the

Figure 3 • 17B   Computer Assoc. Int'l. Inc. (CA): Intermediate Support

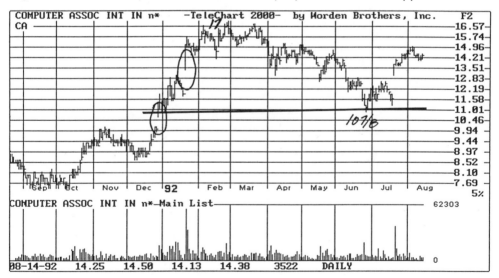

Figure 3 • 18   Santa Fe Pacific Corp. (SFX): Intermediate Support

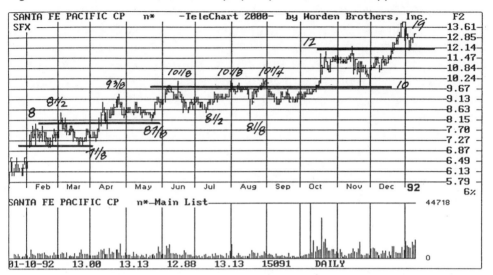

Chart courtesy of TeleChart 2000™ by Worden Brothers, Inc. Used with permission.

stock will stop exactly at support, sometimes a little below, sometimes a little above. Intermediate support, though, gives an investor a guideline for action.

In a previous chart in Figure 3-3 the breakout of Santa Fe Pacific, with the stock gaping above previous highs of 7 1/8, was shown. Figure 3-18 (above) carries it forward.

After the breakout move to 8 1/2, the next decline stops exactly at prior support, as defined by the previous high of 7 1/8. On the next advance the issue rises to 9 3/8. Prior support is defined at 8 1/2. The stock stops at 8 1/8.

One rule for determining the effectiveness of prior highs as support is to take into consideration how decisively the stock moved to new highs. If the stock has not moved to new highs by a large enough margin, say 10%, then the immediate prior high may not be the support.

During the late May rally, Santa Fe did move to new highs, but only closed about a half a point above the previous high of 9 3/8. On the ensuing reaction, the stock fell back to support not at 9 3/8, but back to 8 1/2.

During June, August, and September the stock rose to a series of new highs above the 10 level, 10 1/8, 10 1/8, and 10 1/4, but the advances were not decisive. On the pullbacks, the stock kept falling back to support below 9.

On the other hand, the October 18 move past 10 to 12 was quite decisive.

The stock clearly had moved above 10, and 10 could now be defined as support. Dutifully, the stock fell to support at 10.

On the next advance, the stock moved to 14; on the subsequent decline, the stock stopped at support at 12.

These are not examples of buying low-priced stocks at their exact lows. The intermediate advance/decline sequences can be utilized very profitably by investors who are looking to buy into a rising trend, but at relatively low-risk entry points. Whether low-priced or high-priced, intermediate support is a low-risk buying opportunity.

5. Area Patterns

A stock may form an area reversal pattern at the lows. One common pattern is the descending triangle, with the horizontal bottom line defined by support and a downward sloping top line.

Some technicians label a descending triangle as inherently bearish because the upper line slopes downward, supposedly reflecting less and less buying power. This pattern is common in reversals not only at the top but also at the bottom. Any pattern represents the converging of the demand and supply forces, and the ultimate breakout is a reliable barometer of future stock prices.

Federated Department Stores (see Figure 3-19), emerging from bankruptcy, began trading on a when-issued basis on the NYSE on Wednesday, February 6, 1992, at $17.25. Under the terms of the offering, about 80 million shares were issued during a six-week period starting the week of February 17. The stock did not stay in the upper teens for long. After quickly sinking to 15, FD went into what appeared to be a descending triangle for two weeks, broke to the downside, and started to trade within a large, symmetrical triangular pattern for several more weeks. It then broke sharply to 13 1/2, rallied back to the apex, and continued to skid.

From late April to early June the stock began to form a descending triangle, with the upper line sloping downward. A horizontal lower line reflected buying at 11 1/2. The stock broke out as it moved past the trendline at 12 1/4 – 12 1/2. Support after a breakout in a descending triangle is indicated by the rally highs within the triangle. The late May rally high of 12 7/8 provided support in August and October.

Quaker State, KSF, (Figure 3-20) had the reversal triangle formation at the lows, an ascending triangle. The horizontal top line was defined by resistance at 9 1/2 – 9 3/4. Support developed in a manner that resulted in an upward sloping bottom line. KSF broke sharply above the horizontal top of the triangle and moved to 12 5/8.

Figure 3 • 19 Federated Depart. Stores (FD): Area Patterns

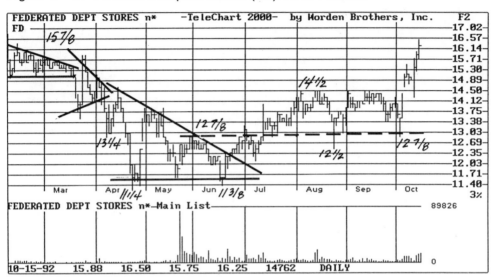

Chart courtesy of TeleChart 2000™ by Worden Brothers, Inc. Used with permission.

Figure 3 • 20 Quaker State Corp. (KSF): Ascending Triangle

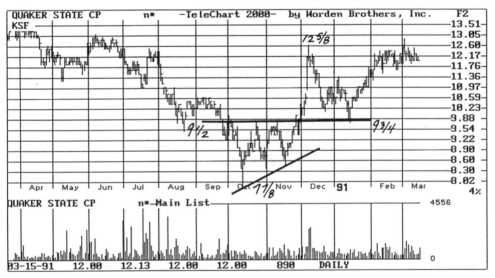

Chart courtesy of TeleChart 2000™ by Worden Brothers, Inc. Used with permission.

Figure 3 • 21   Wheeling Pittsburgh Corp. (WHX): Double Bottom

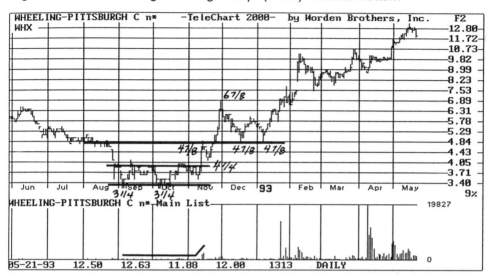

Chart courtesy of TeleChart 2000™ by Worden Brothers, Inc. Used with permission.

On the ensuing pullback, the stock dropped back to support at 9 3/4 as indicated by the horizontal line of the ascending triangle.

Wheeling Pittsburgh (see Figure 3-21 above) had a formation that could be called a double bottom, or perhaps a rectangle.

The stock traded between support at 3 1/4 and resistance at 4 and had a decisive breakout in rising above 4 on very high volume. The rally halted at resistance, 4 7/8, as indicated by the July-August trading range. The stock dipped back to support at 4 1/4, then ensued its advance. Following a November high of 6 7/8, the stock twice declined to support at 4 7/8. Support at 4 7/8 was not only indicated by the mid-November high, but also by the trading range the prior July and August.

While few of the textbook area pattern formations will develop at the exact lows, many of the area formations will develop as part of a consolidation pattern as the stock moves higher.

VF Corp. (see Figure 3-22) hit a low of 11 5/8 on October 18. The stock rallied to 15, and then moved into a rectangle/ascending triangle formation for the next month. The stock traded at support at 13 1/2 – 14 during each of the three reversals. VF Corp. broke out quickly at first in moving above 15. The stock

Figure 3 • 22 VF Corp. (VFC)

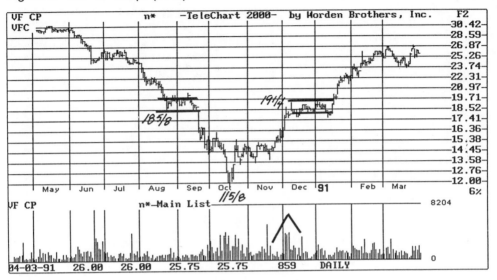

Chart courtesy of TeleChart 2000™ by Worden Brothers, Inc. Used with permission.

encountered resistance as indicated by the trading congestion late September, but quickly moved above as that resistance was overcome.

Note how volume expanded as the stock encountered the next resistance level as defined by the August 24 low of 18 5/8. VF once again moved into a rectangle during the next five weeks. On January 18 the issue broke out in rising past 19 1/4.

Low-priced stocks usually do not form many area patterns at the lows. On the intermediate consolidations that occur as the major trend develops, they can form some well-defined patterns.

6. The Breakout

The breakout is one of the most exciting aspects of technical analysis. In a breakout, resistance is overcome, and the bulls are in charge. The demand/supply equation shifts; the buyers show the greater resolve. Distribution gives way to accumulation. Supply is absorbed. Until something develops to alter the new demand/supply equation, the future course of prices points higher.

The primary characteristics of a breakout are price and volume. A breakout by definition has to be decisive in extent and trading. Sufficient force to push prices into the next tier and to turn bullish trend momentum up a few notches must be present.

With low-priced and depressed issues, the breakout is not always an obvious development. A stock may exhibit different types and degrees of breaking out. In many low-priced stocks, breaking out is not always black and white; it is more subtle.

Investors must be alert to the different types of breakouts and be prepared to buy. Buying on breakouts can be a tricky business because they are not always clear-cut. By the time the breakout is apparent, it is too late and too risky to buy.

By some definitions, a breakout has to be a 3% move. This 3% requirement, added to the extent of the advance preceding the breakout, further adds to the risk of buying high.

In addition, the breakout is not the start of a move. The breakout is confirmation of the trend. A good portion of the move is already over, and investors risk buying late and high by the time the stock has broken out.

While a buy-limit order can sometimes be used to anticipate a breakout move, investors must be careful. A stock can move up on an intraday basis only, taking out the buy-limits and short-selling stops, and then move right back down.

Portec was one of the best winners in early 1993 after the stock finally got underway. Portec (see Figure 3-23) rose off its major lows in moving from 2 3/8 to 4 at the first of the year, and the stock was consolidating between 3 and 4 during much of 1992. Like many low-priced stocks, the issue had a quick rebound off the lows, then bided its time for months.

It was largely dormant during the first half of the year. The action of July 17th was interesting because volume swelled with the stock finishing last on the day. On the following Monday, July 20, the stock rose and closed at a new high of 4 1/4. Was this a breakout? In price, yes. In volume, no.

While the stock closed at new highs, volume declined. For a decisive breakout, volume should swell as the stock makes new highs. At Portec, the increase in volume was not during the breakout. The stock subsequently declined to a new low for the year, 3 1/4.

During the first week of October Portec again moved back to 4 1/4, on a moderate expansion of volume. It fell back again. It did not fall back toward the lows, but held at 3 5/8. The following week the stock rose right back to 4 1/4. The area pattern during October began to resemble an ascending triangle, with resistance at 4 1/4. Increasing bids led to a rising bottom line.

On November 6, Portec decisively moved to new highs by moving past 4 1/4 on heavy volume. A beautiful trendline in this low-priced stock developed after the breakout (see Figure 3-23).

Figure 3 • 23   Portec Inc. (POR)

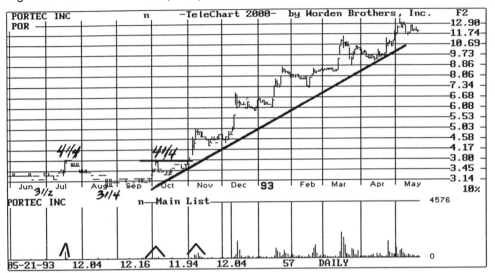

Chart courtesy of TeleChart 2000™ by Worden Brothers, Inc. Used with permission.

Ceridian had a sharp rally on September 27 (see Figure 3-24), breaking a declining trendline dating back several months. The stock quickly ran into resistance at 10 and drifted lower during the next few months. On December 26, Ceridian again broke a trendline. This time the rally carried it above 10 to 10 7/8. Volume was not especially dynamic, but the stock did close 7/8 higher. The breakout was not particularly decisive.

There was no question that the stock's breakout on January 27 and 28 was decisive because the stock rose sharply above the prior high of 10 7/8 on a tremendous increase in volume; it moved to 12 1/2.

On February 27, Ceridian rose again on heavy volume, but was not able to move to decisive new highs, only rising to 12 3/4. Subsequently the issue declined and marked time for seven weeks. The gap breakout on May 27, however, was decisive on both time and points.

With Ceridian a variety of breakouts is seen—from the initial breakout from a declining trendline to signal the start of the major trend moving higher, to breakouts of varying magnitude from area patterns of both minor and intermediate nature.

Breakouts, though, are not always the best time to buy. This is partly due to the problem of "false" or indecisive breakouts, and partly due to the fact that

Figure 3 • 24   Ceridian Corp. (CEN)

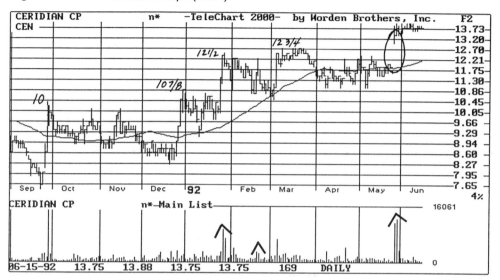

Chart courtesy of TeleChart 2000™ by Worden Brothers, Inc. Used with permission.

in a decisive breakout, the stock has moved sharply higher. Investors who learn what to expect will have plenty of buying opportunities along the way.

7. The Countermove

By definition breakouts should be decisive. It can be risky to chase the stock after it has advanced. Instead, a lower-risk buying opportunity will often be present in a countermove.

The countermove following a breakout can take three versions:

1.   A 40% retracement of the breakout move
2.   Return to trendline
3.   Return to support

For a stock that has broken out, the investor should measure the three countermove possibilities and buy on whichever point occurs first. Often the three guidelines will dovetail but investors cannot be dogmatic.

General Datacomm had a bullish chart during 1992 – 1993, rising nicely from 2 7/8 into the lower teens.

Look at General Datacomm (Figure 3-25), as the stock was in the process of starting its move. Previously, General Datacomm had declined from a March 92 high of 5 1/2. Following the August lows of 2 7/8 the stock moved up nicely to 3 5/8 in September but alone the move did not carry anything more than minor bullish implications.

The mid-October move, though, established that the intermediate trend was bullish; the stock also took out the prior resistance at 4. Buying was in order. The buying point was on the pullback following the move to 4 1/4 of October 14.

A 40% correction is measured from the minor high of 4 1/4 to the preceding minor low of 3 1/4, or one point. A 40% correction of the one-point move was a 3/8 correction to 3 7/8.

A return to a trendline was about 3 3/4. An initial trendline is drawn at a slope parallel to the trendline connecting the two minor highs, 3 5/8 and 4 1/4. A stock can be expected to either decline to the trendline and/or horizontally until it intersects the trendline.

Note that the trendline does not connect the lows of 2 7/8. Trends start at the first lows, by definition, but a stock does not start trending higher until after the breakout. The low preceding the breakout is used for trendline purposes, not the absolute low.

Previous minor support was indicated at 3 5/8. However, support at a previous level of congestion in July and August between 3 3/4 and 3 7/8 was a more significant support area than 3 5/8 and is why the stock traded at 3 7/8 instead of 3 5/8. Looking for a pullback to support is elementary. Investors, though, sometimes have to decipher when the appropriate support is indicated.

For eight days following the 4 1/4 minor high GDC traded at 3 7/8. Either the 40% correction, or a pullback to support, were sufficient guidelines to execute buys.

As these low-priced stocks gather speculative fervor, the degree of self-correcting pullback diminishes. After the move to 4 3/4, the stock had only a one day pullback to prior support at 4 1/4. The stock then marked time at 4 3/4 until the issue encountered the trendline connecting the lows of 3 1/4 and 3 7/8. After the stock rose above 4 3/4, it began to rise exponentially.

Skyline (see Figure 3-26) had a persistent decline to the mid-teens during the summer of 1992, finding support at an intraday low of 14 on July 2, exactly 1/8 higher than the stock's low nearly a year earlier on August 15, 1991. Support levels tend to repeat.

After hitting 14 on July 2, the stock began to work its way higher. At first the advance for Skyline was sluggish. The formation during June and July off the 14 lows resembled a symmetrical triangle to some extent, with the stock's move

Figure 3 • 25   General Datacomm Inds. (GDC)

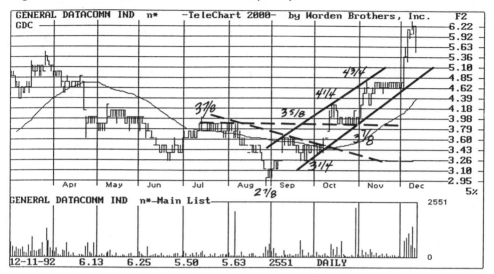

Chart courtesy of TeleChart 2000™ by Worden Brothers, Inc. Used with permission.

Figure 3 • 26   Skyline Corp. (SKY)

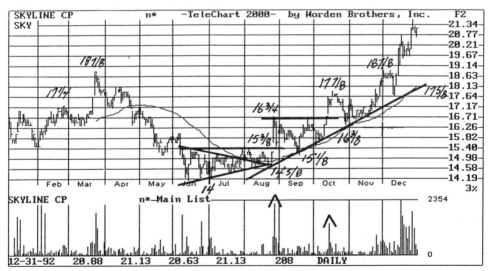

Chart courtesy of TeleChart 2000™ by Worden Brothers, Inc. Used with permission.

to 15 3/8 a breakout from the triangle. In the following two weeks, the stock declined to trade at 14 3/4, the apex of the triangle.

In August the pattern began to resemble an ascending triangle. The leisurely trading price quickly changed, and on August 27 the stock rose sharply higher above 15 to 16 3/4 on very heavy volume.

According to the countermove buying rules, the investor can expect a 40% correction of the move, a return to support, or a return to the trendline. A 40% correction of the move from 14 5/8 to 16 3/4 was 7/8, or a return to 15 7/8. A return to support was a return to 15 3/8.

During the next advance, the stock rose to 16 5/8, but could not move decisively above the earlier high of 16 3/4. Resistance at 16 1/2 defined by the reversal pattern the preceding March and April caused the stock to decline back toward support once again. Instead of declining all the way back to support at 15 3/8 the stock found support at the trendline. The backing and filling took the form of an ascending triangle.

In the week ending October 16 Skyline skyrocketed to new highs, to 17 7/8. A 40% correction of the move, a pullback to support, and the trendline, all coincided nicely at 16 3/4, and positions could be taken.

On the next move during the last week in November, the stock advanced to 18 7/8. During the subsequent dull reaction, the stock did decline back to support at 17 7/8, but did not linger. Speculation was heating up.

During the advance over 20 the week ending December 17, volume soared to the highest level of the year. Buying became feverish. The trend was becoming out of control. Some pullback occurred, but not to any level of support.

As a stock becomes more speculative, and either the issue does not stay long at support and/or begins to move up and away from support, the trend loses its self-correcting feature. When a trend begins to move nearly straight up, investors should see warning signals. Buyers of low-priced stocks aim to speculate when the trend is orderly, self-correcting, when time and space are in balance, but not when the trend becomes speculative and the stocks move up exponentially.

A stock can bottom in any number of ways, breakouts can develop in any number of ways, the countermove or dull reaction can appear in any number of ways. By learning what variations to expect, what to buy and when, an investor can significantly improve the risk/reward ratio. In buying low-priced and depressed stocks, timing is everything.

Setting Stops

Buying depressed and low-priced stocks is definitely bottom fishing, and bottom fishing can be hazardous at best. Investors will not know for a while if they have bought at the bottom. Stocks are depressed for good reasons, and many a depressed stock ends up declining another 50–60–70%, or becomes worthless.

The first thing to decide after making a commitment is when to get out. Investors must decide where to set the stop-loss point.

Many investors set stop-loss orders at a percentage below current prices, say 10%. In buying depressed stocks, any stop loss is better than none. Prior minor lows and sometimes prior highs are better places to set stop losses.

Both the prior minor lows and highs represent some degree of trading concentration in the stock. They have been reversal points and thus support and resistance levels. The stop loss should be set at a computed percentage below those levels.

Brunswick (see Figure 3-27) had all the earmarks of a buy. The trendline was broken during the week ending September 4, and purchases could have been made as the stock crossed 13, or in the following minor pullback at 12 5/8.

Stops would be set a certain point under the low of 12 1/4. How far a stop should be set depends on the measure of volatility, such as beta. The higher the beta, the greater the latitude the investor should give the stock. Brunswick had a high beta of 2.00. If stops are set at 5% under a normal issue, a stop of 10% below the low should be set for Brunswick, or at 11.

Figure 3 • 27   Brunswick Corp. (BC)

Chart courtesy of TeleChart 2000™ by Worden Brothers, Inc. Used with permission.

When the issue advanced to 14 1/8, the conservative investor could move up the stop because another high had been achieved. The low preceding the move to 14 1/8 was the 12 5/8 of September 8. The stop could be raised to 11 3/8.

Stops should not be set too tight. Brunswick drifted lower during early October, and too tight of a stop may have been taken out.

A reasonable buying point for Hancock Fabrics (see Figure 3-28) would have been around 16 in mid-January. The stock was well depressed, down nearly 50%, had moved upward in a minor zigzag bullish wave, and had corrected to support. The stop-loss point for Hancock would be based on its beta of 1.14, or at 5. 7% under its low of 15 1/2 or 14 5/8.

After purchase the stock acted nicely, moving to 19, when it suddenly fell. During the decline the stock dropped to 14 5/8 and the stop order was executed.

A stop certainly could have been put in under the earlier 14 1/4. The decline to the 14 5/8 level might have just been another test of the lows; however, investors must draw the line over how much capital they will risk.

For setting stops, a minor low is well marked. Sometimes it is not. In textbooks on technical analysis the lows always seem to be well marked. In practice the lows do not always jump out. A variety of guidelines or "rules" can help identify the right stop-loss points.

Figure 3 • 28 Hancock Fabrics Inc. (HKF)

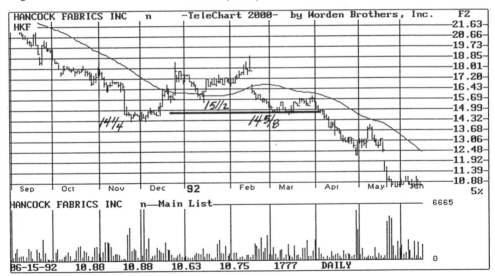

Chart courtesy of TeleChart 2000™ by Worden Brothers, Inc. Used with permission.

One rule is that after a stock has traded higher for three days—that is, the three-day price range is above the high of the daily price range that contained the low—that low can be considered the minor low.

Another rule is that when a stock moves to a new high by 3%, a preceding minor low can be established. Another rule is to set the minor low as the low point in the three to five days preceding the breakout.

As a general guideline, after a stock has broken out and moved to new highs on heavy volume, use the preceding minor low to set stops. Aggressive investors can raise stops whenever a stock again moves to a new high.

Knowing When It Is Too Late To Buy

Low-priced and depressed stocks can rise at great speed after the stock begins to build some steam. Low-priced stocks can very quickly move from oversold to overbought, and investors can end up in the position of having bought too late. Resistance theory can help explain and predict how far and how fast a stock moves and when it becomes too late to buy.

For Portland General (see Figure 3-29), the $16 price level is the pivot point, first as support and then as resistance.

First 16 1/2 was support in January 1991. PGN rallied to a high of 18 7/8 by April 17, entering a trading range that would turn out to be distribution.

From those highs Portland General began to give ground grudgingly. The stock rallied off the lows of 16 1/2 in July and 16 3/8 in September. Bulls kept losing ground. The entire formation from June through September took on the pattern of a descending triangle.

The last ditch rally of late September soon gave way to weakness, with the stock falling to 16 1/2 again. This time support gave way and a panic was on. In just two days, the stock dropped from over 16 to less than 14.

As do many low-priced issues, Portland General rallied nicely as tax-selling pressures began to abate. After just a few days of advances, the stock was off its lows and back up to more than 16. The speed at which a stock rebounds is in part defined by overhead supply or resistance. PGN traded between 14 and 16 for only two days. Relatively little stock was traded on October 22, with the stock dropping to under 15. On October 23 volume exploded as the stock dropped to 13 1/2, and most of the trades probably occurred around the lows. In terms of activity, probably not a lot of stock traded between 14 and 16. The price level was thin, and when PGN was heading back up, not a lot of resistance developed.

At 16 1/2, on the other hand, heavy resistance could be expected. The stock quickly fell back the following week. Not for another six months was Portland General able to finally push above 16 1/2.

Figure 3 • 29   Portland General (PGN)

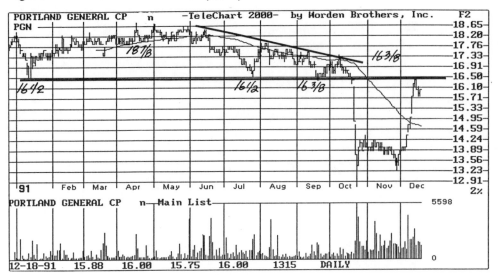

Chart courtesy of TeleChart 2000™ by Worden Brothers, Inc. Used with permission.

Most stocks do not move up as sharply as Portland General, because there is not a panic, but the principles are similar. When a stock rebounds back into resistance, it is not a time an investor wants to buy. Buy at support. Avoid the stock at resistance.

Additional Buying Guidelines

Other guidelines indicate when it is too late to buy. The number of advance/decline sequences or zigzags a stock has completed can be an interesting guideline. The breakout is the signal to buy. The following dull reaction is a time to buy. The dull reaction following the next minor high is a second chance to buy.

After the stock has advanced in three waves in the direction of the intermediate swing, it is getting too late to buy. While this is a somewhat arbitrary number, counting the zigzags will limit buying "high."

Kroger (see Figure 3-30) had an important bottom in 1990 at around $10 a share, and in August 1992 the stock dropped back into that support area. Support levels tend to repeat.

From a panic low of 11 1/4 the stock rebounded to 13, where it encountered resistance. Typically, the stock again began to sag and declined back to 11 3/8.

Figure 3 • 30   Kroger Co. (KR)

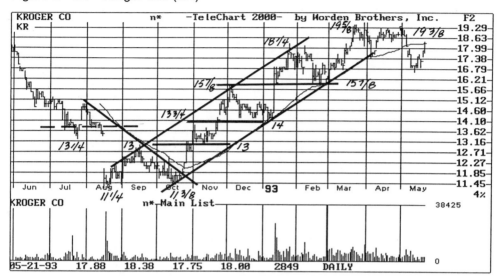

Chart courtesy of TeleChart 2000™ by Worden Brothers, Inc. Used with permission.

The next rally was stronger. The stock broke out above a declining trendline in rising past 12. The stock also broke out from its double bottom and advanced past 13. Volume expanded when the stock rose above 13. Supply from the resistance level at just under 14 came on the market. After hitting 13 7/8, Kroger bided time for two weeks right above support at 13, affording a typical dull reaction buying opportunity.

The next advance carried the issue to a December 4 high of 15 7/8, where it underwent another dull reaction, declining to support at 14, just 1/4 above the previous high. Buying could once again be done between 14 1/4 and 14 3/4.

Kroger had a very strong breakout in moving to yet another high. Wall Street was catching on. Following a high at 18 1/4, it fell back to support. The exact low of the dull reaction was 15 7/8, the exact high of the previous advance.

Under the "buy only twice" rule, should buying still be done?

In the move from the October low of 11 3/8, how many advance/decline sequences had Kroger completed? More to the point, was the move to 15 7/8 of December 4 one advance, or two?

Looking at the overall pattern from the lows of 11 3/8 relative to subsequent trend development, such as pullbacks to the trendline, lends credence to the argument that the October 16 low–December 4 high is one piece.

On the other hand, the move to the November 3 high of 13 3/4 was made up of two minor advances, a dull pullback followed by a breakout on November 20 with the stock moving up to 15 7/8.

Many low-priced stocks tend to have a two-piece action similar to Kroger's October 19–November 3–December 4 advance. Early trend action tends to be "stunted" by resistance, such as that represented by the patterns in July, so the stock cannot fully extend in an intermediate advance or would be expected under subsequent trend development.

A further argument could be made that the move started from the absolute low of August 18 of 11 1/4. However, the bullish trend clearly did not start until the October 16 low of 11 3/8.

Only in textbooks and magazine articles about technical analysis the world perfect. In practice, classification of the trend requires some judgment.

In using the "buy only twice" rule, I regard the move from 11 3/8 to 15 7/8 as two moves. An investor could buy on the reaction to 14 in January following the peak at 15 7/8, but not on the following reaction.

The "buy only twice rule" is not designed to scalp points, buy dips, sell rallies. The rule exists to tell the investor when the best part of the trend has passed. The best buying opportunities are when a trend is getting under way, when the stock is starting its advance.

By the time Kroger had its explosive rise on January 13, the best buying opportunities were gone. At 18 the stock began to encounter serious resistance, the point where the decline had started in earnest, and that is never a favorable place to buy.

Prudent Rule

The last buying guideline is based on what can be expected from normal moves in stock prices over six months. For instance, a $5 stock over a six-month period can be expected to move about 25%; a $10 stock can be expected to move about 20%, a $20 stock 15%, and so on.

If an investor is thinking about buying a stock priced at $20, then buying after the stock has moved 15% higher following the breakout, is buying late in the move.

While low-priced and depressed stocks can achieve some very impressive gains, stocks do move in spurts. If a series of waves has carried the issue beyond the percentage cutoff, wait for the next intermediate correction. The prudent rule tells you that you have missed the prime time to buy.

When To Sell

When to sell is the toughy. Having bought right, how does an investor sell right?

Technical analysis has a host of rules for selling. "Trendlines are made to be broken," goes one saying. In order to put that seemingly logical and simple rule into practice, investors must decide which trendline breaks are significant.

Part of the decision to sell depends on the nature of the stock. If it is a relatively speculative stock, that is, one with a limited capitalization, with fundamentals showing characteristics of cyclicals, with a limited price range during the past couple of years between 5 and 10, a basically low-grade issue, chances are the stock will remain speculative and investors should be prepared to take gains quickly. Selling too soon will be better than selling too late.

The more-speculative stocks tend to flourish for brief periods, with a brief 2-, 3-, or 4-month run up. The advance may start slowly, then quickly show a pickup in momentum as the buying in the stock becomes more speculative. The quick-to-run rules of technical analysis, like the breaking of the trendlines and close progressive stops, are most applicable for the speculative types of stocks.

For stocks that are not only low-priced, but also truly depressed, the fallen blue chips, such as Goodyear, the payoff is likely to take two, three, or more years.

The best gains come from fallen blue chips, as Graham said, that are speculative when purchased, such as Chrysler on February 12, 1991. Moody's had dropped its rating on Chrysler debt to junk levels, and the stock was selling at 10 5/8. Investors in such stock should wait until the stock comes full circle, such as on September 8, 1993, when Moody's raised the ratings back to Investment Grade, and the stock sold at 42 3/8. Chrysler may not necessarily be a sale, but close watch should be kept on any support levels failures.

With such potential, investors don't want to sell every time some trendline is broken. With potential gains of 100%, 200%, 300%, and higher, investors do not want to be caught as a sold-out bull. If technical analysis is used properly to buy the right stocks at the right price, a fair share of winners will be the reward for those who let their profits run.

Relationship Between Fundamental & Technical Analysis

As with the three trends of the market, trends have three phases that coincide with fundamentals.

Robert Rhea in *The Dow Theory* listed the bear market phases as:

1. The first represents the abandonment of the hopes upon which stocks were purchased at inflated prices;
2. The second reflects selling due to decreased business and earnings;
3. The third is caused by distress selling of sound securities, regardless of the value, by those who must find a cash market for at least a portion of their assets.

Bull market phases were described by Rhea as follows:

1. The first is represented by reviving confidence in the future of business;
2. The second is the response of stock prices to the known improvement in corporate earnings;
3. The third is the period when speculation is rampant and inflation apparent—a period when stocks are advanced on hopes and expectations.

Finding Winners emphasizes the third phase of a bear trend: distress selling of securities regardless of value. While many of the securities under review are not exactly sound, the selling is at distress prices. During the subsequent first phase of a bull trend, stocks advance reflecting some improvement in confidence, advancing in some instances on relief that the company will not be going out of business.

In terms of fundamentals, the third phase of a bear decline and the first phase of a bull advance are characterized by a lack of conviction. First, fundamentals may be lacking. With depressed stocks the financial position has taken such a beating that many traditional measures of fundamental analysis are not applicable. Uncertainty regarding the fundamentals with depressed stock can be very high.

Second, research may be lacking. Wall Street tends to be biased toward the buy side. Brokerage house "buy" recommendations on depressed stocks are likely to be few. Fundamental analysis is usually directed toward the stocks with good stories. Stocks down on their luck just don't make good copy. Fundamental analysis on truly depressed stocks is largely lacking. Few Chartered Financial Analysts (CFAs) are writing up fancy reports on them.

The period when a stock moves from the distress selling associated with a major bearish decline to the start of a rebound is not easy to discern from the fundamentals. Stocks tend to move into the first bull phase not due to optimism or an increase in reasons to buy, but just due to the lack of any further negative news. The selling has run its course. All those who held stock for sale have sold.

With few sellers remaining, a lot of buying is not required to tilt the balance toward a rebound. Just the absence of distress selling in a deeply oversold market will allow those few purchases to push the stock higher.

Those few purchases may come from insiders, may come from long-term investors who are buying at support, may come from investors who just like to buy cheap and who like to buy stocks that are down 90%, or may come from speculators priming the pump to see if they can start a rally. Depressed stocks are bought for any number of reasons. In a well-liquidated market just a little conviction can cause some buoyancy in the stock.

Lacking any direction from fundamentals, the clue that investors will be looking for is some incremental uptick in buying—or technical analysis. Technical analysis is how the market reacts to a budding rally. At the key pivotal points, as the final phases of distribution give way to accumulation, the only guideline for individual investors with low-priced and depressed stocks is technical analysis.

"A Great Deal More Can be Known Than Can be Proved"

There are some interesting trends in academia to define technical analysis. Until recently the trend in academia and in the financial industry to some extent as well, has been an effort to debunk technical analysis. "Random Walk" was the operative word. A very lively and down-to-earth discussion of technical analysis, the aforementioned book by Burton G. Malkiel, *A Random Walk Down Wall Street*, takes technical analysis to task.

A *Journal of Finance* article of December 1992, "Simple Technical Trading Rules and the Stochastic Properties of Stock Returns," may indicate a change in academia. The authors tested different versions of several trading methods—moving averages and trading-range breakouts.

The moving average test was designed to measure the effects of the price of the Dow Jones Industrial Average moving above or below different moving averages, including the 200-day moving average. The results were positive and significant.

The trading-range breakout test was a version of the support and resistance concept, with the authors using recent highs as resistance and recent lows as support. The test measured the significance of prices moving above or below the highs or lows. The results were positive, implying the ability to make forecasts of significance.

While in both test cases the authors were testing trading rules, they were in effect testing for the existence of trend. They showed that the very essence of technical analysis, that future prices can be forecasted by past price patterns, is valid.

Most readers of *Finding Winners* are not traders. Neither am I. However, recent research suggests that trends can be classified, and that it is possible, even practical, to be on the right side of the trend, should be of importance to any investor. With even the academic community beginning to accept the notion that stocks move in trends, the most skeptical of investors who seek to find winners cannot afford to overlook the importance of technical analysis.

· 4 ·

The January Effect

An important variation of technical analysis for buyers of depressed, low-priced stocks is the January Effect—the tendency of stocks to provide above-average returns in January. While the January Effect is one of the shortest Chapters in *Finding Winners*, the performance of low-priced stocks in the month of January is so strong that the January Effect demands separate coverage. The January Effect is one of the most important determining factors in finding winners among depressed, low-priced stocks.

The January Effect is a form of seasonality in the stock market. Studies on seasonality have been going on for more than 50 years. Another form of seasonality is the "turn-of-the-month" effect, which suggests that returns are abnormally high the last trading day of the month and the first three days of the following month.

The "day-of-the-week" effect suggests that the market has a tendency to decline on Mondays and gain in strength toward the end of the week.

The "time-of-day" effect shows different returns depending on the time of day. The "holiday" effect suggests above-average returns prior to market holidays.

None of the other seasonalities are as strong, or as much debated, as the January Effect. The presence of a January Effect in the stock market was discussed and debated as early as the 1930s. Dozens of papers have been written on the subject. A book, *The Incredible January Effect: The Stock Market's Unsolved Mystery* (Joseph Lakonishok and R.A. Haugen, Dow Jones Irwin) was published in 1988.

Increasing evidence shows that certain types of stocks, specifically depressed and low-priced stocks, exhibit the strongest January Effect. In "Does the Stock Market Overreact?", (*Journal of Finance*, July 1985) authors De Bondt and Thaler first establish that portfolios of past losers consistently outperform past winners by an average of more than 24.6%. They go on to show that nearly all the "excess" returns of the losers occurred during January (see Figure 4-1).

Figure 4 • 1   January Returns: Losers versus Winners

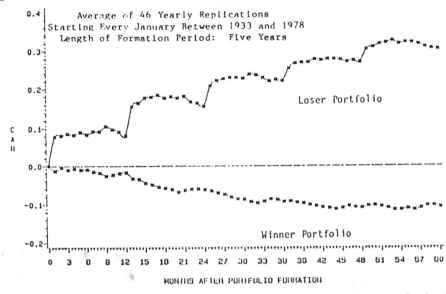

Figure 3. Cumulative Average Residuals for Winner and Loser Portfolios of 35 Stocks (1–60 months into the test period)

Source: *The Journal of Finance*, Vol. XL, No. 3, July 1985. Used with permission.

The January Effect is so strong that it was evident as late as five Januaries after the initial portfolio formation.

In a follow-up paper, aptly titled "Further Evidence On Investors' Overreaction and Stock Market Seasonality," De Bondt and Thaler further explored the relationship between superior returns from losing portfolios and the January Effect.

The authors not only found, using 5-year test periods, that losers outperformed winners by an average of 31.9%, but confirmed that long-term winners perform worse and long-term losers perform better following down market years. For losers, the January Effect is significantly more pronounced following years of market decline.

In summary, the work of De Bondt and Thaler appears to be some of the most convincing in demonstrating that portfolios of losing stocks outperform portfolios of winning stocks, and that the January Effect accounts for nearly all the gains.

The Price Effect

Many of the papers discussing the January Effect reduced it to a small-cap or market-value phenomenon. Some of the studies showed a return of the smaller

Figure 4 • 2 The January Effect–S&P Low-Priced Stock Index 1942 – 1993

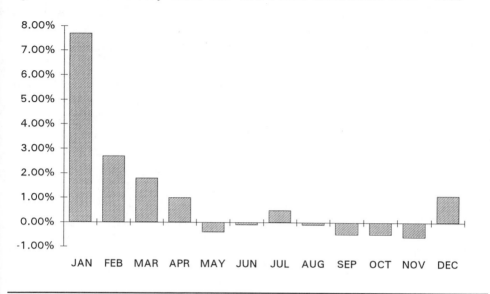

issues over the larger issues of more than 8-to-1. More recent research suggests that the January Effect is not a small-cap effect, but a low-price effect. Several authors found that after adjusting for firm size, the lowest-priced stocks showed the superior returns, and the lower the price, the greater the returns. Findings confirming that the January Effect is primarily a price effect is of prime importance to buyers of low-priced and depressed stocks and is a factor investors familiar with the historical returns of low-priced stocks know only too well (see Figure 4.2).

Historical Performance of Low-Priced Stocks

The S&P Low-Priced Stock Index (LPSI) has been published since 1926. While any index is going to be incomplete in some manner, the LPSI at least provides us with some degree of reference and consistency in understanding the cyclical pormance characteristics of low-priced stocks; the hazards as well as the potentials.

The parameters for the LPSI are stocks under $25. When a stock moves higher, it is a candidate for a change. On the downside, a firm just about has to go out of business in order to cause the common stock to be removed from the LPSI.

The current LPSI is made up of 20 common stocks listed in Table 4-1. The

Index is calculated at the close of the market every Wednesday by taking the market value and dividing by a divisor. On June 30, 1993, the divisor was 72.528.

The S&P Low-Priced Stock Index is truly an index of low-priced stocks. At mid-year 1993 only one stock was over $20, Oak Industries, which recently had a 5-for-1 reverse stock split. Eight issues sold for between $10 and $20 and 11 sold for less than $10. Excluding Oak, the average price was less than $8.875.

Few investment-grade issues are on the list. Only three of the issues had a B+ rating. Two issues were rated B, five were rated B-, and six were rated C.

Four were not rated. Not many investors would be anxious to place these issues in their retirement accounts.

On the other hand, the performance of the stocks within the LPSI attests to the fact that the action is in low-priced stocks. During the last 50 years the average annual capital gain of the LPSI has been 9.21%. Over the same time period, the average annual capital gain from the S&P 500 has been 7.24% (see Figure 4-3).

During the last 20 years, however, the LPSI has really kicked in, advancing on average 14.5% per year, compared to 7.92% for the S&P 500.

Table 4 • 1   Stocks in the S&P Low-Priced Stock Index

	Price 6-30-93	S&P Rating	Market
Anacomp	2 7/8	B-	NY
Champion Enterprises	16 1/8	B	NY
Consolidated Freightways	16	B-	NY
Cray Computer	3	NR	NMS
Fedders	4 7/8	C	NY
Genesco	7 3/4	B-	NY
GenRad	3 1/2	C	NY
Hillhaven	3 1/2	NR	AS
ICN Pharmaceuticals	10 3/4	C	NY
Kaufman & Broad Home	18 5/8	B+	NY
Merry-Go-Round Enterprises	10 7/8	B+	NY
Navistar Int'l	2 1/2	C	NY
Oak Industries	27	B-	NY
Parker Drilling	6 1/2	C	NY
Publicker Industries	1 3/8	C	NY
Rollins Environmental Serv.	7 3/8	B+	NY
Seagate Technology	15 7/8	B-	NMS
Topps	8 7/8	NR	NMS
Tyco Toys	11 5/8	NR	NY
Wendy's Int'l.	14 5/8	B	NY

Figure 4 • 3   S&P Low-Priced Stock Index—1973 – 1993

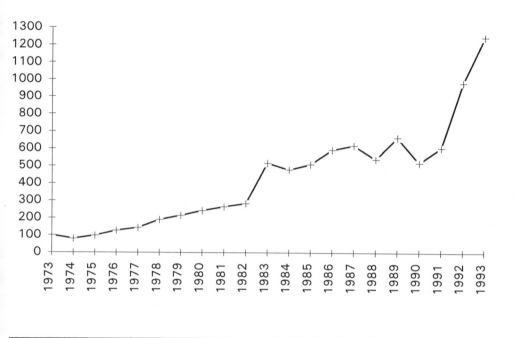

At a time when institutional dominance on Wall Street has grown, the performance of the speculative low-priced stocks, as represented by the LPSI has increased. Either the Standard & Poor's analysts selecting stocks for the LPSI have been very good stock pickers, or the market has been more conducive to advances in low-priced stocks than generally thought.

While the buy-and-hold policy of low-priced stocks has worked out well in past years, providing investors with a return nearly double the overall market, the stocks have been very volatile.

By the very nature of the speculative tone to the stocks, when the market, as measured either by the DJIA or the S&P 500 stubs its toe, the LPSI takes a beating. During market declines, the LPSI decline will be about three times greater than the decline in the overall market.

Table 4-2 lists the decline in low-priced stocks for each year since 1973. In nearly every year there was an annual decline of 10% or more. The average annual decline has been more than 22%.

Table 4 • 2 S&P Low-Priced Stock Index Corrections

Year	Month/ Week		Month/ Week		% Year Decline	% Yr-Yr Decline
1970	1-1	167.0	7-3	95.2	42.98%	
1971	4-4	169.4	11-4	118.6	29.99%	
1972	3-3	162.4	12-2	123.2	24.14%	
1973	1-1	131.2	6-4	84.3	35.72%	
	10-4	106.0	12-4	75.7	28.54%	
1974	3-3	95.1	12-4	53.5	43.69%	
1971-74	4-4-71	169.4	12-4-74	53.5		68.4%
1975	7-3	120.7	12-2	90.8	24.71%	
1976	7-2	141.7	11-2	121.4	14.33%	
1977	7-3	157.9	11-1	133.5	15.45%	
1978	9-2	245.8	11-3	159.9	34.95%	
1979	8-3	247.5	10-4	192.2	28.39%	
1980	2-2	265.6	3-4	190.2	28.39%	
	9-3	284.8	12-2	235.6	17.28%	
1981	6-3	304.5	9-5	221.5	27.26%	
1982	5-2	278.5	8-2	236.1	15.22%	
1981-82	6-3-81	304.5	8-2-82	236.1		22.5%
1983	7-1	608.7	11-2	517.9	14.92%	
1984	1-3	576.2	7-4	399.2	30.72%	
1983-84	7-1	608.7	7-4	399.2		34.4%
1985	7-3	538.6	9-4	467.2	13.26%	
1986	6-3	654.1	8-1	582.2	10.99%	
	8-3	631.7	9-3	527.5	16.50%	
1987	4-2	685.2	5-3	629.7	8.10%	
	8-2	707.6	10-4	403.6	42.96%	
1988	3-4	547.7	5-3	506.1	7.60%	
1989	9-2	746.3	11-4	585.4	21.56%	
1990	1-1	613.0	1-4	542.0	11.58%	
	6-2	612.9	10-3	372.1	39.29%	
1989-90	9-2-89	746.3	10-3-90	372.1		50.1%
1991	11-2	702.3	12-3	635.4	9.53%	
1992	3-4	1053.9	4-2	935.1	11.27%	
	5-13	1018.6	10-1	873.1	14.28%	
				Average	22.67%	43.8%

When a multiyear decline occurred, a bear market in low-priced stocks, such as 1970 – 74, 1981 – 82, 1983 – 84, and 1989 – 90, the average multiyear decline is 43%.

The largest year-to-year decline was the 1971 – 1974 debacle of 68%. The most recent multiyear decline was the period from September 1989 to October 1990, when the LPSI dropped 50%. Generally speaking, the LPSI declines in line with overall major bear markets, but the declines are longer and deeper.

The LPSI tends to correlate better with the Dow Jones Transportation Average, or the NYSE Advance-Decline Line or the NASDAQ, than the major market averages, such as the Dow Jones Industrial Average or the S&P 500. When the newspapers are heralding a new high in the Dow, but the Advance-Decline Line is moving lower, it is usually not a time to be investing in low-priced stocks.

The LPSI also tends to register a far greater setback on a relative percentage basis during declines that are more intermediate or secondary in nature. For instance, during 1992, when the market was characterized by its choppiness, the S&P had several corrections that averaged less than 4%. The LPSI, however, had two declines of more than 12%, and a third decline of about 7%.

In terms of sharpness, the month-to-month declines as they effect low-priced stocks, dollar for dollar, are apt to deliver a greater punch than major bear markets. While the Dow may be down only a few points, any correction that dampens the speculative tone in the market is apt to be felt the greatest in low-priced stocks.

The superior performance returns from buying low-priced stocks are well documented. Investors have a far better opportunity to come up with winners when looking among low-priced stocks.

Since low-priced and depressed stocks are speculative, they will also tend to fall as a group hard and fast. However, the individual investor, who has a good working knowledge of technical analysis, especially support theory and trend analysis, will find timely opportunities in these low-priced stocks and, as we've seen in Figure 4-2, the performance of low-priced stocks in January is extraordinary.

The January Effect Explained

The reasons for the January Effect are widely debated. Tax-loss selling at the end of the year is often mentioned; stocks that are already depressed and low-priced get a further kick from investors looking to take losses to offset any capital gains, as well as to take the loss against ordinary income. These issues, under pressure in tax-selling season, subsequently rebound in a January market void of outside IRS-related pressures.

Window dressing among institutions is another explanation. Money managers liquidate their losers at the end of December so that they do not appear on the books at the end of the quarter. Some argue that positions in the same issues are taken again after the first of the month. So, not only is there a selling effect in December, but a reverse buying effect in January.

The cash-flow theory suggests that both individuals and institutions have new money after the first of the year to invest in stocks; the money is either from bonuses or pension plan contributions.

Additional theories exist. Investors can form their own conclusions from the wealth of available articles. The January Effect is real. It is one of the more powerful anomalies in the stock market, and it is of particular importance when buying low-priced and depressed stocks.

Is The January Effect Practicable?

The debate is not about the existence of a January Effect but about whether investors can exploit it.

Transaction costs can severely limit potential returns. On a percentage basis, the costs of buying and selling low-priced stocks can be quite high.

Of further consideration is the bias in the bid-ask spread in the over-the-counter market. Some evidence suggests that selling in December takes place at the bid, while buying in January takes place at the ask, and that studies using last trade data are overestimating the January Effect. While a market maker can make money on the January Effect, the individual investor may not be able to obtain all the returns suggested by the various studies.

The purpose in discussing the January Effect here is not for short-term trading, such as buying on the last day of the year and selling after the first four days of the next year. Instead, stocks are bought in anticipation of a double or a triple or more increase in price.

Arbitrage or scalping, holding the stocks for a few days or weeks, just for a few points is not of interest here. What is of interest is getting the most advantageous prices and investing at the most advantageous time. The point is to accumulate positions that may be held for several years in order to rack up the profits that are attainable from low-priced and depressed stocks.

Lynch's Sticky Wicket

While those in academia debate the existence of the January Effect and whether it can be useful to the investor, a stock picker of no less caliber than Peter Lynch cuts through the rhetoric in *Beating the Street* (Simon & Schuster, 1993).

He introduces the January Effect in a chapter titled "Art, Science, and Legwork." Lynch states, "In the late fall, which is always when I begin to do my

Barron's homework, annual tax selling by disheartened investors drives the prices of smaller issues to pathetic lows."

In the following paragraph, Lynch continues, "You could make a nice living buying stocks from the low list in November and December during the tax-selling period and then holding them through January, when the prices always seem to rebound. This January Effect, as it is called, is especially powerful with smaller companies, which over the last 60 years have risen 6.86 percent in price in that one month, while stocks in general have risen only 1.6 percent".

Later, Lynch makes further references to the January Effect. In his "Prospecting in Bad News" chapter, he bemoans the fact that the stocks he likes to recommend often get away from him before they appear in *Barron's*: "Here's a tip from the prospectors of year-end anomalies: Act quickly. It doesn't take long for bargain hunters to find the bargains in the stock market these days, and by the time they've finished buying, the stocks aren't bargains anymore. . . . More than once I've identified a likely winner that's been beaten down by the tax sellers in the fall, only to see it soar in price before I could get its name published in *Barron's* two months later."

The January Effect is alive and well. The prime time to buy low-priced and depressed issues is during tax-selling season. The best opportunity for the type of bargains smart investors are looking for among low-priced and depressed stocks is often present in December.

What the January Effect means for the investor in low-priced and depressed stocks is that it is mandatory to be invested by the end of the year. One man's loss will become another man's gain. One man's trash will become another man's treasure. The time to be invested in low-priced and depressed stocks is prior to the January Effect.

The Importance of Technical Analysis

Because the January Effect is so important to success in buying low-priced and depressed stocks, investors must be sure not to be left behind when stocks start to move. Stocks depressed during tax-selling season are extremely oversold, and the speed at which they can rebound cannot be overstressed.

On the other hand, blindly averaging down or trying to guess the bottom in a low-priced stock moving lower during tax-selling season can create instant losses and negate any benefit of the January Effect. Technical analysis becomes of critical importance during the window of opportunity offered by the January Effect because it tells investors when to buy.

Investors must avoid the misfortune of buying too soon, of buying just because the stock has dropped. They must be alert, ready to act at the first sign that tax-selling liquidation has run its course with a tightly-coiled stock poised to surge higher.

The case examples that follow demonstrate the relationship between the January Effect and technical analysis. They illustrate its practicality for the everyday investor. The examples start with stocks that have been winners and look at the route they took in getting to the top. The same principles of technical analysis evident in these case studies surface time and time again.

The January Effect: Case Examples

BancFlorida Financial (BFL)

BancFlorida Financial (see Figure 4-4) was 1992's best performing Big Board issue, up 357.1% for the year. The stock finished the year at 12, up 9 3/8 for the year. One-third of the gain can be attributed to the January Effect.

BancFlorida (BFL), reflecting the plight of the savings and loans (S&Ls), was clearly a depressed stock, down 90% from its all-time high of 25 5/8. Through the early part of the fourth quarter of 1991 the stock drifted lower, but selling quickly picked up as the stock slid to 2 3/8 on October 18 on very heavy volume.

Figure 4 • 4 BancFlorida Financial (BFL)

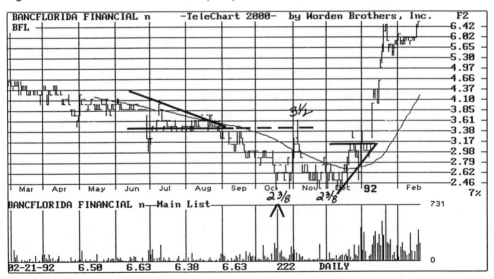

Chart courtesy of TeleChart 2000™ by Worden Brothers, Inc. Used with permission.

The first factor of important technical merit is that the selling panic low of 2 3/8 of October 18 was identical to the stock's low of 2 3/8 of December 31, 1990. Readers of previous Chapters know the importance of previous support levels. In 1991 support for the stock was developing at the same price at which support developed in 1990. Support often develops right around previous support levels. When trying to bottom fish, previous support levels are invaluable.

Resistance, on the other hand, was at 3 1/2. Resistance is defined by a previous level of concentrated trading. The left of the chart shows some of the previous trading range at around 3 1/2. Depressed, low-priced stocks do not spring straight up. They rise to a resistance level, are turned back, then regroup to stage another assault.

On November 1, November 4, and November 5, BFL rallied through its 50-day moving average—a bullish development if taken in the right context—but the stock was moving right into resistance. A stock moving through a moving average is bullish if it is running free and clear. However, when rising right into resistance, especially during tax-selling season, investors have to treat any minor rallies with care, even if they are moving above moving averages. As it was, the stock declined once again to 2 3/8.

By mid-December the 2 3/8 level had been fairly well established, and investors could have bought stock at that price based on support theory. In nine trading days the stock had found support at 2 3/8. Further, BFL was in a trading range—2 3/8 to 2 3/4. On November 29 the issue moved higher, but without volume and follow through. A valid breakout had not occurred.

On December 19 the issue again moved higher, but this time on volume, indicating a valid breakout, and investors could have bought on the breakout.

The advance carried the stock back to resistance at 3 1/2, and BFL stalled for three weeks. The activity took the form of an ascending triangle. In depressed and low-priced stocks, patterns usually do not develop at the lows. However, after a stock has already advanced and is consolidating, a pattern is likely.

What is meant by consolidating? Most investors think of consolidating the gains. Consolidating here reflects a step-up in selling. The most important factor is that consolidating can be expected to develop from identifiable overhead resistance levels.

On January 13 BFL broke out of the pattern on explosive volume. Did the sharp increase in price and heavy volume appear because investors were buying the stock for the January Effect? No. Whenever a stock has successfully breached a level of resistance, it is free and clear until it encounters the next level of resistance.

The January Effect is the interaction of support and resistance levels. A rebounding stock is like a Ping-Pong ball moving between vested interests who want to buy and vested interests who want to sell. By looking at previous trading ranges, an investor can see where the vested interests lie.

When an issue lazily drifts lower, being marked down in price without much volume, not a lot of resistance is evident. When the tax-selling issues start to come off the bottom, they can travel a considerable distance before encountering resistance of any degree. What makes technical analysis useful and practical that you can predict likely stock price action as the stock interacts with these various pockets of vested interests.

Moves for a stock tend to end on high volume. Just like BFL bottomed out on October 18 on very high volume, BFL topped out on January 22 at 6 1/2 on very high volume. High volume on a breakout is bullish. High volume after a move is well underway has to be viewed cautiously since high volume is a characteristic of the end of the move.

WMS Industries (WMS)

The best performer in 1991 was WMS Industries (see Figure 4-5), up 669%. At its low of 3 1/4 on January 7, 1990, the stock was down about 80% from its highs,

Figure 4 • 5   WMS Industries (WMS)

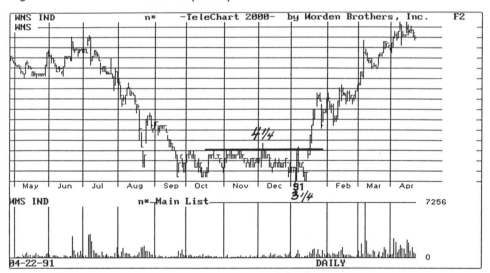

so it certainly qualified as a low-priced, depressed stock. From October through December 1990, the stock appeared trendless, never closing higher than 4 1/4, selling off to 3 1/4 at the beginning of January 1991.

During the week ending January 18, 1991, two important developments occurred. First, the lows of January 7 were tested and held, and second, the stock then broke out above 4 1/4. The trend was bullish, and WMS was on its way to close out the year at 27 7/8, up 24 1/4 points.

Is this discussion too technical for average investors? Investors who expect stocks to deliver gains of 100%+ cannot wait until a stock appears on some analyst's buy list. A stock must be bought when the trend begins to point higher. If the stock is moving up within the January Effect, investors cannot hesitate after the technicals signal a buy.

Allied Products (ADP)

The leader through the first six months of 1993 was Allied Products (see Figure 4-6). From the end of December 1992 through June 30, 1993, Allied Products was up 412.5%, up 12 3/8, from 3 to 15 3/8. This diversified manufacturer got off to a good start with the January Effect.

Figure 4 • 6   Allied Products (ADP)

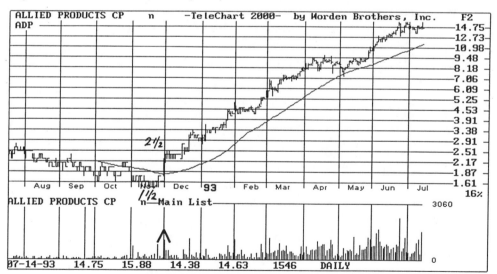

Chart courtesy of TeleChart 2000™ by Worden Brothers, Inc. Used with permission.

Allied Products, through November 31, 1992, had been drifting steadily lower through much of the year. Indeed, Allied Products had been drifting lower for several years. The high in the stock has been 45 1/2 before a series of losses had turned Allied Products into a real depressed stock.

Through most of the fourth quarter of 1992, the stock just drifted. During a rally the week of October 26, the stock crossed the 50-day moving average by rising above 2, but volume was lacking. The stock resumed its decline. For the next three weeks, it traded between 1 1/2 and 1 3/4.

On November 31, the stock broke sharply higher rising to 2 1/2. Volume was heavy; more than 105,000 shares were traded, more than five times the average daily volume of less than 20,000 shares. The stock hesitated for a week, with volume dropping sharply. Then on December 16 it broke sharply higher again.

The trend was obviously bullish by that point, and Allied Products was on its way to being not only the leading issue for the first quarter of 1993, rising 162.5% to 7 7/8, but also the leader for the second quarter, rising 95.2% to 15 3/8. Measured by the November lows, the gain was 683.3%

Did investors have any idea that—as with BancFlorida and WMS Industries—Allied Products was to be the NYSE's leading issue through the first six months of the year? No. Although studies and experience have shown that the potential gain is related to the degree to which a stock is depressed, investors really cannot foresee the magnitude of the coming advance.

However, technical analysis can tell us what, where, and when to buy. Allied Products was depressed, was low-priced, and showed a very decisive breakout on November 31, 1992. According to the standard buying rules of technical analysis, positions can be taken on the dull reaction following a breakout, and buying during the week ended December 11 at 2 1/4 to 2 3/8 was warranted.

Conclusion

The January Effect is alive and well and is one of the more important buying opportunities for investors, especially for those interested in buying low-priced and depressed stocks. The January Effect clearly can also be exploited by the individual investor, not for in-and-out trading, but for taking positions in stocks that have the potential to provide gains substantially more than implied by some trading rule. To capture the big returns available in low-priced and depressed stocks, timing is everything.

Section II

CASE STUDIES

· 5 ·

1993 Winners

During the first half of 1993, the stock market was grudgingly, but persistently, bullish. I say "grudgingly" because money managers and average investors alike were skittish on the market. "Values are scarce," they would say. "P/Es are too high, yields are too low," they complained. As indicated (see Figure 5-1) on the American Association of Individual Investors AAII Investment Sentiment Survey (*AAII Journal*, September 1993), investors were bullish at the start of 1993, but turned

Figure 5 • 1   AAII Investment Sentiment Survey

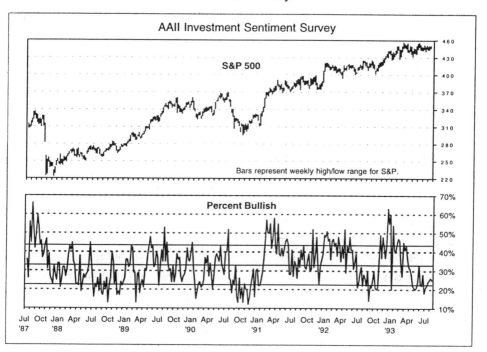

increasingly cautious as the year went on. In spite of a so-so stock market, low-priced stocks saw plenty of action.

During the first quarter of 1993, the S&P gained 3.66%. The 10 stocks showing the best gains averaged 92%. Of those 10 stocks, 7 were priced under $7 per share. As usual, the best gains stemmed from the lowest-priced stocks (see Table 5-1 below).

During the second quarter the market eased lower, with the S&P 500 down

Table 5 • 1   1993 1st-Quarter Winners

	Price ($) 3/31/93	Price ($) 12/31/92	% Change
Allied Products	7.875	3.000	162.5
Western Co. of NA	12.500	5.750	117.4
ICN Pharmaceutical	12.750	6.500	96.2
National-Standard	6.000	3.125	92.0
Callaway Golf	31.500	34.750	81.3
Weirton Steel	6.625	18.000	76.7
General Datacomm	11.250	6.375	76.5
Tesoro Petroleum	5.250	3.000	75.0
Elcor	31.500	18.000	75.0
United Inns	4.125	2.375	73.7
Average		13.56	92.6
w/o Callaway		7.34	93.8

Table 5 • 2   1993 2nd-Quarter Winners

	Price ($) 6/31/93	Price ($) 3/31/93	% Change
Allied Products	15.375	7.875	95.2
Mitel	4.375	2.250	94.4
HMO America	40.750	21.750	87.4
Damon	22.625	12.500	81.0
EMC	22.375	24.657	79.9
Pioneer Financial	8.875	5.250	69.0
Bolt Beranek	8.000	4.750	68.4
Sahara Casino	5.875	3.250	67.9
Standard Brands Paint	3.750	2.250	66.7
Oak Industries	27.000	3.250	66.2
Average		8.80	77.6

1.02%. Although a drifting market affected the gains of the top 10, the average gain among them was still 77.61% (see Table 5.2). Not surprisingly, 7 out of the 10 stocks were priced under $8 per share.

For the entire six months 7 of the best 10 were from the first two lists. As in the first quarter, Callaway Golf was the highest-priced stock on the list, with a beginning price of $34.75. If Callaway is taken out, the average price of the re-

Table 5 • 3   1993 1st-Half Winners

	Price ($) 6/31/93	Price ($) 12/31/92	% Change
Allied Products	15.375	3.000	412.5
National-Standard	9.125	3.125	192.0
Western Co. of NA	15.875	5.750	176.1
Callaway Golf	42.000	34.750	141.7
Weirton Steel	8.750	3.750	133.3
General Datacomm	14.500	6.375	127.5
Oak Industries	27.000	2.375	127.4
Wheeling Pittsburgh	12.750	5.750	121.7
Tejas Gas	47.500	21.594	120.1
Lifetime Corp.	31.625	14.750	114.4
	Average	16.12	166.6
	w/o Callaway	7.38	169.4

Table 5 • 4   1993 Winners

	Price ($) 12/31/92	Price ($) 12/31/93	% Change
Allied Products	3.000	12.500	316.7
United Inns	2.375	7.875	231.6
First USA	23.250	35.750	207.5
Callaway Golf	34.750	53.375	207.2
Wheeling Pittsburgh	5.750	17.125	197.8
Galoob Toys	3.250	9.375	188.5
Pioneer Toys	4.875	14.000	187.2
Prime Hospitality	2.250	6.375	183.3
EMC	23.750	16.500	177.9
Humana	20.500	17.750	177.1
	Average	12.375	207.5

maining nine stocks is $7.38. Seven of those stocks were priced under $7 (see Table 5.3 above).

For the full year, the average price of the 10 top gainers was $12.375, for an average gain of 207%. Five out of the 10 stocks were under $5. The top two gainers were priced at $3 and $2.375.

This Chapter reviews some of the issues that made the best gains. The same technical analysis principles discussed earlier are evident among the 1993 winners.

Allied Products Corp. (ADP)

Allied Products, like many low-priced stocks, started the year out with a bang via the January Effect (see commentary and Figure 4-6 on page 111 in Chapter 4).

Western Company of North America (WSN)

Western Company (see Figure 5-2) was already in a major bull trend dating back to mid-1992 and was trading at support at 4 1/2 in the last quarter of 1992. To start off 1993, the stock had a very nice advance on January 22, rising out of a four-month consolidation to 7 3/8 on a large increase in volume. Purchases on

Figure 5 • 2   Western Company of North America (WSN)

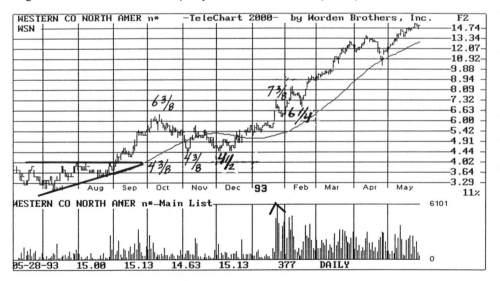

Chart courtesy of TeleChart 2000™ by Worden Brothers, Inc. Used by permission.

the pullback at support, at 6 1/4 – 6 1/2, the week of January 29, could be expected. Following the breakout, the issue would eventually rise to 19 1/4.

Consider the lows of the consolidation, 4 3/8 – 4 1/2 in November and December 1992. Where did they come from?

In mid-1992, Western was rising off its lows. The formation was an ascending triangle, with a series of rising lows, yet a horizontal top line formed at about 4. When Western broke out the week ending September 11, it signaled the start of Western's major bull trend. The previous level of resistance, 4 – 4 1/4, would become support during a later correction. Those who did not buy on the breakout could have bought at those same prices in November and December 1992.

National-Standard Co. (NSD)

National-Standard was a most-depressed stock. From a high of 48 1/4 in 1972, the stock had persistently dropped until it bottomed out at 1 in 1991, a decline of 97.9%, over nearly 20 years. The markets for the firm's wire and other metal products have not been sources for growth.

While 1993 was a banner year, with the stock finishing up the six months ending June 31 at 9 1/8, consider how the trend unfolded at the start of the year.

Figure 5 • 3   National-Standard Co. (NSD)

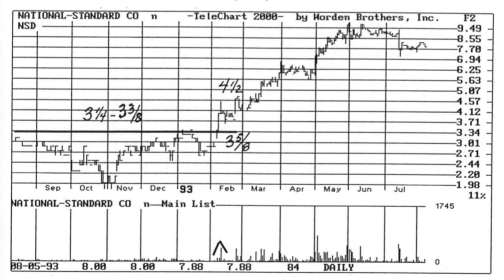

Chart courtesy of TeleChart 2000™ by Worden Brothers, Inc. Used with permission.

The stock was in an established uptrend going into December, but then the trend exploded, driving the issue sharply higher. The 1991 high was 3 1/4. The 1992 high was 3 3/8. Moving past resistance sparked the upsurge in January. Investors could have bought on the dull pullback under 4 in mid-February.

Callaway Golf (ELY)

Callaway Golf was not a low-priced stock. The figures in the chart reflect a 2-for-1 stock split. Nonetheless, note the beautiful self-correcting trendline as it unfolds in nearly straight-line fashion (see Figure 5-4).

Weirton Steel (WS)

Weirton Steel (see Figure 5-5) was listed on the NYSE in June 1989, and it was all downhill for awhile. From a high of 15 3/8 Weirton Steel slid until hitting 3 1/4 in December 1991.

Like many secondary, low-priced stocks, Weirton can lose its gains as quickly as they developed. The stock nearly doubled, from 3 1/4 in December 1991 to

Figure 5 • 4   Callaway Golf (ELY)

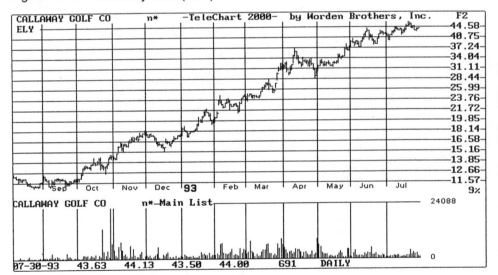

Chart courtesy of TeleChart 2000™ by Worden Brothers, Inc. Used with permission.

6 3/8 in May of 1992, then proceeded to lose all the gains as the stock slid back to 3 3/8 by December 1992.

The first advance off the lows for a depressed stock is not sustained due to overlaying resistance levels. Important resistance for Weirton was present at 6 3/8. These stocks have a better time attacking resistance the second time around.

Following the December 1992 lows of 3 3/8, Weirton Steel advanced in the first couple of months of 1993 back to that resistance level at 6 3/8. Note the high volume at the end of the move in February, reflecting the resistance. The stock then moved higher to close at 7 1/4 on March 12. The stock had surpassed the 1992 resistance level, although not decisively.

The resistance during 1992 was a top. The resistance during 1993 turned out to be a consolidation. Can an investor tell in advance? No. The trend must play out.

In 1992 the formation was a top as the stock broke down with the new lows. In 1993, the stock reacted to 6 1/4 and bounced off those lows for four weeks. The stock was picking up support at the 1992 highs of 6 3/8.

Look at the explosion as the stock broke out and clearly cleared resis- tance. Weirton's advance to 7 1/4 put it on the 10 best list for the first quarter. Weirton's second-quarter advance to 10 put it on the 10 best second-quarter list.

Figure 5 • 5   Weirton Steel (WS)

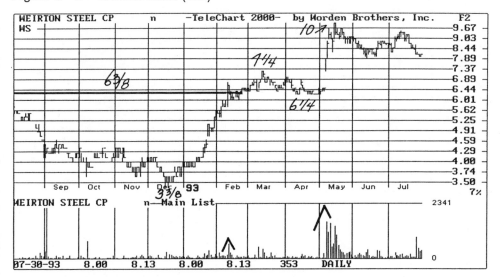

Chart courtesy of TeleChart 2000™ by Worden Brothers, Inc. Used with permission.

Wheeling Pittsburgh Corp. (WHX)

Wheeling Pittsburgh was another steel stock that made the first-half list. The company emerged from six years of bankruptcy proceedings on January 3, 1991. The price on the last day of trading in the old stock was at 3 7/8.

The new stock initially traded on a "when-issued" basis between 7 1/4 and 8. After a high of 13 1/4 in May 1991, the stock proceeded to fall to 3 1/4 by September of 1992 (see Figure 5-6).

During September and October 1992 the stock traded at 3 1/4 several times, marking the lows, in support, of a trading range. On November 12 the stock broke out to 4 7/8 on good volume. Buying on the dull return to 4 1/8 the week of November 20 was in order.

For nearly nine months Wheeling Pittsburgh traded along in textbook self-correcting trend fashion. The breakdown of support the week of July 25, 1993 suggested that the move was over.

General Datacomm Ind. (GDC)

General Datacomm had a beautiful self-correcting zigzag trend from late 1992, as if the stock was walking up a set of stairs. By 1993 the issue had already eaten

Figure 5 • 6   Wheeling Pittsburgh Corp. (WHX)

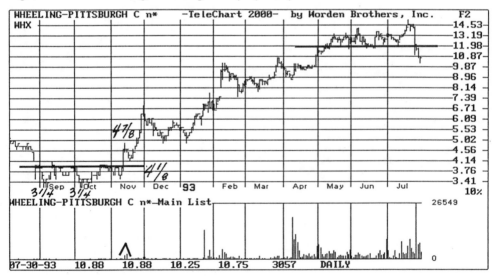

Chart courtesy of TeleChart 2000™ by Worden Brothers, Inc. Used with permission.

up overhanging resistance and was trending higher in very predictable fashion.

A "surprise" of lower-than-expected earnings changed the picture quickly. On July 8 General Datacomm said that earnings would be below estimates of $0.10 – $0.13. The stock fell 3 1/8 to 10 1/4 in a panic.

However, during July General Datacomm started to form a pattern resembling a symmetrical triangle at the lows that formed at support at 10 (see Figure 5-7).

Oak Industries (OAK)

Oak finished up June 1993 at 27. Oak had started the year at 2 3/8. Not only had the issue advanced nicely, a 1-for-5 reverse stock split had taken place (see Figure 5-8).

The stock had been drifting, and drifting, and drifting. When it moved up on December 2, 1992 from 1 1/2 to 1 7/8, the issue rose above a tight eight-week range of trading at 1 1/2 and 1 5/8; it also broke above its downtrend.

Note the slight pullback to support at 1 5/8 on December 14 and 15, 1992. While more money is lost trying to sell at the "top eight" and buy at the "bottom eight," an "eight" was appropriate for Oak Industries.

Figure 5 • 7   General Datacomm Ind. (GDC)

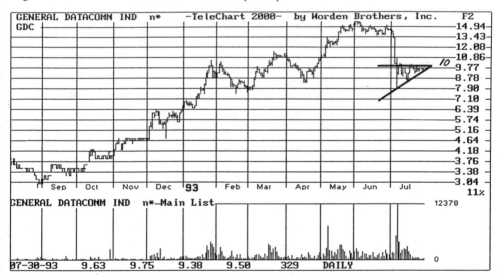

Chart courtesy of TeleChart 2000™ by Worden Brothers, Inc. Used with permission.

Figure 5 • 8   Oak Industries (OAK)

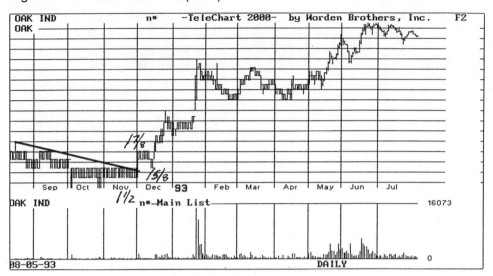

Chart courtesy of TeleChart 2000™ by Worden Brothers, Inc. Used with permission.

Tejas Gas (TEJ)

Tejas Gas (see Figure 5-9) was not a low-priced stock. The stock had already bottomed out in 1991 at 14, about the same support level it had found buyers in 1990 as well as in 1991. By 1993, the stock was in a bull market.

Area patterns tend to occur during consolidations, and in the last quarter of 1992, Tejas was consolidating its gains leading up to the September highs. The formation during October, November, December, and into January resembled an ascending triangle, with resistance at 23.

On the breakout the week ending February 5, volume was very low. Volume picked up, however, on the move during the week ending February 19.

Lifetime Corp. (LFT)

Lifetime Corp. (see Figure 5-10) during the last month of 1992 and the first quarter of 1993 was in a consolidation pattern, having risen from a 1992 low of 9. Resistance was at 17, the rising support levels indicated a pattern resembling an ascending triangle.

The breakout for Lifetime in mid-March was dramatic.

While Tejas and Lifetime were both higher priced stocks in 1993, there are

Figure 5 • 9   Tejas Gas (TEJ)

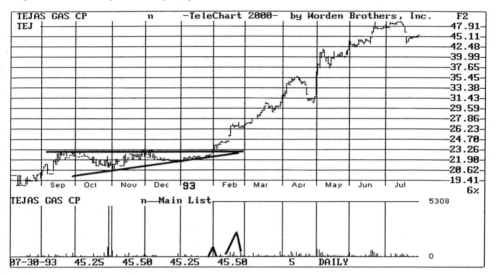

Chart courtesy of TeleChart 2000™ by Worden Brothers, Inc. Used with permission.

Figure 5 • 10   Lifetime Corp. (LFT)

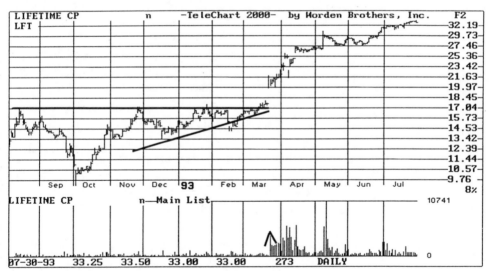

Chart courtesy of TeleChart 2000™ by Worden Brothers, Inc. Used with permission.

a couple of points to be made. For one, both stocks were in the process of rising from low-priced stock status, and the initial upswing in the stock prices was during a period when earnings were poor. The technicals were preceding the fundamentals.

By the time 1993 rolled around, however, earnings were picking up nicely. So, while earnings are often lacking at the lows, and is why investors have to rely on the technicals, the earnings growth is what gives most low-priced stocks their "second-wind" or puts them on "afterburners."

Learn to look for big earnings gains and watch for breakouts from consolidations.

Precious Metals—Gold

One of the best stories for the first half of 1993 was the precious metal stocks. Precious metals had been depressed for several years but sprang to life as the price of gold and silver increased sharply, in large part reflecting some rekindling of inflation fears.

Gold stocks have always had a special place among speculators. A renewed rise in gold stocks during the previous several months had already wetted investors' appetites. When the April report on the producer price index rose 0.6%, nearly three times what had been expected, inflation fears took off. Investors stampeded into gold and silver stocks. Investment analysts declared a new bull market in gold. When fence-sitters heard predictions of a price running up to and over $500, they plunged in.

Investors who had prospected among low-priced stocks had had plenty of indications far earlier about the improving prospects for the gold and silver stocks. Investors who followed technical analysis could have jumped on the bandwagon at far lower prices than those scrambling aboard in mid-May.

LAC Minerals Ltd. (LAC)

Lac Minerals (LAC) is an interesting situation in that the company earns a profit. In January the stock drifted down to a low of 4 1/4 (see Figure 5-11). During the week ending January 29, the stock demonstrated three items of technical note: 1. the stock established that the minor trend was bullish; 2. the stock broke above a very tight trendline; and 3. the rally stalled at resistance at 5.

During the week ending February 5, the technical development continued. The stock broke above its brief resistance at 5, broke above the 50-day moving average, broke above another trendline, and then stalled at resistance at 6. On March 5, LAC moved sharply higher on heavy volume.

The first intermediate advance was eight weeks long, from the lows of January 19 to a high of 7 7/8 on March 19. The correction saw the stock decline to the 50-day moving average. During the week ended April 30, the stock broke out past the highs of March 19 and the previous July. The public would not join in until May 12.

Homestake Mining Co. (HM)

Homestake Mining has had a volatile financial history. Note that the stock's move began about the time the dividend was cut the week of January 15 (Figure 5-12).

Homestake Mining is noteworthy in showing the typical stair-step characteristic of trends. The zigzag patterns come from support and resistance.

Note the stock broke above the 50-day moving average in mid-December which by itself may be bullish. However, the stock moved right into resistance at 12.

The value of the 50-day moving average depends in large part on its relationship to the underlying trend and support and resistance levels. In mid-December, the 50-day moving average is not reflecting very well the trending down of Homestake. The 50-day moving average is too far away from the downtrend and too close to resistance.

Figure 5 • 11   Lac Minerals Ltd. (LAC)

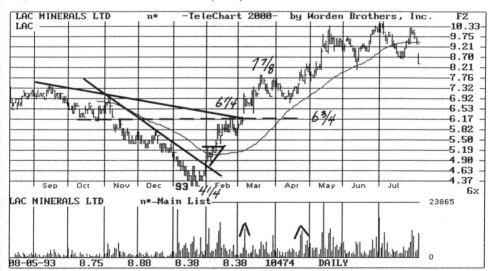

Chart courtesy of TeleChart 2000™ by Worden Brothers, Inc. Used with permission.

In January on the other hand, the 50-day is hugging the trend and thus a breakout is more reliable than in December.

Buying picks up as the stock clears the previous minor high in December, 11 3/4, but runs into the resistance between 12 and 13.

The countermove provides a buying opportunity. In March the stock had declined 40% of the previous advance and had also declined to support. Investors who did not buy on the breakout at the lows in late January could have bought on the reaction in March.

As buying in the precious metals picks up, the stock begins to move away from its self-correction pattern. As gold stocks were being touted in May, the stock was beginning to assume "late in the trend" characteristics as it loses upside momentum.

By May 12 the stock had already advanced past the "buy only twice" rule—stocks can be bought on the pullbacks following the first two minor advances, but not following the third.

Thus, a buy could have been made in March and April, but certainly not in May.

Instead of buying late into the intermediate trend, the next buying opportunity is after a more significant correction. Where might a more significant correction take the stock? Back to significant support, to 14-15.

Figure 5 • 12   Homestake Mining Co. (HM)

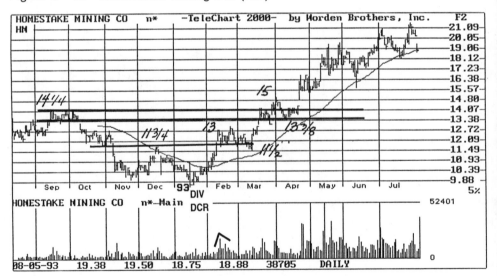

Coeur D' Alene Mines Co. (CDE)

Buying Coeur D' Alene Mines (CDE) at 9 7/8 was not indicated, but when the stock broke above 11 on January 20, it established that the minor trend was bullish (see Figure 5-13).

The only one bullish minor trend during the previous six months was on August 3 but without volume. It takes volume to make breakouts reliable. On January 20 volume picked up nicely.

Minor trends can be deceptive. Investors buying during the buying panic of May 12 were buying at the end of the move. However, a bullish minor zigzag like in January after an extensive decline can be very significant.

During the week of January 29, the stock had a 40% correction, had declined to support, and had declined to the trendline. All three countermove buying guidelines suggested buying at 11.

On February 8 the stock advanced sharply, with volume soaring. The countermove following a very explosive breakout may not return to the immediate preceding support, but will correct 40% of the previous advance and just mark time until it hits the trendline. Buying was in order at 12 1/2 – 13.

Figure 5 • 13   Coeur D' Alene Mines Co. (CDE)

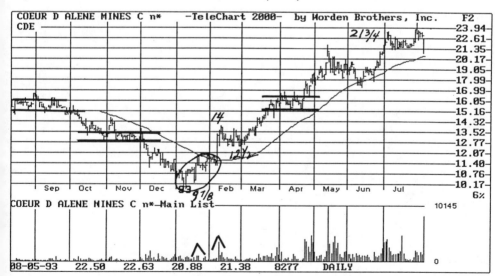

Chart courtesy of TeleChart 2000™ by Worden Brothers, Inc. Used with permission.

Hecla Mining Co. (HL)

The $9 level for Hecla (see Figure 5-14) was support during August and September 1992, but when price slipped under 9 on September 28, 9 would become resistance.

On the rallies in November and February, 9 would be resistance. In mid-March, however, the stock broke past 9 on good volume. A two-day minor countermove to support at 9 followed. Note how the volume diminished. The next buying opportunity did not develop until April.

At the bottom 7 1/2 was the support for the stock during the majority of trading sessions for nearly two months. During the height of the tax-selling season bids did sink to 7 1/4 for a couple of weeks, but bids promptly moved back up to 7 1/2 after tax selling ran its course. The stock began to edge higher, and, when on the minor rally broke a new high on January 20, it was clear that the trend was bullish.

Some simple rules of technical analysis signaled that the trend for the precious metals had turned bullish. Long before they became the talk of Wall Street experts, investors had plenty of opportunities to take positions in the precious metal stocks.

Figure 5 • 14   Hecla Mining Co. (HL)

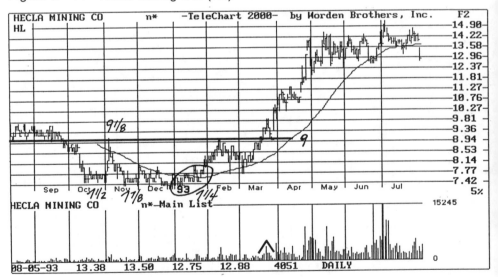

Chart courtesy of TeleChart 2000™ by Worden Brothers, Inc. Used with permission.

· 6 ·

The 100% Club:
The Top 10 Winners For 1992

In 1992 each of the top 50 percentage winners on the NYSE had returns of more than 100%. While the S&P 500 was up 4.46% for the year, 50 stocks showed gains of 100% or more.

Picking a stock showing a gain of 100% or more represents either a lot of hard work, or a lot of luck, or some combination of both. Picking stocks destined for this exclusive 100% club is a game of chance to be sure. Do parameters exist that might improve the picker's odds?

Price is the number one factor. Simply, the lower the price, the greater the chance of landing a winner. The average price of all common stocks traded on the NYSE in 1992 was $34. The average price of the top 50 winners was far less: $13.89.

Averages sometimes lie. The table below ranks the 50 in terms of percentage gain.

NYSE Top 50
12/31/91 to 12/31/92

	Average Gain (%)	Average Price ($)
1 - 10	229.8	5.35
11 - 20	157.7	10.96
21 - 30	130.5	9.71
31 - 40	116.9	23.75
41 - 50	106.7	21.62

The results indicate that the best winners came from the lowest-priced stocks, not necessarily the smallest stocks, as is commonly thought, but the lowest-priced stocks.

Figure 6-1 charts the price range and percentage gains of the 1992 NYSE 50 Top Performers.

The best winners came from the lowest-priced stocks. Stocks priced less than

Figure 6 • 1   1992 NYSE Percent Gains: Top 50 Performers

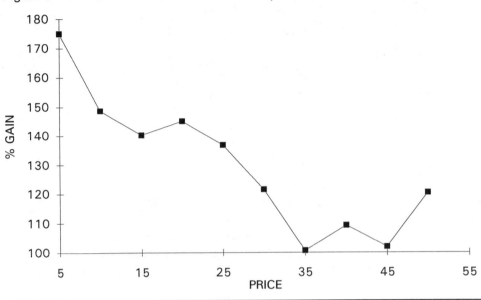

$5 were the largest group by far (34%) and provided the best gains (175%). Stocks less than $10 accounted for exactly one-half of the total winners.

Because low-priced stocks accounted for the best gains, this Chapter examines some of the issues that performed best in 1992. Many investors would not consider a stock below $10, much less one under $5, but knowing more about the type of issues that became best winners in 1992 might lessen investor's fears.

Winning Characteristics

The first characteristic of these winners is that the majority were depressed. Most were not just down from previous highs, but truly depressed—down 60, 70, 80%. The average decline was 81.1%.

Notice in the accompanying stock charts how persistent the declines are and for how long stocks declined from previous highs. In a few cases the stocks had been dragging sideways, as if the stock were hibernating. But in most of the cases, the stocks had been in a steady decline for at least several years.

The average length of decline was 45 months, measured from the high price to the low price. In the majority of the cases, the stocks spent 12 to 18 months at the lows before advancing.

A second characteristic of the majority is that they were selling at less than book value, if not at the time, nearly always at less than book value before a series of write-offs lopped off book values. Generally, in depressed stocks, book values also decline. A drop in price to less than book value does not mean that a stock is depressed. However, the winners were depressed and selling at less than book.

A third characteristic of the 100% club is that many of the stocks represented weakness in an entire group. In many of the case examples that follow the cause of the financial misfortunes was related to the industry. Thus investors will tend to find depressed issues on an industrywide basis. Several issues reviewed are from banking, manufactured housing, technology, and retailing. In some of the examples the reasons why a stock becomes depressed is specific to the company itself. The company simply was not able to compete for one reason or another.

Among the top 50 performing issues, no less than 10 represented banking—BancFlorida, Equimark, Northeast Federal, MNC Financial, Continental Bank, Bank of Boston, Fidelity National of Florida, Citicorp, Leucadia National, and Hibernia.

Many times the problems in the industry are so widespread that depressed stocks are typical of the industry. In terms of technical analysis, an investor can often find the best winners when a group as a whole begins to move ahead.

The fourth and last characteristic of the majority of the 10 best winners of 1992 is that their stock prices broke the downward momentum, or broke out of a period of dormancy, and began trending upward. While this statement sounds inane, don't underestimate its importance.

In his chapter, "Price Movement and Other Market Action Factors," Loeb states, "For example, consistent strength and volume in a particular issue, occurring after a long general decline, will usually turn out to be an extremely bullish indication on the individual stock in question."

In depressed stocks in particular, the technicals are about all investors have to go on. When a firm has experienced a string of losses, has a deficit book value, and is on the verge of financial collapse, when even management doesn't really know what the next day will bring, how can its stock be valued? Intrinsic value may work for the firms at the top of *Fortune's* most admired list; but for the firms at the bottom, it is all guesswork.

While determining whether a price is high, or low, or fair, can be exceedingly difficult, an investor can determine trend. At the earliest stages of a depressed stock's recovery, technicals nearly always lead the fundamentals. A review of the 10 best winners for 1992 follows.

The First Six Winners

BancFlorida Financial (BFL)

The biggest winner on the NYSE was BancFlorida Financial, up 357.1%. BancFlorida Financial (see Figure 6-2), the holding company for BancFlorida, FSB (formerly named Naples Federal Savings & Loan Association) was representative of the savings & loan (S & L) crisis. After experiencing a period of rapid growth, the number of substandard loans began to rise as did the loan loss provisions. Earnings, which peaked in 1988, slid continuously, cumulating in a loss of $4.98 per share for the year ended September 30, 1991. Dividends were cut in 1988 and again in 1990, and were omitted in 1991. BancFlorida Financial had not been a very positive investment.

The stock price action was typical of the S&Ls. From a high of 25 5/8 in 1987, the stock persistently declined until it bottomed out at 2 3/8, a 90.7% drop.

What were the clues that BancFlorida was ready to rebound off its low of 2 3/8? One factor was that the low of 2 3/8 was support. During 1990 the stock was on the last leg of its plunge, continuing a drop that had started in October 1989 at 12, to close at 2 3/8 in December 1990. The stock rallied into February 1991, then it proceeded to slip.

For the first seven months in 1991 BancFlorida drifted lower. The last of the holders-on were ready to bail out, and on October 18, 1991, a selling climax occurred on extraordinary volume of more than 67,000 shares. It dropped to 2 3/8.

After briefly touching 2 3/8 on October 31, the issue rallied for about three weeks, closing at 3 1/4 on November 6. Subsequently the issue drifted lower, until it hit 2 3/8 again on November 22.

The price of 2 3/8 was beginning to take on some meaning. The stock had buyers at 2 3/8. BancFlorida bounced off 2 3/8 a half-dozen times during December. Based on the tape action, speculative buying could have been executed at 2 1/2 or under.

During the week ended December 20 BancFlorida moved up again, establishing a new closing high for the quarter at 3 3/8 on December 25. Exactly a week later, on Wednesday, January 1, the stock fell back to 2 1/2 on heavy volume, but by week's end, on Friday, the issue was back at 3 3/8.

The range was formed. Support kept coming on the market at 2 3/8, and resistance was defined at 3 3/8. On January 13 the stock broke through the resistance on a substantial increase in volume. BancFlorida Financial was on its way to becoming the 1992 leader with a gain of 357%.

Figure 6 • 2   BancFlorida Financial (BFL): March 1991 – February 1992

The entire banking group was in the process of being upgraded by investors. On January 13, the day of BancFlorida's breakout, Citicorp was the most active issue, up 1 1/2 points on volume of more than 6 million.

While banks and the S&Ls could still be considered depressed, the opinion that the worst might be over for the financial issues was growing. As more large banks reported higher-than-expected earnings, momentum picked up considerably for the financials, and BancFlorida was on its way to $15.

Equimark Corp. (EQK)

Equimark's principal subsidiary, Equibank—the third largest bank in Pittsburgh—merged into Integra Financial Corp. in mid-1992.

Equimark's stock pattern is typical of many low-priced and depressed situations at the lows. The stock did little for extensive periods—just drifting.

The primary lows of 1 3/8 for Equimark were set back on January 25, 1991. The stock advanced nicely for a month, then it settled back, closing at 1 3/4 on April 12, 1991. After a quick rally to 4 on April 26 the stock just drifted lower next 9 months (see Figure 6-3).

Many low-priced, depressed stocks spend extensive time at the bottom. Little is written about these issues, and a lot of sellers jump in on every rally. In

Figure 6 • 3   Equimark Corp. (EQK): March 1991 – February 1992

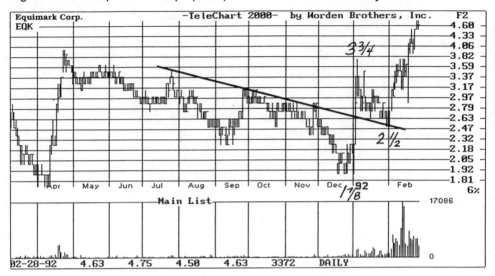

Chart courtesy of TeleChart 2000™ by Worden Brothers, Inc. Used with permission.

December 1991 Equimark once again moved below 2. The lows of 1 7/8 during December may not have been the final lows, but support had arisen twice before as the stock moved below 2. A speculative buy was warranted.

The stock jumped sharply higher on January 6, 1992, and hit 3 3/4 intraday the following day, both days with volume running higher than it had for the preceding year. A spike is obviously bullish. There is an aggressive buyer. While an investor should not chase a spike, a dull pullback to support is a buy opportunity.

On the move to 3 3/4, the stock had broken a down trendline. After a stock breaks above the trendline, the trendline represents support. The stock pulled back to the trendline at 2 1/2 the first week of February.

Tandycrafts Inc. (TAC)

Tandycrafts was not a depressed stock. It was dormant. For years Tandycrafts had traded between the lower and upper teens. During November 1991 the stock was trading at 13 1/2.

Once Tandycrafts started to move, there was no looking back. The stock hesitated at the upper teens where it had been turned back before. With an explosive move to 25 the stock moved past its historical resistance level. Tandycrafts had entered a new level; it was trading in clear air.

Northeast Federal Corp. (NSB)

Northeast Federal is a holding company for Northeast Savings, one of the largest thrifts in New England. When the stock was listed on the NYSE in 1987, prospects were bright and the stock traded at more than $25 a share. Like the other financials on the list, the firm's and the stock's move to depressed status was a long one, falling to an eventual low of 1 1/4 in December 1990. Also like the other financials, the stock rallied in early 1991, then fell back to the earlier lows in December 1991. On January 8 the stock broke upside and moved to 5 7/8.

Western Digital Corp. (WDC)

Western Digital, a manufacturer of disk drives for personal computers, had seen some troubled times. Earnings fell from a record $1.78 per share in 1987 to a hefty loss of $4.59 per share by the year ending June 30, 1991 (see Table 6-1). Operating losses and a series of restructuring changes, including bank debt restructuring, saw book value shrink to under $4 per share by the fiscal year ending June 30, 1992.

Losses and liquidity woes saw the stock sink to a low of 2 by December 1991, down 93.8% from 1987's high of 32 5/8.

What indicated that Western Digital would move ahead so strongly in 1992?

Western Digital traded at 2 for three straight trading days, December 12, 13, and 16, then started to move right back up. Often as the January Effect comes into play, investors do not have a lot of time to take positions after a stock begins to move.

The breakout was the December 26, 1991 move to 2 3/4, with volume picking up nicely. The move higher snapped the downward momentum of the previous six months (see Figure 6-4A).

At 2 3/4 the stock hesitated, and so might have the investor. While the rally broke a declining trendline, it looked similar to the one in August, where after a nice push up on heavy volume, the stock went on to lose another 50%.

However, on January 2, 1992 the issue moved right to the next breakout point, 2 3/4, and on the following day, moved up to 3 1/4 on heavy volume.

Rather than just a minor counterrally against a bearish trend, two back-to-back minor rallies established a bullish trend.

Note in Table 6-1 the highs and lows of previous years' price ranges. The previous year's low had been 4. A longer-term chart would indicate that a substantial amount of stock was traded at 4 and 5.

Table 6 • 1   Western Digital Earnings and High/Low Prices 1986 – 1993

	Earnings	Price	
	(June)	High	Low
1986	0.96	20	9
1987	1.57	32	11
1988	1.51	17	11
1989	1.18	15	5
1990	0.82	14	4
1991	−4.59	6	2
1992	−2.49	6	2
1993	−0.78	6	2

An investor could have assumed, based on resistance, that the stock's quick move to 4 – 5 would finish the move for the time being. Look at the very heavy volume as the stock hit 4 5/8 on January 17 and was turned back.

As noted earlier, moving averages are only effective to the extent that they correctly measure resistance. With Western Digital most of the resistance, based on actual transactions, was between 4 and 5. While the breaking of the 200-day moving average at 3 1/2 was bullish to the extent that the stock moved through one measure of resistance based solely on price, it was limited because the stock was moving right into resistance as defined by previous volume as well as price. The stock did peak out at 4 3/4 on February 14 and began to slide down.

Western Digital: The Pattern

When a stock breaks out of a declining trendline, like Western Digital did in December, the focus point of support is not as easily identified as if the stock had broken out of a pattern. In a rectangle, for instance, a level of trading concentration is well-established.

Patterns form in low-priced stocks, but often not at the lows. They form only after the stock has started to trend higher. In these cases, the combination of pockets of trading can give a clue. For instance, during Western Digital's downtrend preceding the low at December 12, 1991 the widest trading level developed during much of October.

That level of trading—at 3 to 3 3/8—in turn is the reason that on the move subsequent to the December lows, the widest trading level occurred the week of January 6 and the first few days of the following week, again at 3 to 3 3/8. Together, these two areas of trading defined support for Western Digital as it corrected from its highs of 4 5/8 on February 13.

Figure 6 • 4A Western Digital Corp. (WDC): February 1991 – January 1992

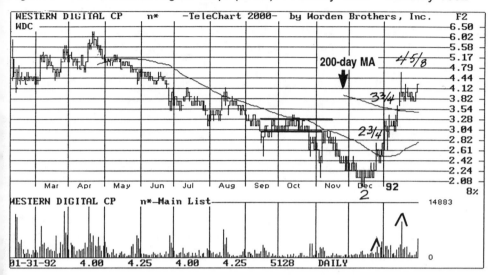

Chart courtesy of TeleChart 2000™ by Worden Brothers, Inc. Used with permission.

Figure 6 • 4B Western Digital Corp. (WDC): January 1992 – January 1993

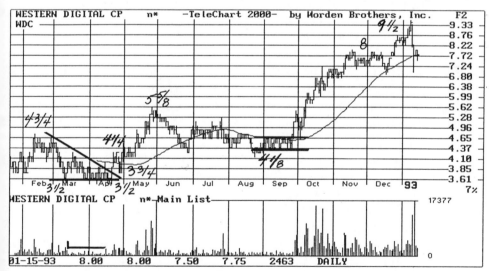

Chart courtesy of TeleChart 2000™ by Worden Brothers, Inc. Used with permission.

The 200-day moving average, with its limitations, can also help approximate the level. A stock's correction should fall just short of the 200-day moving average. Considered with volume and any other patterns, like the trading areas described in the previous paragraph, these guidelines can help an investor buy into a stock.

Western Digital quickly declined after hitting 4 3/4. The first support occurred at 3 1/2 on March 12 (see Figure 6-4B). After a minor rally, Western Digital sank to 3 1/2 again on April 8, rallied, and then sank to 3 1/2 again on April 19. Western Digital then traded at 3 1/2 on three successive days.

At 3 1/2 Western Digital was forming a descending triangle. The top prices kept declining, while the bottom prices formed at 3 1/2. The entire formation was taking place with volume declining sharply. Investors could have bought in anticipation of a breakout.

On April 22 and 23, Western Digital broke to the upside, quickly rising to a high of 4 1/4. On April 28 Western Digital had the customary throwback to 3 3/4 and traded there for three days. Investors who missed the breakout were given three more chances to buy at 3 3/4.

Western Digital: The Trends

By year end 1992 Western Digital had risen to more than 8. The advance happened in a series of trends.

The major trend was from a low of 2 in December 1991 to a high of 8 in December 1992.

The major trend was made up of intermediate trends. The first was from a low of 2 in December to a high of 4 3/4 in February. Another intermediate trend was from a low of 3 1/2 in April to a high of 5 5/8 in May. The third intermediate trend was from a low of 4 1/8 in August to a high of 8 in December.

Each intermediate trend was made up of minor trends. On the move from 4 1/8 to 8, five distinct minor trend moves occurred, each with an advance and pullback.

Note where the intermediate correction in July-August-September took place. When the stock was moving from the December 1991 lows, it did not have a well-defined support area. By the summer of 1992, a support area was defined by the four high-volume days in February. The stock closed at 4, 4 1/4, 4 5/8, and 4 1/4. The average was just about 4 1/4.

Where did the stock find support during the correction following the May 20 highs? Support was at 4 1/4 and volume was down sharply.

Prices fluctuated between 4 3/8 and 4 5/8 during a very tight formation for the four weeks through September 25. Western Digital had a nice volume breakout during the three days ending September 30, followed by the customary pullback on the three days ending October 6. Then Western Digital was again off and running. There was nothing "random" about how Western Digital became one of the top-performing low-priced stocks in 1992.

Salant Corp. (SLT)

Salant is a good example of how stocks rise out of the ashes of bankruptcy. Salant, an apparel designer and manufacturer, suffered a combination of mushrooming debt plus a slippage in sales volume. As recently as 1989 it was trading for 28 7/8 per share. A more than six-fold increase in debt to fund an acquisition was the firm's unraveling. As cash flow dried up, Salant was unable to pay interest and declared bankruptcy.

The low point on the stock was recorded in December 1990; the stock traded at 1 1/4. By December 1990 it had lost approximately 95.6% of its value.

Salant rallied to 4 1/4 by March 1991, then proceeded to drift. After a low of 2 1/8 in June, the stock rallied for four weeks to 3 1/2, then drifted for the duration of the year (see Figure 6-5). Many depressed stocks under the burden of continuing financial losses will drift for months after an initial rebound rally.

If an investor knows what to look for, the pattern can be very bullish. Look for a stock holding above the panic lows. If the bear trend was still intact, the stock would be moving to new lows. The downtrend has been broken, and the stock is more or less treading water. Take positions at support, or watch for a breakout. What is sometimes difficult is knowing whether or not a breakout has occurred. In late 1991 Salant was to begin its 1992 advance.

After hitting a low in June 1991, Salant trended higher through October. However, the stock kept moving up against resistance at 3 1/2.

On October 22 the stock moved to 3 3/8 on a pickup of volume. By itself, the move was positive. Was it a decisive breakout?

On a decisive breakout, volume increases to at least double the preceding average daily volume; in addition, the stock closes at new highs by over 3%.

On the October 22 move volume increased, and the stock traded higher on an intraday basis, but it did not close at a new high. A few days later the stock advanced and closed at 3 3/8, but on little volume.

First it advanced on an increase of volume, but it was not a closing high. Then there was a new closing high, but on low volume, and the new high was only higher by 1/8.

Technical analysis asks the question: How is the stock acting? That question can be answered only by reference to past price and volume patterns. It is not always clear. A decisive breakout should be obvious. Salant's move to 3 3/8 of

Figure 6 • 5   Salant Corp. (SLT): April 1991 – March 1992

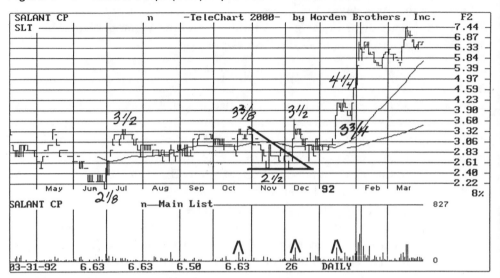

Chart courtesy of TeleChart 2000™ by Worden Brothers, Inc. Used with permission.

October 22 raised so many questions, the advance had to be discounted. Subsequently, the stock drifted to 2 1/2.

On December 9 the stock had a nice rise on pretty heavy volume, closing at 3 1/2. The move had more of the qualities of a breakout.

During the next two weeks Salant drifted back to 3 and stayed there through the week of January 6. The pattern from the December 6 lows of 2 1/2 to the December 11 highs of 3 3/8 was a carbon copy of the move from the December lows of 1 1/4 to the March 1991 highs of 4 1/4—an advance on volume, then a dull reaction—just on a different scale.

When Salant rose explosively away from 3 on January 16, moving past 3 1/2, then to above 4, the breakout was unquestioned.

As is customary, Salant pulled back for a couple of days on very low volume, allowing investors a low-risk buying entry at 3 3/4. In the next few days, it skyrocketed.

The Last Four Winners

The next two largest winners, Coachman Industries and Carriage Industries, up 200% and 189% respectively, and two issues further down on the list, Winnebago Industries, up 116.1%, and Clayton Homes, up 108.3%, represent the manufactured housing industry. Coachman makes motor homes and travel trailers;

Carriage makes carpets for manufactured housing; Winnebago and Clayton make motor homes.

The manufactured housing industry has had its ups and downs. The industry had suffered the proverbial seven years of bad luck through 1992. In 1986 these stocks were selling at 2 to 2 1/2 times book value. By the end of 1991 they were selling at one-half book value.

Coachman Industries (COA)

Coachman's low was 3 1/2 in 1990. In 1991 the issue declined to that vicinity again, trading twice at a low of 4 1/8. The stock showed textbook staircase zigzag patterns in rising off the lows and offered plenty of buying opportunities.

Carriage Industries (CGE)

Carriage Industries had several interesting characteristics. First, the stock was very thinly traded, with a float of only 2.3 million shares. Trading was very tight. Even after factoring in higher volume in April, the average daily volume was only 5,700 shares.

Second, the price range of the last four years was 3 – 6, 3 – 6, 3 – 5, and 3 – 5. When Carriage moved above 6 in April, it signaled that a major move was underway.

Carriage had not been a dynamic mover and required some patience. It broke out on December 24, 1991. An investor did not need to have a chart to know what was happening with Carriage.

Winnebago Industries (WGO)

Winnebago followed in the footsteps of the other issues. The tight price range was from November 8 to December 20, 1991 at around 3 1/4. Winnebago would have been a solid January Effect selection (see Figure 6-6).

Clayton Homes (CMH)

Clayton Homes, the highest priced of the four, broke out of its doldrums in the second half of 1990. At the beginning of 1992, Clayton was already in the midst of a major bull market. Clayton showed the least gains among the manufactured housing stocks and was also the highest priced.

Conclusion

I could go on and discuss some additional issues in the 100% Club. Some of the names on the 100% Club list are well known, others are not known at all (see

Table 6-2). However, the principles of technical analysis are just about the same for all of them.

Table 6 • 2   NYSE Percent Leaders for 1992

	Price 12/31/91	Price 12/31/92	% Change
BancFlorida Financial	2.625	12.000	357.1
Equimark	2.250	8.125	261.1
Tandycrafts	16.000	28.875	260.9
Northeast Federal	2.000	6.625	231.3
Western Digital	2.625	8.625	228.6
Salant	3.125	9.500	204.0
Coachman Industries	5.750	17.250	200.0
Carriage Industries	4.625	13.375	189.2
EMC	12.500	23.750	185.0
Diana	2.000	5.375	181.3
Paxar	11.000	24.250	156.6
Chrysler	11.750	32.000	172.3
Mueller	8.500	22.875	169.1
MNC Financial	4.875	12.875	164.1
Kysor Industrial	7.000	18.250	160.7
Jackpot Enterprise	7.875	19.375	158.3
Volunteer Capital	2.625	6.750	157.1
Promus	22.000	55.000	150.0
Unisys	4.125	10.125	145.5
BIC	29.875	36.375	143.5
Chaus Bernard	2.875	7.000	143.5
Best Buy	16.500	39.000	136.4
Par Technology	2.625	6.125	133.3
Scientific-Atlanta	16.375	25.375	132.4
Continental Bank	9.375	21.625	130.7
IMCO Recycle	6.625	15.125	128.3
GenRad	2.250	5.125	127.8
Magma Copper	5.875	13.375	127.7
Circuit City Store	23.125	51.570	123.8
Bank of Boston	11.500	25.500	121.7
XTRA	28.875	64.000	121.6
International Game Tech.	46.000	50.875	121.2
Marvel Entertainment	45.750	25.125	119.7
Fidelity National	18.000	26.625	116.9
Winnebago	3.875	8.375	116.1
Universal Matchbox	3.875	8.375	116.1
Solectron	34.750	37.375	115.1
Citicorp	10.375	22.250	114.5
Leucadia National	36.875	79.000	114.2
Timberland A	9.125	19.500	113.7
Hibernia	2.750	8.875	113.6
Healthsource	27.250	38.250	110.5
Value Health	28.250	39.625	110.4
Continuum	12.250	25.750	110.2
Clayton Homes	15.375	25.625	108.3
Portec	3.625	6.750	104.9
Winn-Dixie Stores	37.500	76.625	104.3
Service Merchandise	10.750	14.500	102.3
Louisiana Pacific	44.375	59.750	102.0
CML Group	34.125	32.250	100.7

· 7 ·

Big Winners Among
NYSE Fallen Blue Chips

Reviewed in this Chapter are three of the biggest winners among the most widely held and traded stocks on the NYSE: Chrysler, 9 1/8 to 58 3/8, for a gain of 539%; Unisys, 2 1/8 to 13 7/8, for a gain of 552%; Citicorp, 8 5/8 to 39 3/4, for a gain of 360%. As is the theme of this book, among the most extraordinary gains arise from fallen blue chips.

The Chrysler Advantage

One of the best-performing stocks on the NYSE in 1993 was Chrysler. The stock entered 1993 at 32 and closed out the year over 50. Of the 25 most active issues, Chrysler was number one in terms of percentage gain.

Like many stocks that fare well in a calendar year, Chrysler's 1993 advance was part of a major bull market in the stock that started on December 19, 1991, at 9 1/8. Taken from the beginning, Chrysler's gain was even better, up over 500%. Chrysler represents the epitome of what investors should look for in a low-priced and depressed stock.

First, the company was well-known. With nearly 300 million shares outstanding, Chrysler was one of the most widely held. The very essence of the model low-priced, depressed stock is one high on name recognition. Chrysler met the recognition requirement squarely.

Second, Chrysler was out of favor, an additional essence of the model low-priced, depressed stock. At the time Chrysler was not the most enamored of American corporations. In *Fortune*'s 1992 annual survey of America's Most Admired Corporations, Chrysler rated a scant 4.27, a ranking of 294 out of 307 companies, 14 placed from the bottom. Chrysler's prospects were considered poor.

In terms of price, Chrysler was depressed by any standard. At the stock's lows the issue had fallen nearly 80% from its previous highs. After hitting $48 per share on August 25, 1987, Chrysler began its persistent decline for four straight years until it finally bottomed out at a little under $10 a share in December 1991. At its lows Chrysler was selling for 1/3 of book value, and the stock had an alpha rating of -2.11.

Certainly shareholders were depressed, both those who had ridden the stock down, as well as those who had tried to guess the bottom, only to see the stock continue to fall.

When the stock was trading around 10 in December, how could the investor have foreseen that Chrysler was at the lows and about to embark on a significant advance?

Several technical considerations are important. First, and foremost, however, Chrysler on December 19, 1991, was trading at major support. (See Figure 7-2).

Chrysler had traded at 9 3/4 just the previous September, as the stock traded on September 30. Expecting Chrysler to find support at 9 3/4 in December, during tax-selling season, was logical given the formation the previous September. However, the 9-10 level posed considerably greater significance because the stock previously found support at that level on September 28, 1990, when it began to advance after hitting a low for the year of 9 1/8. (See Figure 7-1).

The bottom for Chrysler was the low of 9 1/8 on September 28, 1990. However, the bull trend in Chrysler started on December 19, 1991.

Most bull trends do not start from the absolute lows of a decline. Stocks hit a low and rebound. Sellers take advantage of the rise. The stock declines. If anything, the bear trend is still intact or, at best, the trend is neutral. Not until a stock successfully moves through a level of resistance and the issue begins to trend higher, does the bull trend in fact develop. For that reason trendlines are *not* drawn from the absolute lows but usually from the low where the bullish momentum or mark up actually begins to assert itself.

It took Chrysler a year to build the groundwork for its dynamic advance, a characteristic not uncommon for depressed stocks struggling to rebound. Few investment buyers were buying Chrysler. During 1990 and 1991 Chrysler was running red ink, the dividend was cut, and the outlook for the stock was bleak by every standard. The only buyers of Chrysler were bottom fishers and speculators, hoping to scalp a few points. On the other hand, a lot of sellers were waiting to bail out of the stock, to cut their losses short, to just get Chrysler off the books.

Resistance theory spotlights where selling should be expected to surface. The net effect is that the initial rallies off the lows are apt to be short-circuited along the way, with the stock moving back toward its lows after just a few months or even a year. With a truly depressed stock, such as Chrysler, it takes time to attack the resistance before the stock can advance in earnest. It took time to build the base necessary to sustain Chrysler's solid bull run.

Chrysler (C): 9/28/90 - 12/20/90

A review of the Chrysler bull market should start with the lows of September 29, 1990 (See Figure 7-1 on pages 148). From a technical analysis point of view, Chrysler's trend pattern was classic.

At first glance the most important number on the chart is the September 29, 1990, low of 9 1/8. While 9 1/8 is the most important for statistical purposes, other numbers are more important from a trend standpoint.

Keep the number 15 in mind. Support and resistance are defined by a trading range, of a level of concentration. Chrysler kept bouncing off 15 in May, June, and July 1990.

In technical pattern parlance, Chrysler was forming a downward sloping triangle, with support at 15 forming the lower edge of the triangle, but with increasing resistance keeping downward pressure on the stock.

At that time, 15 was support. After a stock declines below support, that support trading range becomes resistance. When Chrysler moved below 15 the week ending August 3, 15 became resistance. That one week move will define the lid for Chrysler during the entire next year.

Fifteen is just the edge of the resistance. The focal point is determined by the volume of trading. While 15 represented the edge of the level, the volume of trading suggested that the greatest concentration occurred between 16 and 17. The four largest volume days during the first six months of the year took place at prices between 15 7/8 and 17 3/8. The concentrations of turnover activity came into play later.

After bottoming out at 9 1/8, the stock began to move higher in a series of minor advance/declines. First an advance to 11 1/4, then a decline to 10 1/2, then an advance to 11 3/4, then a decline to 11. With a combination of two minor advance/decline movements, the intermediate trend in Chrysler could have been classified as up.

Note the low of 11 7/8 of August 24. That low defines a minor level of resistance, and that is why the stock stopped its advance on the week of October 22 at 11 3/4. Support and resistance patterns come in three sizes: minor, intermediate, and major. They all play a role in stock price patterns.

Investors could have taken speculative positions during the pullback from the rally, as the stock traded at 11 and volume diminished. Positions could also have been taken as the issue moved above the 50-day moving average on November 14.

Figure 7 • 1 Chrysler Corp. (C): February 1990 – January 1991

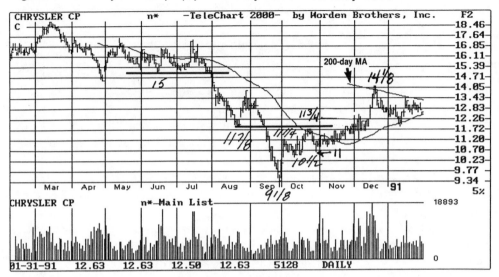

The rally was slowing approaching resistance at 15. The closer to 15 the stock moved, the more likely the end of the current advance and the higher the risk of buying high.

Just as resistance theory would imply, Chrysler, in a burst of climactic buying in the week ended December 21, reversed at 14 1/8 and began to move lower again. The high of 14 1/8 happened to coincide with the 200-day moving average.

Using pattern areas of concentration in conjunction with volume analysis is the preferred method for determining support and resistance levels. By definition the 200-day moving average, however, represents support and resistance because there are 200 trading days.

For classification purposes the move from September 28 to December 20 was a bullish intermediate advance in what has to be considered a major bear market for Chrysler. After the intermediate advance, with the issue turned back at resistance, a stock can be expected to sink back to its lows, which Chrysler did.

Chrysler (C): 12/20/90 - 9/30/91

The next rally was less orderly. After the stock bottomed out at 10 5/8 on February 13, 1991, it rallied for a few days, then shot up. An intraday high of

Figure 7 • 2 Chrysler Corp. (C): January 1991 - December 1991

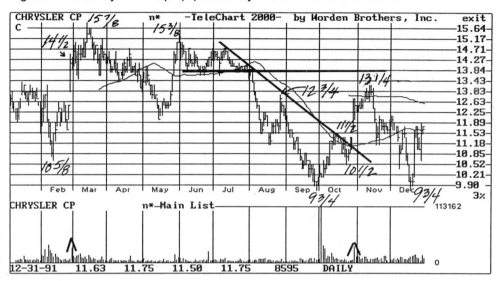

Chart courtesy of TeleChart 2000™ by Worden Brothers, Inc. Used with permission.

14 1/2 occurred on February 28 on very heavy volume because of Wall Street recommendations (see Figure 7-2 above).

Three major brokerage firms had recommended all the auto issues—GM, Ford, and Chrysler—on the theory that car sales would improve along with consumer confidence because the Persian Gulf war was over. The auto stocks were in the news.

The move higher was a breakout of sorts. The stock moved above the previous intermediate high of 14 1/8. However, it was not a solid, dependable breakout. It was part of a buying panic. The best gains from low-priced land depressed stocks stem from greater institutional support for a stock. This occurs as a stock moves from a low-priced, depressed, speculative status, step by step, to an earned semi-investment status among the institutions. On the other hand, buying into the face of a buying panic is a riskier proposition. When institutions are pushing and shoving to get into a stock, it is usually not a buying opportunity for investors.

But of more importance was that the stock was running right back into overhead resistance. As discussed earlier, the 15-17 range was an area of heavy past trading, and investors seeking to cut their losses short would no doubt be ready sellers as the issue worked its way higher. Not everyone would be buying the Wall Street line that the autos were buys.

Following the breakout, nimble investors could have bought on the pullback at 14 or under, protected by a stop, but buying stocks so much in play can often cut both ways because support tends to be more faddish/emotional than fundamental.

The resistance was too much for the advance, and as Wall Street's initial jubilation gave way to the realities of lower sales and earnings, Chrysler began to erode again. One more rally happened in June, back to 15 3/8, but faded as well. While Wall Street was ballyhooing the autos, Chrysler had formed a major pattern of distribution commonly known as a head-and-shoulders.

The move in Chrysler that would result in 1992's dynamic advance was about to begin.

Chrysler (C): 9/30/91 – 12/19/91

Not once, but twice during late 1991, Chrysler bottomed out at just under 10 a share, reflecting the same level of support that had surfaced in 1990. Investors have every reason to take speculative positions at support, or they can wait for some bullish technicals to develop when the stock is at support. Note that on the 4-1/2-week decline from 12 3/4 on August 28 to the September 30 low no bullish minor advance/decline sequence developed. Every minor rally was followed by declines to new lows.

Following September 30, the stock began a bullish minor advance/decline sequence—rallies to new minor highs, declines stopping at support. Positions could have been taken also when the stock's downward momentum of the previous 4 1/2 weeks was broken as the issue rose above 11 during the week ending October 4.

In addition, old-fashioned tape readers would find merit in the market's reaction to Chrysler's sale of stock. The very heavy 11.3 million share volume on October 1, reflected in part the sale of 35 million shares of stock on that day. Chrysler had planned to offer 33 million shares, but sold a greater number of shares at a higher-than-expected price.

The action of the stock in response to the stock sale was bullish in that the market was willing and able to absorb increased stock in a firm that had suffered such extensive selling pressures. Technically speaking, the market was well liquidated and void of stock.

Buying on declines can be hazardous. Bottom fishing is hardly foolproof. In the case of Chrysler, the stock found support where it should, reversed the bearish momentum of the previous month, and absorbed a significant amount of stock.

Nothing guaranteed that 9 3/4 would prove to be the bottom. Technical analysis gives some clues as to where to buy. To be safe, investors should put in stop-loss orders under support.

The stock rallied nicely off the lows, stopped briefly by resistance at 11 1/2, which in turn could be traced back to the lows of the formation of August 23. Buying could have been done on the following dull pullback to 10 1/2 the week ended October 25.

The stock began to move higher, and on October 30 shot up 1 5/8 on very heavy volume of more than 3.2 million shares. Chrysler had reported a loss of $82 million for the third quarter, much smaller than the expected loss of $225 million. However, the stock was moving right into resistance.

Seeing a stock rise sharply on heavy volume is bullish when the stock is breaking out free and clear. Investors have to be careful, though, when the stock is moving right into overhead resistance. Investors who had bought Chrysler based on the newly found Wall Street bullishness had about a 1/2-point gain for a week or so, but the gain quickly developed into a loss.

Tensions concerning the deteriorating economy no doubt caused Chrysler to sink lower than otherwise could have been expected after the stock backed off from its highs of 13 1/4. The overall market cracked 120 points on November 15, supposedly due to a plan to lower interest rates on credit cards. A buckling market took down stocks across the board, Chrysler included. Chrysler's decline ended at support at 9 3/4.

December 19 was not especially noteworthy. Trading was a bit heavier than usual; Chrysler traded at 9 3/4, but closed unchanged at 10. A fair amount of tax-loss selling and window dressing probably occurred. As noted in Chapter 4, the resulting January Effect is one of the strongest anomalies in the stock market. Chrysler was poised to commence its outstanding 1992 advance.

Chrysler (C): 1992

Technically, Chrysler from that point began to show a splendid orderly advance. The issue moved up in a self-correcting trend, a series of alternating minor advances and declines, just like walking up a flight of stairs, an advance on increased volume, followed by a decline on lighter volume, an advance on increased volume, followed by a decline on lighter volume. Buying can be done on the pullbacks.

These minor advance/decline series lead to the most dependable patterns, especially when compared to various spikes in the stock due to a deluge of Wall

Figure 7 • 3   Chrysler Corp. (C): January 1992 – December 1992

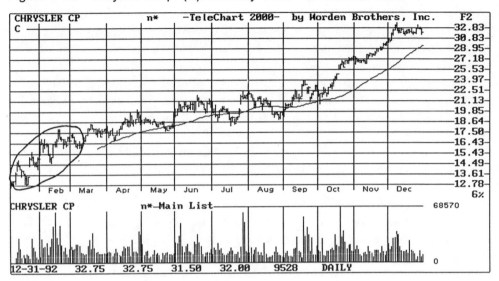

Chart courtesy of TeleChart 2000™ by Worden Brothers, Inc. Used with permission.

Street brokerage house buy recommendations based on news external to the company.

During the first three months of the year, Chrysler moved steadily higher. The final taking out of resistance above 15 was of great significance. The important supply of stock at 15 – 17 was absorbed and finally free to move higher (see Figure 7-3 above).

No formula can determine when a stock will be able to push through an area of resistance. On occasion, an outside stimulus, such as the surprise lowering of the Discount Rate on December 20, 1991, creates the type of bullish climate that will jump start market momentum. In the last seven trading days of 1991, the resultant money-manger buying panic raised up the Dow 254.47 points, and a lot of stocks, including depressed issues like Chrysler, went right along.

As shown through earlier examples, low-priced and depressed stocks usually do not overcome resistance on the first try and neither did Chrysler. The first intermediate advance from the lows is not the advance that starts the bull trend in earnest.

On the other hand, the more shares traded at the resistance level the first time, the more time and points and volume a stock spends at resistance, the greater the probability that when the stock makes it through, the stock is in a major bull trend. Thus, after the second test of the lows, at support, buying on the minor-trend advance/decline sequence is in order.

The 1992 percentage move of 172% (from 11 1/2 to 32) may seem a bit spellbinding, but the investor should look at the textbook pattern in the stock, advance on high volume, pullback on low volume, advance on high volume, pullback on low volume—the self-correcting zigzag, the basic pattern of technical analysis. Few patterns are more perfect.

About the only item of technical note is why the stock soared during the fourth quarter. Was it because the stock was steadily gaining support from the money mangers? Chrysler's financial health had improved, and all through 1992 sales and earnings steadily advanced. Chrysler was once again acceptable. The transition in status from that of a low-priced and depressed stock to an issue worthy of consideration by money managers and mutual funds provides an important boost.

However, looking from late 1987 to the end of 1989 Chrysler was in a trading range that centered around 24. As Chrysler moved first to 18, then to 20, then to 22, then to 24, the stock was moving up through that body of sellers. After Chrysler cleared the resistance, it was free and clear.

The *Fortune* annual survey of Most Admired Corporations was published in the February 8, 1993, edition. Chrysler was not at the top. It occupied position 232 out of 311. By moving from a position of 294, 14 slots from the bottom, to 232, Chrysler had the distinction of being number one on the 10 most improved list!

The Unisys Renaissance

Unisys has been a major winner among NYSE stocks, up over 500% from its 1991 lows of 2 1/8 through its 1993 highs. Investors had ample opportunities to buy into Unisys early in the move.

Unisys displayed many of the typical traits of a depressed, low-priced stock. In addition, it was widely held and had a large following on Wall Street. The Unisys story will be presented from start to finish, highlighting the technical pattern in tandem with Wall Street opinion.

Unisys: The Decline

As recently as 1987 Unisys was in top form. The stock traded as high as 48 3/8 in August 1987. It enjoyed widespread grades from analysts, had an impressive run during the preceding 12 months, and split 3-for-1.

Wall Street was endorsing Chairman and CEO W. Michael Blumenthal's strategy to combine Sperry Corp. with Burroughs. The theory was that combined, the two together would effectively compete against industry leaders, such as Digital Equipment and IBM.

The new Unisys looked very good to Wall Street analysts. However, marketing problems began for Unisys from the need for continued software development on two basically different systems—Sperry's and Burroughs's—while at the same time keeping current customers satisfied and trying to integrate the two systems.

Further compounding the problem, Unisys fell behind on hardware technology. While Wall Street continued its praise, the computer market reacted to Unisys's awkward strategy of trying to make diverse profit lines work together.

Unisys unraveled over several quarters. Record sales and earnings were reported for 1988. By 1989 Unisys plunged deep into the red, losing $3.25 per share for the year. In 1990 the dividend was cut from $1.00 to $0.50, and in 1991 the company eliminated the dividend. Increased cash flow problems at Unisys caused the market to begin to focus on the firm's hefty debt load.

Unisys stock never quite recovered from the 1987 crash. In the last half of 1988, it began to lose ground and by the last half of 1989, the stock was in a free-fall. The stock stopped at what had been major support, around 10. When that support level was taken out in the summer of 1990, the free fall accelerated (see Figure 7-4).

By the time the selling panic subsided, Unisys was beyond being a depressed stock. The low of the year was 1 3/4 on October 26, 1990 and closed at 2 1/4. The stock had been in a major bear market for three years, down an incredible 96%. It was trading at only 0.14 of book value and the alpha was -3.28. Unisys gave depressed new meaning.

MBAs gave up on the stock. Just a few years earlier they were giving it accolades. By the time of the February 1992, *Fortune* survey of America's Most Admired, Unisys had sunk to just five positions from the bottom. Out of 307 companies, Unisys was able to beat out only Crossland Savings, Continental Airlines, Home Federal, and Wang Labs. Chrysler beat out Unisys. Unisys was given up for dead.

The News About Unisys

A review of the official news about Unisys will help the investor understand the psychology of low-priced, depressed stocks. The review will start with Unisys's plunge to its lows.

By September 1990 Unisys was already a very weak stock, and investors had been shaken by a fall in stock price from 15 7/8 on June 1 to $7 a share by mid-September. Investors were being reassured by management, but credibility problems

Figure 7 • 4 Unisys Corp. (UIS): March 1990 – February 1991

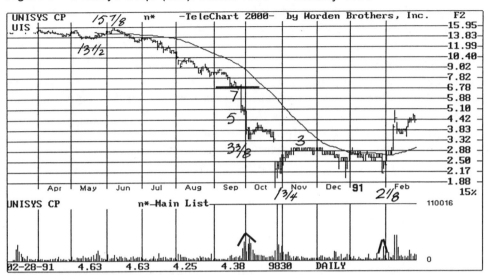

Chart courtesy of TeleChart 2000™ by Worden Brothers, Inc. Used with permission.

had developed. Then shaken investors heard a series of negative developments. A wholesale selling panic began.

A review of the Unisys panic will also give investors who like to bottom fish plenty to think about. Trying to peg the bottom price of a fallen blue chip can be extremely unprofitable. Buying on the basis of high yield/low price, for instance, can lead to some real big losses if you don't know what you are doing. Only by tracking the stock price action can investors have any clue as to when to take a stake.

The panic began with the September 27 announcement of a dividend omission. Of probably greater consequence was the announcement by the Chief Executive Officer (CEO) James Unruh that he was backing away from earlier assurances that Unisys would be profitable for the full year. The company reiterated that it expected a profitable fourth quarter, but the CEO added that predicting was becoming more hazardous.

Investors threw in the towel on September 27. Unisys stock dropped 1 5/8 to 5 3/8 on volume of 2.28 million. The 1 5/8 drop was a 23% cut. After the drop Unisys had a market value of only $800 million, compared to $10 billion in annual sales. It truly qualified as a depressed stock.

A few days later the stock plunged further. Moody's downgraded its rating on Unisys debt to below investment grade, raising fears of a liquidity crunch. The downgrade effectively eliminated Unisys from the commercial paper markets. The issue fell another 1 1/2 or 22.5% to close at 3 7/8. One analyst opined that the Unisys situation looked "ugly." To investors who owned the stock, "disaster" was more fitting.

Until the very end Unisys was still labeled investment quality by the rating services. The rating services have their function, but overall they lag far behind what the stock price is saying quite clearly.

Investors often hold or buy into a technically weak stock just because the stock or debt is low and is rated investment grade. The rating services, due to the nature of the process, are based on past, not current, performance, and especially not future performance.

Unisys had a brief reprieve for a few weeks in October. After all the heavy selling, the stock traded at just under $4 a share.

The final price plunge came when the company reported on October 25, 1990, a $356.8 million loss for the third quarter. The situation was worsening. Management stated that the fourth quarter would probably show a loss as well. Just the previous month Unisys had said it would show a profit in the fourth quarter.

Management changed. Michael Bluementhal, who largely had shaped Unisys's strategy, announced his resignation. Jim Unruh, Unisys's chief executive, became Chairman. Unruh assured Wall Street that, while the current outlook was poor, the firm was taking steps to put its business back in order.

Wall Street's real concern was the financial viability of the firm. Could Unisys stay solvent? Standard & Poor's Corp. cut its rating on Unisys debt on October 25, 1990, based on third-quarter results, citing a concern that cash flow would continue to be under severe pressure. The very next day, Moody's, for the second time in a month, downgraded Unisys across the board, cutting the rating on the long-term debt to Ba-3, the convertible subordinated debt to single B-2 from Ba-3, and the preferred stocks to single B-3 from single B-1.

The combination of an already weak stock, further losses, plus downgrades in debt was enough to cause the last holders of Unisys to cash out. The stock fell 33% on October 26, 1990, to close at 2 1/4, down 1 1/8 on the day. The low of the day was 1 3/4. Unisys was the most actively traded stock on October 26, with more than 11 million shares trading hands. More than a few money managers probably wished they had never heard of Unisys.

The overall state of the stock market contributed to the extreme weakness of Unisys. Wall Street was very bearish. By October 26, 1990, the stock market had fallen sharply from its July highs of 3000 to below 2400. The outlook for stocks in general was very pessimistic. On the day that Unisys made its low, only one stock on the NYSE made a new high—Dean Foods; 137 made new lows.

Further adding to the gloom about Unisys was a bond market in retreat as well. "Big U.S. Debt Sales Spook Bond Investors" headlined the "Credit Markets" report in the *Wall Street Journal* on Monday, October 29th. The downgrade in Unisys debt did not sit well with an already skittish bond market.

By October 26, though, the lows of the stock market had already been seen. The Unisys stock low had already been seen. The bond market low had already been seen. At the time, investors couldn't give their stock away fast enough.

On October 3, 1990, 4.2 million shares had traded as low as 3 3/8. On October 26, the stock traded as low as 1 3/4, with volume of more than 11 million shares. Combined with other days when volume was more than 2 million shares, massive liquidation between 2 and 4 a share had occurred.

For the next few months Unisys traded in listless fashion, between 2 and 3, with most transactions closer to 3. The stock market was uncertain. The news had little to say about Unisys. The stock was dead in the water.

Unisys stock showed a renewed weakness on Wednesday, January 30, 1991, dropping 1/2 to 2 1/8 on volume of 2.6 million shares. A day earlier the firm announced a larger-than-expected fourth-quarter loss of more than $436 million. The stock, however, bounced back nicely to the 3 level in just a few days. All the selling in Unisys was over.

The Unisys Turnaround

One of the greatest turnaround stories on record was about to begin. What can technical analysis tell us about what was to happen?

On Friday, February 8, 1991, on volume of 4.8 million, Unisys broke out, sharply rising 1 1/8 to 4 per share (see Figure 7-5). There was not any particularly significant news. The firm had announced an agreement with European Amadeus Development S.A. to provide microcomputer equipment. Rumors that Unisys was planning asset sales were continuing.

On the following Monday, February 11, 1991, Unisys was up again, closing 1/2 point higher at 4 1/2, hitting 5 intraday. Unisys was the second most active issue with volume of 4.7 million. The news of the day was that Unisys suspended dividends on its preferred stock, a further indication that the firm was trying to deal with its debt load. Continuing speculation regarding asset sales resulted in a 5-point jump in Unisys 8% Senior notes.

The rise of the stock was puzzling to Wall Street. Newspaper accounts of Unisys were bearish, saying that the cut in the dividend reflected the "depth of the trouble in which Unisys finds itself."

Figure 7•5   Unisys Corp. (UIS): January 1991 – December 1991

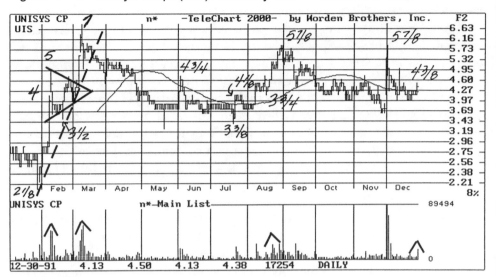

As to the asset sales, the Wall Street conclusion was that Unisys had been talking about asset sales for several quarters and that a deteriorating economy was making it more difficult to get the prices it sought.

While Wall Street was uncertain over the reason for the move, the technicals were positive. Buying pressures were stronger than the selling pressures. The stock broke out of a three-month period of listless trading. The breakout was decisive. The trend was unquestionably bullish.

On the following day, Tuesday, February 12, 1991, the stock gave back 5/8 of a point on volume of 2.5 million shares. The news of the day was Standard & Poor's announcement that it may lower its rating on $4 billion of Unisys debt following the company's suspension of its preferred dividends.

Mum was largely the word at Unisys for the next few weeks. On March 1 the firm named two new directors. On March 7 it introduced a new mainframe computer, the A19, with some fanfare, but some analysts thought prospects might be hurt by worries over Unisys's financial health. On the same date, a former Unisys marketing executive pleaded guilty in a defense contract case. Overall, the news was neutral.

Technically, the stock was doing what it should have done following a breakout. Following the advance to 5, the issue pulled back on very low volume, trading at 3 1/2 – 3 3/4 for several days. The time to buy a stock in classic technical analysis is on the dull reaction following a breakout. Investors could have bought at 3 3/4.

The next week Unisys started to work its way back toward 5. Some additional selling that surfaced at 4 1/2 in late February took the stock back to 4, but volume on the decline was light. The overall pattern following the initial pullback after the advance to 5 was one of slowly firming strength.

Unisys was forming a fairly well-defined symmetrical triangle. Because patterns tend to be formed by support and resistance levels, they are sometimes useful in helping analyze the forces of support and resistance at work.

Symmetrical triangles often represent continuation patterns, with buying and selling pressures gradually coming together, with prices tightening up and volume drying up. While the symmetrical pattern in Unisys was bullish in that it suggested some further gains, the lack of a similar formation after the advance to 7 was less bullish.

On March 7, 1991, Unisys again jumped sharply, up 1 1/8, breaking above 5, to 5 1/2. Investors could have bought on a limit order when the symmetrical triangle was broken out of at 4 3/4, or on the breakout above 5.

On Friday, March 8, Unisys was up another 3/4 to 6, the second most active stock. No "media" reason was given for the advance. The reason for the move was that Unisys had absorbed the body of sellers at 5. The stock attacked the resistance at 5 once, then again, and on the third time, succeeded in moving past 5. After a resistance point is broken, a stock normally moves ahead rapidly on volume.

Why 5? Refer back to Figure 7-4. The low of the panic days on September 27 and 28, 1990, was 5. After a stock moves below a panic low, those lows always provide resistance. Those who thought Unisys to be a bargain at 5, only to see it drop to 2, probably were happy to have a chance to get out at 5.

On Monday, March 11, Unisys led the most active list, on volume of 5.7 million shares. The stock hit an intraday high of 7, but finished down 1/4 of a point on the day, at 6.

A March 12 article in the *Wall Street Journal* suggested that analysts who follow the stock were having a difficult time accounting for the jump in price. Almost as an afterthought, the article noted that Unisys, from a technical point of view was ready to break out of its rut. In all the news accounts on Unisys and analysts' reports, beginning with the stock's precipitous fall from the 1987 highs through its sustained rebound in 1993, this was the only mention of technical analysis.

The stock's decline followed familiar patterns of distribution, and the stock's eventual rebound showed familiar patterns of accumulation. Only the stock action itself provided the clues as to when or when not to buy. Technical analysis alone could decipher these clues.

At a later stage in Unisys's rebound, fundamental analysis would become more important, playing a critical role in making Unisys into a big winner by generating support among Wall Street institutional money managers. At key turning points in the stock, technical analysis provided the only clue to its potential turnaround.

The review of Unisys is lengthy but important because in many turnaround situations, the fundamentals are mixed at best, with many uncertainties. Analysts tend to favor the companies at the top of *Fortune*'s Most Admired list and not those, such as Unisys, at the bottom.

In the early days of February 1991 the trend in Unisys turned bullish. Buyers of Unisys at those levels probably had no idea the stock was about to become one of the best performers on the NYSE during the next two years. Given the very heavy liquidation in Unisys in September and October 1990, it would not take a lot of conviction to move the issue higher.

Technically, Unisys had its most important development on the breakout on February 8, 1991. Buying could have been done as Unisys was rising above 3, which had been the edge of resistance the previous three months, or on the pullback to 3 1/2 subsequent to the breakout.

The move during February and March from 3 to 7 was an intermediate advance. I look for a stock to move in three moves in the primary direction. Unisys had just two advances.

The reason for only two moves to 7 is that the stock hit resistance. Resistance theory will tell us where the selling should come into play.

Resistance levels are defined by key lows. Going back to October 1990, to the point where Unisys was trading before its selling panic, the low of that prepanic trading range was 7. Panics, both buying and selling, nearly always develop as a break from a trading range. Thus, the price level preceding a panic plunge like October 26, 1990, often becomes a focal point of subsequent resistance.

Another characteristic of sharp drops like that of October 26 is that few shares were traded between 7 and 5. Five was the price at which the greatest volume occurred. So the issue's first advance, on February 8 and 9, halted at one area of resistance, 5.

The next advance, once through 5, showed a very rapid advance. Little resistance occurred between 5 and 7. Many investors were impressed with Unisys's sharp advance. The stock was operating in a vacuum. After it hit the expected resistance at 7, it stopped dead in its tracks.

Investors might consider the buying opportunities in Unisys. Buying could have been done on the breakout above 3. A buy limit could have been set at 3 1/4. Investors could also have bought on the dull pullback following the initial breakout, when, after the stock hit 5, the dull reaction carried the issue to 3 1/2 during the weeks of February 15 and February 22.

Finally, investors could have bought either on the breakout from the symmetrical triangle formation that developed during the four weeks prior to the March 8, 1991, advance, as the stock crossed 4 3/4, or as it broke above 5 1/4.

The further away a stock is purchased from its initial breakout, the greater the risk. Another very good rule is not to buy a stock after it has advanced 10% to 15% from the breakout. This rule suggests that buying above 3 1/2 would have been too risky.

In the Unisys advance from 2 1/8 to 7 the stock showed a very tight trend. The lows of January 30, 1991, 2 1/8; February 21, 3 1/2; and March 1, 4, made up a fairly well-defined trendline.

Trendlines form at support. Thus, trend analysis suggested that the stock should have held at 5 3/8 on or about March 22. When Unisys slipped below that point, it suggested that the entire intermediate move from 2 1/8 to 7 was completed and would be corrected.

As noted earlier, important bottoms or bases tend to take time. In depressed issues, there is a lot of uncertainty, based on fundamentals, and there is a lot of overhead supply. Even with improving fundamentals, it takes time and volume to eat through the resistance. Unisys was no different.

During May, June, July, and August 1991, Unysis traded mostly between 3 1/2 and 4. Support was formed right above the trading range of the last 2 months of 1990 and January 1991. Buying in the stock could have been done on any number of days as the stock waffled right above 3 during May, June, and July.

Unisys broke out on June 4. Buying could have been done as the stock crossed 4, or on the pullback following the breakout. The stock pulled back entirely to 3 1/2. The June 4 breakout was false in the sense that a bullish trend did not develop. However, buyers at 4 would not have been hurt badly and would have been in the stock for its later sustained advance.

The action of the stock on July 24 was encouraging. Unisys had declined to 3 3/8 on July 22, probably in anticipation of a further loss. However, when the $1.3 billion loss was reported, the stock rose to 4 1/8 on good volume.

Investors generally were becoming more optimistic after the firm's latest series of job reductions and changes. In the bond market greater certainty that Unisys could pay off a bond issue due in September added to the optimism. Unisys had won a new agreement with the banks. Investors seemed to realize that Unisys was being given some breathing room. The fundamentals were beginning to give some explanation on why the stock was acting better.

That one-day move to 4 1/8 was also the start of an intermediate trend that would carry the issue to 5 7/8 during the next six weeks. Buying could have been done on the pullback the week of August 2 at 3 3/4. However, after the typical three moves in the primary direction, the stock broke lower in September and Unisys again settled back toward 4.

The next surge was not a breakout. It was all news. On December 2 Unisys surged 1 3/8 to close at 5 1/4 on speculation that Charterhouse Bank Ltd., a London merchant bank, was working on a takeover plan. Neither Charterhouse or Unisys commented on the rumor.

Investors who chased Unisys got burned. After reversing the following day at 5 7/8, the same resistance point where it was turned back on August 26 on high volume, Unisys again settled back to 4.

Through the end of 1991 Unisys was a difficult stock. The advances kept fizzling. The rallies indicated that support kept developing around 4. Unisys seemed listless most of the time, but its major trend was bullish. The stock had risen in a well-defined intermediate trend wave from the lows the previous year.

Support was present, and positions could have been taken. Despite what seemed to be failed advances, the overhead resistance was being attacked. Unisys during the dull trading in December was an excellent choice for the January Effect.

The 1992 Unisys Move

The advance on December 30, 1991, began the move, with the stock going to 4 3/8 on volume of more than 1.7 million shares. The move was not big. It was not reported in the *Wall Street Journal*. The volume was the largest of any day during the previous three months, with the exception of the volume induced by the takeover speculation. Some important money had moved into the stock. Volume on the stock's advance to a new high at 4 5/8 on January 2 was not especially impressive, but when Unisys advanced past 5 to close at 5 1/8 on January 7, 1992, volume expanded nicely to 2.1 million shares (see Figure 7-6).

Unisys, without much fanfare, began to trace out a very bullish pattern: minor advances with increased volume, followed by pullbacks on low volume, pullbacks that stopped at support.

On the decline from the January 2, 1992 advance, the stock closed at 4 3/8, the December 30, 1991, top. On the decline from the January 7 advance, the stock closed at 4 5/8, the January 2 top. Subsequent to the next advance to 5 3/4, the

Figure 7 • 6 Unisys Corp. (UIS): December 1991 – November 1992

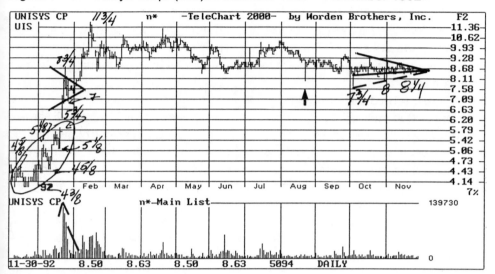

stock retreated to 5 1/8, the January 7 top, and stopped. The stock was tracing out perfect trend development based on support levels.

Unisys made little news as it began its move. On January 15 volume picked up nicely to 2.2 million with the stock advancing to close at 5 1/4. No mention was made in the *Wall Street Journal*. Unisys was up the following day, closing at 5 1/2 on volume of 3.2 million shares. No mention was made in the *Wall Street Journal*.

The overall market was strong, rising very sharply during the last two weeks of December 1991, sparked by the Federal Reserve cutting interest rates on December 20. Not only was Unisys rising in a bullish market, but the stock was quickly gaining relative strength versus the market.

On January 22, 1992, Unisys rose sharply to close at 5 3/4 on volume of 2.7 million shares. Unisys was up against the same price level at which the stock had been turned back in August and December the preceding year. Would the advance be a sustained breakout, or just another false alarm?

On Thursday, January 23, a day with the Dow down some 29 points, Unisys soared on volume of 13.9 million, leading the most active list, up 1 1/4 on the day to close at 7. Unisys had a decisive breakout.

The breakout was attributed in the papers to the earnings gains, with the firm reporting a better-than-expected fourth-quarter profit of $0.31 per share.

After eight quarters of losses and broken promises, Unisys was beginning to regain some respectability.

Two considerations are of technical merit. First, the stock had twice encountered strong resistance at 5 7/8. If an issue is able to move past the point where so much supply existed, it should be able to move freely. Overcoming resistance explains the gaps.

Second, large short interest no doubt helped propel the stock higher. For the reporting period ended January 15, Unisys's short interest was 11.7 million shares, up from 11.3 million shares sold short the previous period ending December 13. Short interest was 25 times the average daily volume. The large short interest was about to fuel an afterburn to the stock's new rise.

(Citicorp had the largest short position for the period ending January 15, and Chrysler occupied the 8th position.)

On Friday, January 24, Unisys led the most active list again, rising 1 point to 8 on volume of 11.2 million. The following Monday, after hitting 8 3/4, Unisys had a reversal and closed down on the day.

Investors who waited to buy until the fundamentals improved at Unisys were still going to make a profit for the year. Buying stocks in the news can be a tricky proposition. Much of the move is already over by the time the news is announced.

Considering the earlier technical action of the stock, investors were justified in buying at lower prices—around 3 or a bit above, during the last quarter of 1990, around 4 or a bit above during most of 1991, or when Unisys started walking up its staircase in January 1992. Any number of technical patterns suggested buying when the stock was $5 or less.

Last minute investors were given only one opportunity to buy, in the dull reaction to 7, during the week of January 31 following the stock's advance to 8 3/4. Right in line with the prior high of 7 on March 11. Technically, the pennant- and flag-type reactions occur as mast formations as they develop at the end of a very sharp surge (the mast) in price. These formations occur in very rapid markets and the reactions tend to be very brief. Volume during their formation declines sharply. Pennants and flags often occur when a stock's overall move is one-half over. They provide about the last, although not the best, opportunity to buy.

The rule is: Buy during the fourth to sixth reversal point, providing volume has declined sharply. In the five trading days following the January 27, 1992 reversal, Unisys sagged in a very tight formation, with volume drying up. Investors could have bought on the fifth day following the reversal at 7 3/8, or on February 4, as the stock broke the downward momentum and began to move higher. Waiting for the stock to surge to new highs, as on February 10, was not a low-risk buying opportunity.

Unisys had another major jump on February 14, up 1 1/4 to 10 3/4 on very high volume of 5.3 million. The news was that Unisys was nearing an agreement with its banks on a new line of credit. Unisys was the second most active stock the following Tuesday, up 3/4 to 11 1/2. On Wednesday, February 19, Unisys's dynamic advance ended with the stock falling 1 point to 10 1/2 on volume of 5.7 million.

The year 1992 started out with a bang. The January Effect certainly seemed to have played a part with Unisys. Nearly all the Unisys advance took place during just a few weeks at the beginning of the year. For the remainder of 1992, the stock drifted. Whether or not investors benefited from the issue's 145% advance depended exactly on where and when in the trend they purchased stock.

The volume characteristics of Unisys in 1992 are also instructive. First, the largest volume in the stock occurred during the four trading days ending January 21, 1992, as the stock traded at and around 8, reflecting that the stock moved past resistance as earlier defined at 7. A large concentration of volume helps define potential support and resistance levels. In the stock's decline throughout 1992, the issue found support at 8. Volume during just four days in January defined 8 as important support.

Unisys formed some interesting patterns. The October – November 1992 pattern could be described as a symmetrical triangle; support was generally rising, with the descending line of the triangle reflecting a tightening of prices. The large intraday drops of October 6 to 7 3/4 and November 30 to 8, reflected support (see Figure 7-7).

Prices were tightening and volume was low, indicating the convergence of buyers and sellers, right where the stock should be supported, at 8. After trading in a convergence pattern for more than two months, Unisys broke out on December 1, 1992, on very heavy volume. The stock rose to 9 3/4, up 1 1/8, on volume of 4.4 million. The stock was up on the highest volume in more than six months.

The following day Unisys was the most actively traded issue, at 6.9 million shares up 1/2, closing at 10 1/4. Unisys was setting the stage for another robust intermediate advance during the first quarter of the year.

Unisys showed the typical three minor rallies in the direction of the primary trend during the first quarter of the year. It advanced in three waves from a late November 1992 low of 8 1/2 to a high of 13 7/8 by March 1993 (see Figure 7-7).

Unisys was turned back when the stock crossed 13 on several different occasions. Finally, it lapsed into another extensive intermediate correction.

Figure 7 • 7   Unisys Corp. (UIS): July 1992 – June 1993

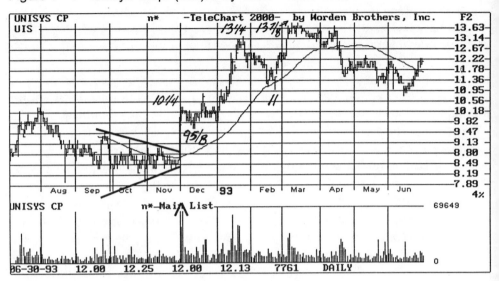

Chart courtesy of TeleChart 2000™ by Worden Brothers, Inc. Used with permission.

This occurred at 13 because 13 3/8 and 13 1/2 were the lows of the trading range formation that dominated the stock during the first half of 1990 (Figure 7-4). The advance in early 1993 should have stopped at that level of resistance, and it did.

While looking at the intermediate advances/declines for Unisys, and the minor advances/declines making up the intermediate trends, major trend continues. There is still plenty of room on the upside at Unisys if bought right.

Citicorp (CCI)

Citicorp has been one of the best performers among the NYSE most active stocks, up 360% from its lows. While Citicorp has made all-time highs in 1993, the Citicorp story began several years ago.

Citicorp is a good example of how a highly regarded stock becomes depressed. It was one of Wall Street's favorites as late as 1989. The company had had its share of write-offs, but its reputation on Wall Street was still high. *Barron's* often featured one or another money manager who owned several million shares expounding on why Citicorp had tremendous potential. I was so impressed that I bought some stock for my children.

Citicorp (Figure 7-8) in summer 1989 looked great. The stock traded to new all-time highs, and the cash dividend had just been increased. Through the summer the stock had traded between 31 and 34, and when during the last week in September, Citicorp moved above 34, the trend could not have looked more bullish.

The market's 190-point drop on October 13, 1989, disrupted a lot of stock patterns, including Citicorp's. Nonetheless, it quickly gathered itself at the support previously present at 31. Citicorp's picture still looked bullish.

After an initial rebound to 32, Citicorp slid down past support at 31 to 28 3/8. After many months and tests of 31, Citicorp had violated that key support level. It was a significant breakdown. At the time certainly no one could imagine Citicorp moving below $10 a share, but the trend had turned bearish.

After a stock moves below a support level it becomes a resistance level. In the weeks following the decline through 31, Citicorp rallied on several occasions back to 31, sometimes a bit above, sometimes a bit below, but was turned back every time. The former focal point of support was now resistance.

During its decline over the next two years the stock found support on several occasions and a new bull trend could have been started. A couple of attempts were made during the first half of 1990.

Figure 7 • 8   Citicorp (CCI): August 1989 – July 1990

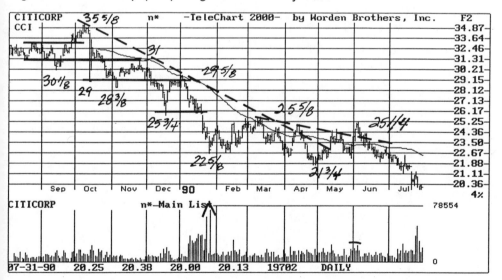

Chart courtesy of TeleChart 2000™ by Worden Brothers, Inc. Used with permission.

Citicorp: 1990

Following Citicorp's break under support at 31, the stock declined persistently until it hit 22 5/8 per share during the selling climax on January 26, 1990. For a stock where the average daily volume was under 1 million, a 7+ million share day was a sign that someone had thrown in the towel. As is often the case following a persistent decline, the large-volume selling climax indicated the end of the decline for the time being.

The stock rallied in a minor advance/decline sequence off the lows of 22 5/8 to an eventual high of 25 5/8 the week of March 12. Coming on the heels of such a drastic decline, the rally found a ready supply of sellers looking to unload their positions. The first sequence of minor advance/declines off panic lows is usually not sustained.

The advance from the April 27, 1990, lows of 21 3/4 was an interesting pattern. A series of higher highs and higher lows was bullish. A trendline drawn along the highs of March 9, April 13, and May 17, suggested a breakout point around 24. The stock also broke a longer trendline dating back to October 10. In the week ending June 1, Citicorp moved to 25, rising above the previous minor high and the trendline.

Taken alone, the sequence from April 27 to June 6 was bullish. On the other hand, the breakout was not inspiring. Volume on breakouts should increase 100%, 200%, 300%, and more. The volume on the new high was higher, but not by a lot. The advance had again moved right up to resistance as indicated by the minor panic low of 25 3/4 of December 19, 1989. Panic lows always have to be given ample respect because the relatively large volume of the panic, by definition, indicates a significant support or resistance level. Because Citicorp subsequently moved below 25 3/4, that panic low represented resistance.

Citicorp had formed a bullish minor advance/decline sequence, a positive formation after persistent declines, and had broken through a declining trendline, an event that suggested that downward momentum had been broken. However, the stock could not rise above the resistance at just above 25.

By July 1990 it became apparent that Citicorp was again headed lower. The lack of even minor support forming along the way from July through October 1990 should have kept buyers with any degree of familiarity with price patterns on the sidelines (see Figure 7-9).

From July to October 1990, Citicorp lost 50% of its value. Earnings were down but were still positive. Bullish recommendations kept being published. Yet, the stock just continued to slide. Extensive declines do not end on a vacuum. They end in a selling climax. Volume soared as money managers could not get rid of their stock fast enough.

Figure 7 • 9   Citicorp (CCI): June 1990 – May 1991

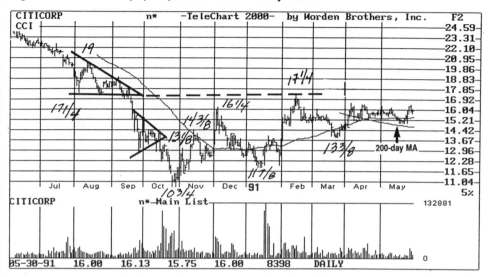

At the end of an extensive decline, investors are warranted to take speculative positions in a stock with any strength. There were no buy recommendations on Citicorp, but the stock had just fallen 50% and a huge selling climax had taken place. Citicorp had fallen to its 1982 lows, 10 3/4.

The stock had been flushed out of weak hands. Some rebound rally could be expected. Following the lows of 10 3/4 on both October 26 and October 30, Citicorp began a minor advance/decline sequence.

While the first rally off panic lows, following an extensive decline, breaks the momentum, it is not likely to be the start of a major bullish trend. The stock will eventually bump up to resistance and perhaps be turned back.

The last major area pattern resistance was in the low 20s as in Figure 7-8. Any bullish minor advance/decline sequence should be used as an opportunity to take positions in stocks that have had extensive declines.

If an investor buys at the start of a trend, the investor will benefit from an uptrend. Stops should be set so as not to get hurt too badly if the stock collapses and moves lower.

The first minor rally carried Citicorp to 13 1/8, where the stock had a slight pullback of just a couple of days. The second minor rally carried to 14 3/8, approximately to the apex of the symmetrical trading formation that had developed in late September. A third minor rally carried the stock to 16 1/4, where the resistance came from a pattern that formed in August; it looked like a descending triangle. Seventeen at that time was support, not resistance.

The Citicorp 1987 panic lows were also coming into play. The absolute low in 1987 was 15 7/8, but a lot of stock was traded at 16 – 17. The 1987 panic lows help explain why the 16 – 18 area would prove so much resistance over the next 18 months.

The three minor rallies constituted an intermediate uptrend. The rule of thumb is to expect three. After three moves in the primary direction, it is too late to buy, and investors should wait for the next intermediate reaction. Citicorp subsequently declined over the next six weeks to 11 7/8.

Citicorp: 1991

Citicorp advanced through January, 1991 and had a couple of nice moves into early February. By February 15 the stock was up against resistance at 17 1/4.

When buying low-priced and depressed stocks, it is critical to buy when an advance is getting underway, when the minor advance/decline sequence is bullish, either after panic lows, such as after the lows of 10 3/4, or after an intermediate reaction, such as after the lows of 11 7/8.

Buying at 17, as the stock is trying to fight its way through resistance, and when the stock is already up more than 50%, is risky. Widely held, depressed blue chips, such as Citicorp, because there is so much resistance, often retreat to their lows months after the first panic lows. Citicorp retreated and then some.

Following the rally to 17 1/4, Citicorp declined to 13 3/8, rebounded slightly, and spent the next three months trading in the range of 14 – 15. While the initial focus of attention on the chart is the panic decline in Citicorp, with the stock dropping to 8 1/2 later in the year, investors should keep the number 14 in mind. It represented an important level of support, then resistance, and then support again (see Figure 7-10).

On October 3, 1991, on a pickup in volume, Citicorp opened under 14, thereby breaking below the tight 14 – 15 range in which the stock had traded the previous three weeks. It continued to decline, rallied sharply back toward 14 on October 15, but closed lower on the day. The rout was on.

The sharp reversal on October 15 was due to a Citicorp announcement of a $885 million third-quarter loss—a deficit exceeding most analysts' expectations—and a suspension of the quarterly dividend. The loss, on top of an already weak capital structure, prompted Standard & Poor's to downgrade Citicorp's rating to triple B+ from single A–. Citicorp stock closed lower on the day by 7/8 to 12 3/4, the most actively traded issue on 4.1 million shares. Volume swelled

Figure 7 • 10 Citicorp (CCI): May 1991 – April 1992

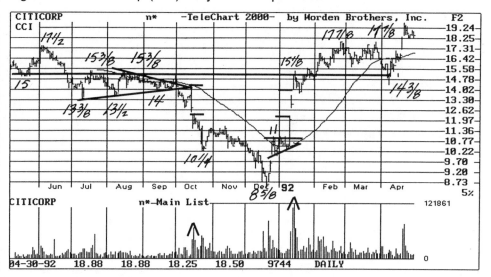

Chart courtesy of TeleChart 2000™ by Worden Brothers, Inc. Used with permission.

the following day with Citicorp down another 1 to 11.75. The stock continued to slide toward 10.

The stock rallied at 10 1/4 on October 25 for four days to close at 11 1/2 on October 31 but could not hold the gains. It slipped below 10 on December 10. Citicorp was the most active stock on volume of 8.2 million shares as it hit its closing low of 8 5/8 on Friday, December 22, 1991, exactly 1/8 of a point higher than its low of 8 1/2 during its 1977-1982 trading range. At the lows the stock was selling for about 40% of book value.

That same Friday the Federal Reserve had dropped the discount rate to 3.5%, the first full 1-point drop in 10 years. An explosive gain in stock prices followed. In the last seven trading days in December 1991 the market rose by more than 250 points. Citicorp's fortunes rose as well.

Citicorp: 1992

Nonetheless, while technical analysis is in large part how a stock reacts to public psychology, close inspection of Citicorp indicates how the stock reacts to "vested" interests.

Following the low of 8 5/8 the stock rallied on the interest rate cut, but came to a halt at 11. What was coming into play was the selling panic of October

16, when Citicorp fell to 11 1/2 on extraordinarily high volume of 6.85 million shares. Panic bottoms, since they represent high volume, always provide resistance when a stock is trying to move back up. Such as the case with Citicorp in early January. The area pattern resembled an ascending triangle, and on January 13, Citicorp broke out to the upside. The trend was bullish for Citicorp once again.

The reason for the advance was attributed to Citicorp Chairman John Reed. When he announced on January 13, 1992, that earnings for the fourth quarter would be in the red, the stock rallied sharply, up 1 1/2 to close at 12. Apparently analysts were relieved the results were no worse.

Technical analysis in its simplest definition is how investors react to general market conditions, to the news, to developments as they occur at any one company, to the action of the stock itself. In just a few weeks the psychology regarding Citicorp made a turnaround.

The stock tacked on another 1 to 13 the following day on 11.2 million shares, with Citicorp being the most active stock of the day. Banks were a strong group in a market that had risen 66 points to a new record. The next day, Wednesday, January 15, volume increased again, to 12.1 million shares; Citicorp advanced 2 1/8 to close at 15 1/8. Goldman Sachs reportedly put the stock on its recommended list.

In terms of technical analysis, however, the sharp advance reflects the lack of trading, or resistance, between 12 and 14 as shown in the panic drop the week of October 18. Perhaps part of the move was due to Goldman Sachs, but the lack of sellers had something to do with the advance as well.

While Citicorp was again becoming a Wall Street favorite after the stock had nearly doubled, it once again was butting up against resistance. The 14 – 15 level of resistance the previous July–August–September, is where and why the stock stalled in the institutional panic.

After a brief sell-off, the rally continued but eventually encountered its resistance at 17, the level which the stock could not overcome all through the previous year (see Figure 7-9). First it rose to 17 7/8 on February 26 but faltered and sold off mildly. A month later it again rose to 17 7/8, but faltered again. This time the stock declined a little more extensively.

Investors looking to buy Citicorp were to find that the 15 level would come into play on more than one occasion. It had been resistance during July, August, and September of 1991 and was resistance in the week of January 13. After the stock rose back above resistance at 15 in February, 15 again changed places and became support.

Fifteen also took on significance because it represented a panic buying high. Consider the tremendous volume as the stock hit 15 the week of January 13.

Volume defines significance. Citicorp was now in a trading range where 15 represented support, 17 resistance.

At 15 demand proved to have the upper hand, and the stock subsequently moved higher. Momentum seems to be the standard operating procedure on Wall Street. Some of the money managers who sold at 15 wanted to climb back aboard.

Fifteen first came into play as support during the week ending April 10, the decline from the February–March high ended as the stock closed at 15 on April 7 (see Figure 7-11).

Note the expanded volume as the stock subsequently rose in mid-April past the resistance represented by previous twin highs of 17 7/8 as well as the highs in the 17 range during June of 1991. The bull trend in Citicorp was fairly evident. Also note the typical dull pullback after the advance to 19 3/4. Support now should now be at 17 7/8. On May 1, after the stock hit 18 1/8, the issue began to rally, a rally that would eventually carry the stock to the next level of resistance.

To determine the next level of resistance, look at Figure 7-8 on page 167. The low of the formation that ran from January through June was 21 3/4 on April 27. What should be the high of the advance taking place two years later, during the first half of 1992? The high of the advance was 21 3/4 on July 3, 1992 (see Figure 7-11).

Figure 7 • 11   Citicorp (CCI): January 1992 – December 1992

Chart courtesy of TeleChart 2000™ by Worden Brothers, Inc. Used with permission.

Technical analysis is not exact, certainly not down to 1/8. Resistance theory held that the 1992 advance would top out somewhere in the low 20s. As Citicorp rose in 1992, it became more and more recommended. However, anyone who bought Citicorp as it approached the low 20s was buying in a high-risk area.

Figure 7-11 also shows the subsequent intermediate decline in Citicorp. It ended at 14 3/8 in early October 1992. While not quite as exact as the preceding top, support theory held that the decline should level out at about 15.

After bottoming out at 14 3/8 on October 9, Citicorp staged a tremendous rally, finishing the year out at 22.25, up 114.5%, to enable the issue to be among the best winners on the NYSE in 1992. Citicorp's trend at the end of 1992 was bullish. Where would it take the stock?

If you go back to December 29, 1989, you'll find that 31 was an important trading range. However, once the stock declined in October 1989 to under 31, 31 was redefined as resistance.

Citicorp had an exceptional move from the October lows, doubling in just about six months. The rally stalled at 30 7/8 for 3 months, April–May–June 1993, before pushing on.

· 8 ·

Dow Jones Winners

Industrial Average's Biggest Winners

Union Carbide: Runner Up at 289%

Union Carbide (UK) has been one of the top winners in the Dow Jones Industrial Average providing a return of 289% during its current bull market. Union Carbide was up some 91.88%. In one year alone, 1992, investors received the spin-off of Praxair in July, and the stock further rose to a 5-year high in 1993.

Three years ago, at the beginning of 1991, Union Carbide was priced at 20 1/4. Two Dow stocks were priced lower: Bethlehem Steel at 14 and Westinghouse at 18. Bethlehem ended the year up 14%, but Westinghouse dropped another 25%. Being a low-priced stock hardly guarantees a gain, with or without a high dividend. The stock must be trending up. In any depressed issue, the potential is present. As a group, these three low-priced Dow stocks rose 23.6%, compared to a return on the Dow of 4.17%.

Union Carbide's story did not begin on January 1, 1991. Carbide's Dow-leading advance has been part of a major bull market that began in Union Carbide on September 26, 1990.

During the major part of 1989 and 1990 Union Carbide had been declining. The issue dropped from a high of 33 3/8 on February 16, 1989, to a low of 14 1/8 on September 26, 1990. Carbide lost 57% in a 19-month period.

At the September lows Union Carbide was selling under its book value of $16 per share. It was about to follow in the footsteps of Goodyear, 1991's big winner in showing that winners do come from stocks selling for less than book value.

Following the lows, Union Carbide would base over the next few months. After important intermediate and major declines, many stocks follow the three-fan principle. If after an extensive decline, the stock breaks three consecutive fans, it can be purchased. The first fan (see Figure 8-1) is drawn from the July 27, 1990,

Figure 8 • 1 Union Carbide Corp. (UK): January 1990 – December 1990

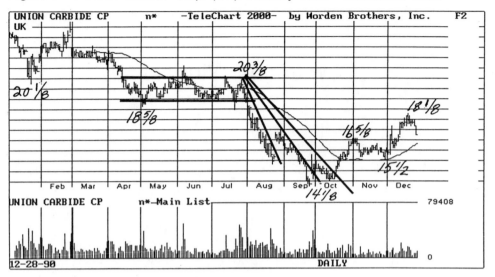

Chart courtesy of TeleChart 2000™ by Worden Brothers, Inc. Used with permission.

highs of 20 3/8 and is broken on the August 27 rise. The second fan is drawn from the July 27 highs and is broken on the September 27 advance. The third fan is drawn from the July 27 highs and is broken on the October 19 rise. Based on the three-fan principles, purchases of Union Carbide could have been executed as the stock was crossing 15.

The three-fan principle works in patterns where a base is being formed. The three-fan principle simply reflects momentum as it shifts from bearish to bullish. Often it takes time and volume for a depressed stock to overcome a big decline. Substantial bearish sentiment had settled in. It took time for support to form once again.

Normally, after an extensive decline, a stock will thrash about, reflecting interaction between support and resistance. These include diverging market interests, speculators buying in anticipation of recovery, and investment groups selling on every opportunity.

For Union Carbide, the three-fan principle suggested that important support was entering Union Carbide. Positions could have been taken at 15 or shortly thereafter.

Technical analysis did not indicate that 14 1/8 of September 26 would be the low. All that could have been inferred was that the stock was gathering enough

Figure 8 • 2   Union Carbide (UK): January 1991 – December 1991

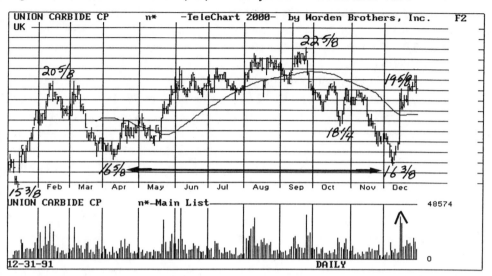

support to perhaps move higher on an intermediate basis. Perhaps support would fuel it up to resistance.

Resistance is defined by a previous trading range. In the case of Union Carbide, 19 – 20 was an important level of trading. The stock first bounced off that level in January of 1990, then declined after a fashion to the 20 level again. It traded on or about 20 from late April to mid-July. Based on resistance, a rally off the September 26 lows of 14 1/8, to about 20, was in order.

Union Carbide had a nearly atypical intermediate-trend rally, composed of three minor-trend rallies. It ended during the week ending February 15, 1991 with the high, 18 1/8, just short of the 18 5/8 low the prior May.

The only unusual formation during the intermediate advance was the decline during the week of January 18, 1991 (see Figure 8-2 above). Based on support levels, the minor decline during late December—early January should have found support around the previous minor high—16 5/8.

Union Carbide, like all other stocks, fell sharply over the uncertainties regarding Desert Storm in early January. It fell to 15 3/8. A few days later, however, with Allied victory so swift, stocks, including Union Carbide, were back on track, sparked by a stampede of 117 points on the Dow.

Desert Storm merely short-circuited a support level during a minor reaction in January. Note where the stock ended its fall during the more significant intermediate reaction that developed during March and April. The reaction corrected the entire move from the January 16 lows of 15 1/2 to the February 14 highs of 20 5/8, right at support—at 16 5/8. It is not unusual for these types of stocks to correct back 2/3 or so to the first support level.

The next move in Union Carbide saw the stock rise off those lows of 16 5/8 in a typical intermediate uptrend to 22 5/8 on September 25, 1991.

From 22 5/8 a normal correction in Union Carbide would have taken the stock back to around 18 – 20. The stock initially did begin to find support and bounce around after hitting 18 1/4 on October 24. However, when the overall market broke, with growing economic concerns leading to a one-day drop on the Dow of 120 points on November 15, all stocks, including Union Carbide, sold off sharply.

On the other hand, after the stock broke 18, the stock did find support at a familiar and more significant support level—16. It closed at 16 3/8 on December 9. Many times the same levels of support come into play.

Normally some ebb-and-flow basing action, like the three-fan principle, would have followed. On Monday, December 16, 1991, Union Carbide caught Wall Street by surprise, announcing a restructuring plan to spin off its industrial gases business to shareholders and a sell-off of $500 million in assets to reduce debt. Stock action was electric. Union Carbide was up 2 1/4 to 19 5/8 on volume of 1.5 million.

Nineteen out of 20 "news" rallies are followed by a dull reaction. Just a couple of days later, however, Alan Greenspan announced a surprise discount rate cut—from 4.5% to 3.5%. The result was a surge in the Dow of more than 88 points.

The entire list was lifted by the Fed's action. The discount rate cut designed to jump start the economy was thought to be especially beneficial to the cyclical issues, such as Union Carbide. Union Carbide advanced 3/4 to close at 20 3/8. The restructuring, plus a positive market environment, had jump-started Union Carbide to the top of the Dow's best-performing stocks in 1992 (see Figure 8-3).

Investors who bought Union Carbide at support at 16 during tax-selling season had a nice gain. Nimble investors could have bought on the very slight pullback following the December 16 advance at 19 1/4 – 19 1/2. However, after the stock had risen in January above its previous highs at 22 1/4 – 22 5/8, one buying opportunity at support opened up the week of April 10, another the week of June 31, another the week of October 16.

During the balance of 1992 Union Carbide was picture perfect. Its major bull trend was made up of alternating intermediate advances/reactions. Every intermediate correction pulled up right to support.

Figure 8 • 3   Union Carbide (UK): January 1992 – December 1992

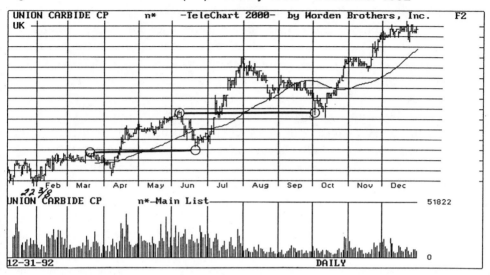

Goodyear Tire & Rubber: The Hands-Down Winner

This far in the decade of the 90's, Goodyear Tire & Rubber has been the "hands-down" winner. Goodyear (GT), though, was not a "winning" company in 1990. It recorded a loss and ended the year with an announcement that the quarterly dividend was being reduced from $0.45 to $0.10.

Goodyear was to become the leading Dow Jones Industrial stock in 1991, up 183.44%, up 34 5/8 points from the start of the year at 18 7/8, to close at 53 1/2. The Dow, in comparison, was up approximately 20%.

The winning 1991 performance was only part of the story. The bull market in Goodyear started at 12 7/8 on November 12, 1990, and as 1993 came to a close, Goodyear was still rising. Adjusting for a 2-for-1 split in May, Goodyear was up 632% from its 1990 lows to its 1993 high.

Goodyear had all the earmarks of a stock that was depressed—not just down, but depressed. The stock's high in 1987 was 76. In 1988 the high was 67; in 1989 the high was 59. In 1990 the stock collapsed, falling from 46 to 12 7/8. Extent and duration defines a truly depressed stock, and by late 1991 the stock had fallen 83% over a period of just over four years. At the lows the stock was selling for only one-third of book value, and Goodyear was about to demonstrate that the best gains come from stocks selling under book value.

Time and points can readily identify the degree to which a stock is depressed. Can technical analysis be of any help in highlighting a depressed stock that is about to achieve the best gains of any Dow stock for the following year?

The degree to which a stock is depressed will influence the degree of potential gain. No form of analysis, of any type, could have signaled to investors that Goodyear, after hitting an intraday low of 12 7/8 on November 12, 1990, was on its way back up to its 1987 highs, hitting 76 1/8 on April 24, 1992, for a gain of 491%, and then moving higher.

What technical analysis can do is to indicate when the trend is changing from bearish to bullish, or when the stock is in the process of rebounding. The degree of decline can suggest the potential of gain; technical analysis will spotlight when to take a position.

For Goodyear the major trend is the stock falling from 76 1/2 in 1987 to 12 7/8 by 1990, then back up and past 76 in April 1992. It pays to be on the right side of the major trends.

As previously discussed, the intermediate trend is probably the most important in making technical analysis practical. The intermediate trend will best define the opportunities.

Goodyear's decline during the months of July, August, September, and October 1990 was an intermediate bearish trend (see Figure 8-4). The advance after 12 7/8 was the start of an intermediate bullish trend. Successful technical analysis is being able to identify these intermediate swings early on.

Intermediate swings unfold in three phases. An intermediate decline starts with the stock gradually rolling over, as its upward or neutral momentum shifts to the sell side. Second, the stock enters the markdown phase, where the steepest part of the decline occurs. Third, the stock begins to show some buoyancy as support enters the picture and the stock begins to flatten out.

The Goodyear chart (see Figure 8-4) shows typical intermediate trend action. Following the sharp late-February to early-March rally, from 32 7/8 to 38 3/4, Goodyear settled into the mid-30s range for several months. Investors would not know until either 38 3/4 was penetrated to the upside, or 32 7/8 was broken on the downside, whether the intermediate trend was either up or down. The correct presumption was that the bearish major trend was still in effect.

The mid-30s, incidentally, reflected the same level of support as the stock attracted during the 1987 crash, when Goodyear declined to 35. The same interests that moved into Goodyear in 1987 were moving into Goodyear in the summer of 1990.

Support can "just develop" in a stock. Investors know that support tends to develop at previous highs. The last major bull market top in Goodyear was in

Figure 8 • 4   Goodyear Tire & Rubber (GT): January 1990 – December 1990

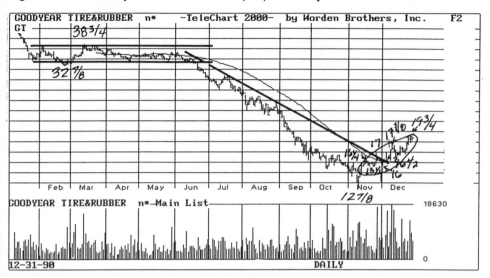

Chart courtesy of TeleChart 2000™ by Worden Brothers, Inc. Used with permission.

1982 – 1983. The absolute highs were 36 7/8 in 1982 and 36 3/8 in 1983. Volume showed that most of the trading look place in the low 30s. So, the low 30s was a likely area for support to redevelop.

Support levels can be broken, and after Goodyear broke major support in the low 30s, panic selling was expected. As Goodyear broke 32 7/8, on June 21, the stock entered the second phase of the intermediate decline, the markdown phase, where most of the damage is typically done. Not only had intermediate support been broken, but also major support had been broken. The stock would drop more than 50%.

The decline was persistent until Goodyear showed some buoyancy after hitting its low of 12 7/8. Support began to form.

How can the formation of buoyancy be measured? A trendline drawn from the early June highs, connecting the minor highs along the intermediate downtrend, form a channel. After the stock's low of 12 7/8 on November 12, the issue began to move sideways, and the downtrend was broken.

One buy rule is that after a stock has had a persistent decline and is beginning to show some buoyancy, indicating that some buying is being done for some reason, it is one time to buy, in anticipation of a bullish intermediate trend.

A bullish intermediate trend may not develop. Back in March 1990 Goodyear had a long decline, but all that occurred was one minor rally. And, even if a bullish intermediate trend began, all that could have been expected was a rally to the upper-30s, where the stock would have encountered resistance. Some knowledge of the phases of intermediate trends helps to define the price levels where investors can establish speculative positions.

This is not all that technical analysis involves. Technical analysis has some fairly intense areas. Understanding the typical characteristics of trends is its most practical area.

A stock such as Goodyear became so depressed because it had a major trend. Whether the advance off the November 12, 1990 lows was the start of a major rebound could not be determined from the available information. Investors had a reason to buy the stock, based on typical trend patterns, as the issue moved out from 12 7/8.

The Goodyear chart in Figure 8-5 shows how the intermediate trend unfolded. Goodyear nearly doubled from 12 7/8 on November 12 to 24 3/4 by March 1991. It then rose to 31 3/8 by June, nearly a tripling. It did this by typical trend development, just like walking up a flight of stairs. First, a series of bullish minor zigzags composed an intermediate trend. Then a series of bullish intermediate trends composed the major trend. If investors take the time, technical analysis is not mystical or difficult.

As shown in Figure 8-4, following the 12 7/8 of November 12, 1990, Goodyear had a minor rally to 16 1/4 on November 16. The stock declined to 15 1/4 the next week on very light volume. Then on November 28, Goodyear broke to new highs on robust volume, moving ahead to 17. In moving above the November 16 high of 16 1/4, the intermediate trend became bullish, and investors could buy on the next pullback to support.

Support is defined by the existence of a previous high. The previous high was 16 1/4, so investors could buy on the pullback to support at 16 following the November 28 rally. On December 11 the stock again broke out on heavy volume, rising to 17 7/8 then declined back to support at 16 1/2. On December 25 the issue again broke out to new highs to 19 3/4, then declined to support.

After months of persistently declining stock prices, a textbook bullish intermediate trend—a series of minor zigzags—was developing in Goodyear. Investors had ample early opportunities to buy into a depressed stock on the recurring pullbacks to support.

Did investors have any assurance that 12 7/8 was the bottom? It could have been just another intermediate bottom, as was 32 7/8 back on February 23. Because bottom fishing is an educated guess at best, investors can set stops just under support.

When Goodyear moved to new minor highs on November 28, stops could have been put in right under the previous support level, at about 15. When Goodyear moved to a new high on December 11, the stops could have been upped to the next level of support.

Goodyear's intermediate advance from November 12 to March 6 was made up of several minor bullish zigzags, then breakouts and returns to support (see Figure 8-5). The advance took approximately 120 calendar days, just a few days longer than the typical bullish primary intermediate swing. The precise extent and duration of intermediate swings are determined by interacting support and resistance levels, many of which can be predetermined.

Goodyear also moved above its 50-day moving average on the November 28 breakout. After long, persistent declines, a stock rising above its declining 50-day moving average may spotlight a breakout as well. Moving averages can be next to useless in many situations, whipsawing investors; on the other hand, they can help formulate the correct appraisal of a stock's trend if used in the right context.

On February 8, 1991, Goodyear cut its dividend from $0.45 to $0.10. The stock dropped sharply to support at 17 3/4. One test of the technicals for any stock is to take a reading on the rally following a minor panic such as that of the dividend cut.

For the next five days Goodyear had the typical rebound. The test of the

Figure 8 • 5   Goodyear Tire & Rubber (GT): January 1991 – December 1991

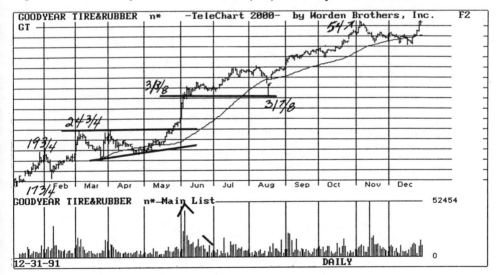

Chart courtesy of TeleChart 2000™ by Worden Brothers, Inc. Used with permission.

trend would be the week of February 17. The stock treaded water, then began to edge back up toward the previous highs. The test following the dividend panic proved successful as the stock rose in March to 24 3/4.

During March and April Goodyear's intermediate correctional pattern took the form of an ascending triangle, where the resistance at 24 3/4 was being defined by the congestion of trading between 23 and 26 back in August the previous year. After a couple of months trading under that resistance level, Goodyear broke out on May 28 and was again off and running. The major trend for Goodyear now definitely was bullish.

Where could investors expect the next level of resistance? A very wide trading range in the mid-30s ran from February through June of the previous year. As the stock surged higher, more than just a few investors could be expected to cut their losses short. The mid-30s was expected resistance.

June 4, 1991 brought very heavy volume of more than 1.2 million shares. Goodyear Chairman Tom Barrett had quit the previous day. The market took the resignation positively, rising 3 1/8. It closed at 30 1/8, and rose another 1 1/4 the next day to close at 31 3/8 on volume of more than 2 million shares.

Buyers of those 2.2 million shares ran right into overhead. A better buying opportunity surfaced during the dull reaction the week ending June 28, as prices on low volume drifted back right to the top of the high-volume move the week of June 7. The highs of the buying panic had set up a level of support at 32.

On Friday, July 26, 1991, Goodyear announced earnings of $0.38, compared to a year-earlier loss. The stock doubled after its positive earnings announcement; but Goodyear was already up nearly 200%.

Goodyear's pattern for the balance of 1991 was about as typical as could be (see Figures 8-5 and 8-6). The only unusual activity was the drop of 1 5/8 points on Monday, August 19, 1991, when Goodyear dropped in line with the 69.99 decline on the Dow in the midst of the Gorbachev coup. Support developed again at about 32.

After moving up through resistance in the low-30s, Goodyear rose in nearly a straight line. It was investment-grade material. Scorned at under 20, the stock now looked good at 40. Investors had had ample opportunities to buy into a depressed stock early in its bull move. The stock would rise to record highs in 1993 and be split 2-for-1.

The Dow Jones Transportation Average

When most investors think of market averages, few think of the Dow Jones Transportation Average. When most financial experts think of market indexes, few think of the Dow Jones Transportation Average.

Figure 8 • 6   Goodyear Tire & Rubber (GT): January 1992 – December 1992

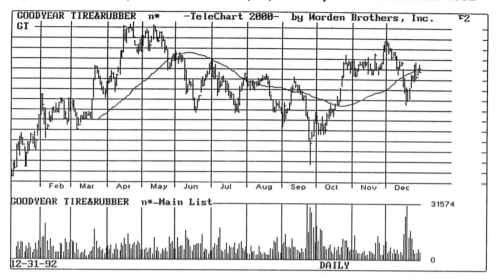

Chart courtesy of TeleChart 2000™ by Worden Brothers, Inc. Used with permission.

The Transports have been in the best bull market of them all. In addition, the forecasting implications of the Transports can be exceedingly helpful.

A forerunner of the current Transportation Average was the first of the Dow Jones Averages. Charles Dow's initial index in his Customer's Afternoon Letter in 1884 was of 11 stocks; 9 were railroads. Over time, more stocks were added to the Railroad Index. In 1970 the Index became a blend of railroad, airline, and trucking issues.

The issues comprising the Transportation Average provide insight into some key sectors of the economy. The airlines give a glimpse of discretionary spending. Trucking companies reflect shipments of light manufactured and finished goods. Railroads carry industrial products and raw materials and shipping reflects export activity.

The Transports serve analysis on many fronts. One of the original Dow theory tenets is the tenet of confirmation: The action of the Industrials and the Transports must be taken together. If the action of one Average is not confirmed by the other, the forecasting significance of the first diminishes.

In significant market movements the Industrial and Transportation Averages nearly always move together. The 30 Industrials represent the production of goods and services. The Transports represent the movement of goods. The confirmation tenet makes sense.

The Transports have some additional attributes that are important. Because the shipment of goods is more sensitive to expectations, the Transports are generally a good barometer of future growth. Being more responsive to growth, the Transports are also more cyclical, reflecting the ups and downs of the economy. This characteristic has important forecasting implications, not only for the economy, but also for the stock market as a whole.

The Transports have been in a major bull market longer than most of the major market averages. The major bull market of the 80s is considered to have started with the August 1982 explosion in stock prices, with the Dow coming off an August low of 776.92 and finishing out the year at record highs.

The trend-setting Transports, however, had already been in a dynamic bull market, doubling in price between 1979 and 1981. Before the bull market in the blue-chips even got started, the Transports were giving a green light to a broad advance in equities.

An expose on the Dow theory is not intended. I have written extensively on the Dow theory and the confirmation tenet. Few analysts really understand this critical element of Dow's theory. On the other hand, the success of the average investor is very much subject to the workings of the Dow theory. Because finding and successfully exploiting low-priced and depressed issues depends in large part on the tone of the market, taking a reading of the Transports is critical.

Because the Transports are a leading index, the last time an investor should buy is when the Transports are beginning to falter and diverge from the Industrials. On the other hand, the best buying opportunities are when the Transports, after a correction, begin to show strength relative to the Industrials.

Further, buyers of low-priced and depressed issues will find issues among those comprising the Transportation Index itself. The Transportation Index tends to be more volatile, and thus investors have the potential to find a large number of big percentage gainers among its members.

As indicated in Table 8-1, the Transports have a tendency to advance 56% more than the Industrials and decline 39% more than the Industrials. Stocks that have greater volatility and upside potential are fertile ground for technical analysis. Note, though, that for both the Industrials and Transports, the higher percent low-to-high relative to the percent high-to-low is in keeping with the major bullish trend of the markets.

A good number of opportunities in finding winners among low-priced and depressed issues will be in the Transportation Index itself.

The last major advance in the Transportation Index started in the last quarter

Table 8 • 1   Industrials versus Transports Percent Advances/Declines

	Industrials		% Low	% High	Transports		% Low	% High
	High	Low	to High	to Low	High	Low	to High	to Low
1992	3413.21	3136.58	8.8%	8.1%	1467.68	1204.40	21.9%	17.9%
1991	3168.83	2470.30	28.3%	22.0%	1358.00	894.30	51.9%	34.1%
1990	2999.75	2365.10	26.8%	21.2%	1212.77	821.93	47.6%	32.2%
1989	2783.52	2144.64	29.9%	23.0%	1532.01	959.95	59.6%	37.3%
1988	2783.50	1879.14	16.2%	13.9%	973.61	737.57	32.0%	24.2%
1987	2722.42	1738.74	56.6%	36.1%	1101.16	661.00	66.6%	40.0%
1986	1955.57	1502.29	30.2%	23.2%	866.74	686.97	26.2%	20.7%
1985	1553.10	1184.96	31.1%	23.7%	723.31	553.05	30.8%	23.5%
1984	1286.64	1086.57	18.4%	15.5%	612.63	444.03	38.0%	27.5%
1983	1287.20	1027.04	25.3%	20.2%	612.57	434.24	41.1%	29.1%
1982	1070.55	776.92	37.8%	27.4%	464.55	292.12	59.0%	37.1%
1981	1024.05	824.04	24.3%	19.5%	447.38	335.48	33.4%	25.0%
1980	1000.17	759.13	31.8%	24.1%	425.68	233.69	82.2%	45.1%
1979	897.61	796.67	12.7%	11.2%	271.77	205.78	32.1%	24.3%
1978	907.74	742.12	22.3%	18.2%	261.49	199.31	31.2%	23.8%
1977	999.75	800.85	24.8%	19.9%	246.64	199.60	23.6%	19.1%
1976	1014.79	858.71	18.2%	15.4%	237.03	175.69	34.9%	25.9%
1975	881.81	632.04	39.5%	28.3%	174.57	146.47	19.2%	16.1%
1974	891.66	577.60	54.4%	35.2%	202.45	125.93	60.8%	37.8%
1973	1051.70	788.31	33.4%	25.0%	228.10	151.97	50.1%	33.4%
1972	1036.27	889.15	16.5%	14.2%	275.71	212.24	29.9%	23.0%
1971	950.82	797.97	19.2%	16.1%	248.33	169.70	46.3%	31.7%
1970	842.00	631.16	33.4%	25.0%	183.31	116.69	57.1%	36.3%
1969	968.85	769.93	25.8%	20.5%	279.88	169.03	65.6%	39.6%
1968	985.21	825.13	19.4%	16.2%	279.48	214.58	30.2%	23.2%

Difference Low to High = 56.3%   Difference High to Low = 39.1%

of 1990, as the transportation issues were rising out of the ashes of the takeover mania of 1989. The Transports were trending steadily higher after the 87 crash, but began to soar in the last half of 1989 on takeover fever in the airlines (see Figure 8-7). The Transports spiked at 1532.01, with issues like United Airlines (UAL) doubling in a matter of months to $294 per share.

Figure 8 • 7   Dow Jones Transportation: 1989 – December 1993

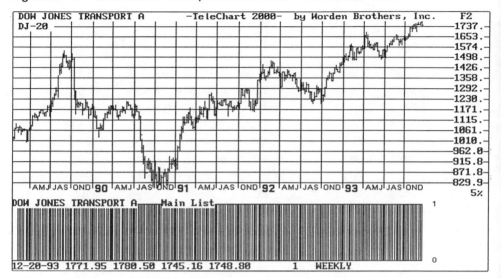

Chart courtesy of TeleChart 2000™ by Worden Brothers, Inc. Used with permission.

When the takeover speculation in the airlines came to a halt nearly all the Transportation issues, not only UAL, came tumbling down. They did not get back on steady ground until the last quarter of 1990.

After the Transports found steadier footing, it became all bull market. From the lows of 821.93 of October 17, 1990, the Transports have been unstoppable, doubling, hitting new records in 1993.

The stocks behind the bull market in the Transports were all low-priced and depressed. When the Transports were doubling, just a handful of stocks accounted for the majority of the gains. Not surprisingly, they were the low-priced stocks (see Table 8-2).

Just four low-priced issues, with an average price of $10.28—American President Companies, Santa Fe Pacific, Southwest Air, and XTRA—accounted for nearly half the gain of the overall Index.

The two issues that achieved gains topping 500%, Southwest Air and XTRA, were priced at $12.75 and $13, respectively.

The average price of the individual stocks in the Transportation Index at the time the Transports began to trend higher was $26.23. Stocks priced less than $26.24 advanced on average 210.6%, stocks more than $26.23 advanced 85.4%.

Table 8 • 2   Dow Jones Transportation Average: Percent Gainers

| | Price ($) | | | |
	Low	Split-Adjust	6-30-93 Price ($)	Gain/Loss
Southwest Air	12.750	6.375	43.625	584.3%
XTRA (2-for-1 '93)	13.000	6.500	42.750	557.7%
American President Companies	10.375	–	56.875	448.2%
Santa Fe Pacific	5.000	–	18.375	267.5%
Consolidated Rail (2-for-1 '91)	32.500	16.250	53.625	230.0%
CSX	26.000	–	71.500	175.0%
Ryder Systems	12.250	–	31.250	155.1%
Burlington Northern	22.250	–	53.625	141.0%
Roadway Services	27.250	–	58.000	112.8%
Union Pacific (2-for-1 '91)	61.250	30.750	61.000	98.4%
Norfolk Southern	35.000	–	65.125	86.1%
Airborne Freight	13.500	–	25.000	85.2%
AMR	39.750	–	63.250	59.1%
Federal Express	29.500	–	46.625	58.1%
Consolidated Freightways	10.750	–	16.000	48.8%
UAL	84.250	–	123.250	46.3%
USAir	12.625	–	16.500	30.7%
Carolina Freight	10.250	–	12.875	25.6%
Alaska Air	13.875	–	15.000	8.1%
Delta Air Lines	52.500	–	48.375	–7.9%
	26.231			160.5%

Nearly all the best performers were less than $15. Stocks priced less than $15 advanced 221.1%; stocks more than $15 advanced 99.9%.

The stocks that achieved gains of 100% or more were priced at $17.93. The stocks that achieved gains less than 100% were priced at $33.02.

The weighing toward price of the Dow Jones Transportation Index itself tells a story, with the price-weighted Index up 88.5%, but an unweighted index of the 20 stocks up 160.5%. The winners were to be found among the low-priced and depressed stocks.

Review of Four Transport Winners

American President Companies (APS)

American President Companies (see Figure 8-8) at its low of 10 3/8 on October 26, 1990, was down 79.5% from its 1987 highs of 51, a decline that had lasted just about three years. At 10 3/8 the stock was selling for one third of book value.

The stock did not have much of a float, only 15 million shares. The limited number of shares outstanding and limited number of shares traded during the decline probably accounted for the ability of APS to move up steadily from its lows. During the move up the stock stalled at every level of resistance, but only momentarily.

Stock charts often have a symmetrical look. The symmetry comes from support and resistance levels. Where there are significant trading levels on the way down, the stock will stop at those levels on the way back up.

With American President the decline was fairly uniform from June through October 1990, an absence of significant trading levels. On the rebound, the stock moved up freely until it encountered resistance represented by the trading range marked by a July 3, 1990 low of 20 3/4.

Figure 8 • 8   American President Cos. (APS): May 1990 – April 1991

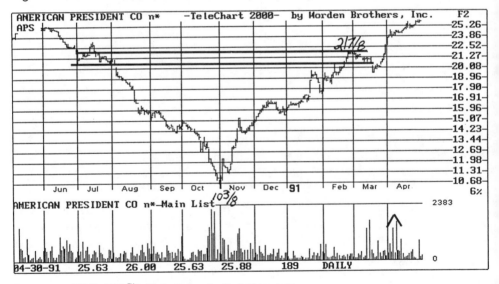

Chart courtesy of TeleChart 2000™ by Worden Brothers, Inc. Used with permission.

Santa Fe Pacific (SFX)

Santa Fe Pacific (see Figure 8-9) at its lows of 5 1/2 on October 26, 1990, was selling right at book value. The firm had had a couple of spin-offs, so calculating the degree of loss was more complicated. However, a decline of more than 50% in the six-month period from June to October certainly classifies the stock as down.

Santa Fe Pacific had several interesting formations. In the decline from the June 1990 highs of 10 7/8. Every decline moved to new lows.

The initial rally to 6 7/8 resulted in new minor highs, and the following decline held above previous lows. That minor advance/decline sequence was very bullish after such an extensive decline the previous six months.

On January 14, 1991, the stock traded intraday at new lows, at 5 1/8, but the stock did not close at new lows. The volume dropped very low on that decline as well. Volume picked up on the following advance.

Volume determines what price levels will be resistance. Seven was resistance for Santa Fe. Back on September 13, 1990, there was very heavy volume of more than 200,000 shares at 7 – 7 1/8. When the stock finally breached 7 on February 5, the stock advanced sharply. In crossing 7, 7 then became a support level.

The stock subsequently pulled back to support at 7, advanced to 8 1/2, but

Figure 8 • 9   Santa Fe Pacific (SFX): November 1990 – October 1991

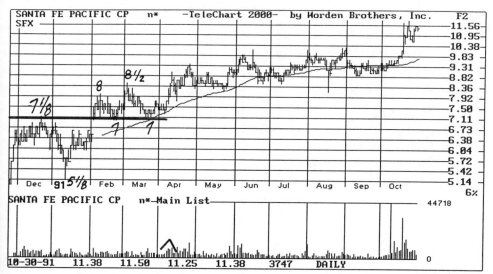

then fell back into support. The next rally on heavier volume took the issue higher.

Southwest Airlines (LUV)

Southwest Airlines (see Figure 8-10) was not depressed at its lows of 12 3/4 on September 27, 1990. The stock was low-priced and down from its highs of 18 7/8 three months earlier.

The stock was also in a trading range dating back many years, with the top of the range marked by resistance at 20 and the bottom in the lower teens.

In late October 1990 when the market and most issues were falling to new lows, Southwest Airlines moved ahead and was trading well above its lows of September 27. A stock beginning to trade higher while the market is trending lower is technically bullish.

When the stock approached resistance at 20 the week of December 7, 1990, the stock was turned back on heavy volume. However, the trend was decidedly bullish, with two complete advance/decline sequences from the lows of 12 3/4.

When Southwest Airlines cleared resistance at 20 on January 17, 1991, the stock gapped and volume exploded.

Figure 8 • 10   Southwest Airlines (LUV): May 1990 – April 1991

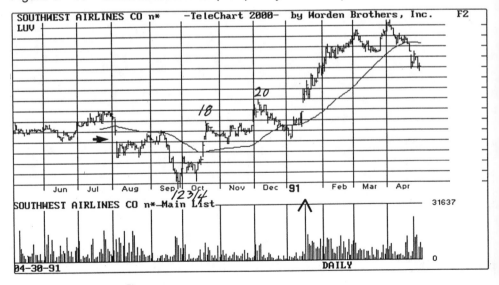

Chart courtesy of TeleChart 2000™ by Worden Brothers, Inc. Used with permission.

XTRA (XTR)

XTRA had an extensive decline. At the lows of 13 in mid-November 1990 the stock had declined 70% from its 1989 highs and was selling at about $2 over book. During the summer of 1990 there was a string of insider buys as well as higher earnings. Both were positive but the trend of the stock was still bearish.

The stock traded between 13 and 14 for a month, then moved sharply higher in a rally to 16 1/8 the week ending December 21, 1990 (see Figure 8-11). After the customary dull pullback to support at 14 1/4, the stock moved rapidly higher once past resistance.

Not all low-priced and depressed stocks in the Dow Jones Transportation Average were winners. However, all the big winners during the advance in the Transports were low-priced stocks, and most of them were depressed. Investors needed to observe how these stocks were acting and ask the simple question: "Are they acting better, are they acting worse?" The opportunity to purchase the four stocks that led the Transportation Index to record heights would have followed.

The Dow Jones Utilities

For many years the utilities have been thought of as "widow and orphan" stocks: not very exciting, but solid, income-producing investments for conservative

Figure 8 • 11   XTRA Corp. (XTR): May 1990 – April 1991

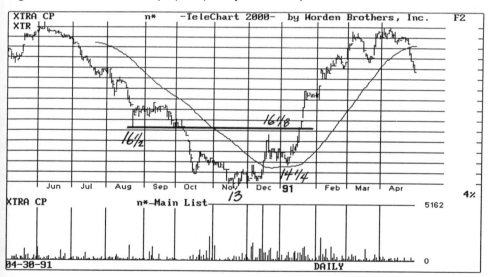

Chart courtesy of TeleChart 2000™ by Worden Brothers, Inc. Used with permission.

accounts. More recently, the utilities have also provided a fair share of capital gains. For instance, from 1988 to date, which encompasses the current bull market in the utilities, the Dow Jones Utilities advanced from a 1988 low of 167.08 to a record high on September 13, 1993 of 256.46 (see Figure 8-12).

Because utilities are interest sensitive in large part they reflect the ebbs and flows of interest rates. Concurrent with the current bull market advance in the utilities has been the decline in interest rates. A prime interest rate of 11.5% at the beginning of 1989 steadily fell to a low of 6% by the last half of 1992. Conservative investors have enjoyed the best of both worlds, high yield plus capital appreciation.

But falling interest rates do not tell the whole story. Of the gain in the Dow Jones Utilities since 1988, just a handful of stocks account for the majority. And, as if readers have to be prompted, the gains were primarily achieved by the lower-priced utilities.

In 1988, the average price of a Dow Jones Utilities stock was a little over $20 per share (see Table 8-3). However, the two largest gainers, Detroit Edison and Pacific Gas & Electric, were priced at $12 and $14 respectively. The issues priced under $15 a share at the beginning of the advance in 1988 account for about 40% of the entire advance of the utilities: Detroit Edison, $12; Niagara Mohawk Power, $12; Centerior Energy, $12.25; and Pacific Gas & Electric, $14.

Figure 8 • 12   Dow Jones Utilities: 1989 – December 1993

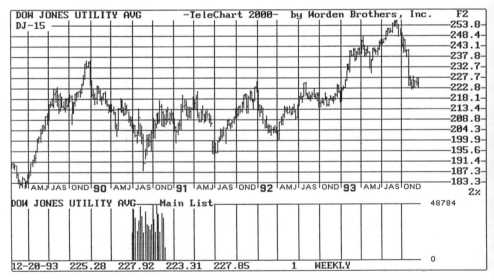

Chart courtesy of TeleChart 2000™ by Worden Brothers, Inc. Used with permission.

The Two Biggest Winners Among Utilities

Detroit Edison was the biggest winner, rising from a 1988 low of 12 to a close of 32 3/4 at the end of 1992, for a gain of 172.9%. At the 1988 lows Detroit Edison was not exactly depressed, with the stock only down about a third from its highs.

However, Detroit Edison was still down from its highs, reflecting upcoming write-offs associated with its troubled Fermi 2 nuclear plant. At the lows, before the 1988 write-offs, Detroit Edison was selling for about 60% of book value.

Pacific Gas & Electric was the second biggest winner, up 136.6%, from 14 to 33 1/8. In early 1987 the utility had traded at all-time highs, but anxieties regarding utilities with nuclear construction and write-offs over its Diablo Canyon nuclear power plant caused the stock to drop just about 50% into mid-1988. Prior to the decline Pacific Gas & Electric traded at a 45% premium to book value. At the lows, the stock traded at about 30% under book value.

Detroit Edison and Pacific Gas & Electric are just two of many low-priced stock opportunities that developed over the years among the utilities. One of the first was Consolidated Edison Company of New York.

TABLE 8 • 3   Dow Jones Utilities: Percent Gainers

	Price 12-31-92	Price 1988	Gain
Detroit Edison	32.750	12.000	172.9%
Niagara Mohawk Power	19.125	12.000	59.4%
Centerior Energy	19.875	12.250	62.2%
Pacific Gas & Electric	33.125	14.000	136.6%
Peoples Energy	30.125	15.350	96.6%
Philadelphia Electric	26.125	16.875	54.8%
Arkla	8.500	17.750	−52.1%
Consolidated Edison	32.625	20.375	60.1%
Panhandle Eastern	16.750	21.000	−20.2%
Public Service Enterprise	30.875	22.000	40.3%
Commonwealth Edison	23.250	22.750	2.2%
American Electric Power	33.125	25.875	28.0%
Houston Industries	45.875	26.625	72.3%
SCE Corp.	44.000	29.125	51.1%
Consolidated Natural Gas	45.500	33.750	34.8%

Other Utilities Opportunities

Consolidated Edison Company of New York (ED)

Consolidated Edison today, and at times in the past, has been considered the Dean of the utilities industry, not only due to exemplary service but also because of its usually solid financial integrity. However, the Dean has had some bumps and bruises along the way.

Consolidated Edison's heyday, and probably the utilities in general, was until 1965. Utilities had enjoyed a tremendous bull market from the lows in 1942. Since then utilities became known as growth stocks. Price-earnings ratios in the 20s reflected just how much investors valued the utility issues.

However, as inflation in the Great Society era began to heat up, the utility industry, by its very nature, could not keep track. Costs were rising more rapidly than in other industries. The price of oil rose rapidly, while the ability of utilities to pass on their cost increases was limited by the regulatory apparatus. Shrinking profit margins resulted, and, in the case of Consolidated Edison, much worse.

Consolidated Edison topped out in 1965 with the stock selling at 49 1/4, or 1.75 times book value. For the next 10 years the stock would consistently drift lower, reflecting a price-earnings ratio which was moving down from 20, then into the upper teens, then the lower teens, then into the single digit range, as investors marked down the value of the shares.

However, the really electrifying jolt to shareholders occurred in 1974, when solid, reliable, good-ol' Consolidated Edison cut its dividend. On the news of the dividend cut, the stock dropped 50% at one fell swoop.

I recall at the time of the dividend cut a fellow Rotarian remarked: "What is the world coming to with Consolidated Edison on the verge of bankruptcy." The stock continued to erode, not bottoming out until it hit $6. At the lows the stock was selling for about 20% of book.

Technically, however, Consolidated Edison at the lows had about as perfect a bottom technical formation as could be asked for, with the stock consistently finding support at 6. Investors kept liquidating their positions on every rally, but the stock kept finding support at 6. The range of the stock was converging at 6.

At the first of the year, 1975, the stock broke decisively out of the formation to the upside. For three straight years the stock moved higher in nearly a perfect trendline. The stock leveled off at resistance at 20 for several years, but in 1981, broke to the upside once again and has been moving up ever since. From the lows of 1974, the stock has advanced by a factor of 21.75. Buying a depressed Consolidated Edison certainly has worked out nicely.

Buying low-priced utility issues is not for the fainthearted, of course. Many investors thought that 20 was the bottom for Consolidated Edison, with the stock down over 50% already, only to see the dividend slashed and the stock drop another 85%.

On the other hand, the utilities share several characteristics that make them excellent depressed stocks. Utilities seem to have 9-lives to the extent that they tend to stay in business. No matter how uncooperative a state commission may be, they are not going to let a utility go out of business. No matter how much trouble a utility gets into, the utilities have always managed to survive and rebound.

There are frequently bargains in low-priced and depressed utility stocks. Investors just have to know what side of the trend they are standing on, that is, when to stand aside and when to buy.

General Public Utilities (GPU)

Other notable utilities have emerged along the way. Most investors remember General Public Utilities (GPU). The Three Mile Island debacle took the stock from $21 a share in 1977 to $3 3/8 in 1980. At the lows the stock was selling for about 10% of book value.

While it took several years for GPU to work out its problems, the stock bounced along at support 4, in late 1979 and early 1981 and then began to trend higher in mid-1981.

If investors would take a moment to study GPU's pattern, they would see GPU's action as typical of many depressed issues, not just utilities, but many stocks.

First, a stock gradually loses ground, as in 1978. Then panic strikes. Then the stock begins to bottom out as distress selling is running its course and speculators are beginning to accumulate positions.

As the stock begins to saucer out higher there is no guarantee that purchases will lead to profits. However, if there is a major recovery under way—and a major recovery in GPU was under way in 1981 with GPU stock eventually rising to 50 and splitting—buying when the issue begins to show some bullish action is the correct time to buy. Bullish action shows itself as some buoyancy following a panic.

Readers do not have to be Chartered Financial Analysts, or Chartered Technical Analysts, or PhDs in mathematics, to understand the stock cycle, from distribution, to markdown, to accumulation, to markup, etc. The process represented by GPU is occurring in some stock or groups of stocks every trading day of the year.

There are a host of other utilities which have fallen in the past into disrepute among Wall Street analysts, only to rebound a year or two down the road, such as: Entergy (formerly Middle South Utilities), Niagara Mohawk Power, Gulf States Utilities, Long Island Lighting, PSI Resources (formerly Public Service of Indiana), and Philadelphia Electric.

Today, several utilities have problems to work out. The following utilities are all down from previous highs, to varying degrees. However, all the stocks have shaved their dividends: CMS Energy, Midwest Resources, Pacific Enterprises, Portland General, Public Service of New Mexico, and Sierra Pacific Resources.

Of all the utilities which are down and out, Tucson Electric Power is the most depressed—by a landslide.

Tucson Electric Power (TEP)

Tucson Electric Power (TEP) is one of the most depressed, down some 97% from a high of $65. The dividend was first cut in the September quarter of 1989 and then omitted in the first quarter 1990. Tucson Electric Power stock is truly depressed. However, look at the stock's technicals. The stock is working to establish an uptrend (see Figure 8-13).

On the heels of the selling panic of December 14 and December 15, 1992, TEP rebounded slightly at first, then picked up strength and advanced right into resistance at 3 3/4. Subsequently the stock eased lower to a trading range just under 3.

During the week ending May 14 the issue broke out, moving to a new high (and resistance, again) of 3 3/4 by the following week. After the customary dull pullback, TEP broke past 4 on high volume the week of June 25, closing at a high of 4 5/8 on July 8.

I doubt that this advance is the one which is going to carry TEP back to respectability. Much uncertainty exists regarding the outlook at TEP. Several more rallies will be needed over a period of months to absorb the resistance. As could be expected, TEP drifted back to support at 3 3/4, right above the prior trading range.

Not only does TEP have work of its own to do, but the more speculative utilities have been too hot. The relative strength leaders CMS, Niagara Mohawk Power, NIPSCO Industries, Portland General, and Pinnacle West are hardly the highest investment-grade issues.

Investor demand for utilities has been so strong that the more speculative-grade issues are leading the pack and we all know what that means. TEP will be a good speculation after some of the "froth" is off the utilities, and the stock is just quietly trading right above support.

Figure 8 • 13   Tucson Electric Power (TEP): October 1992 – September 1993

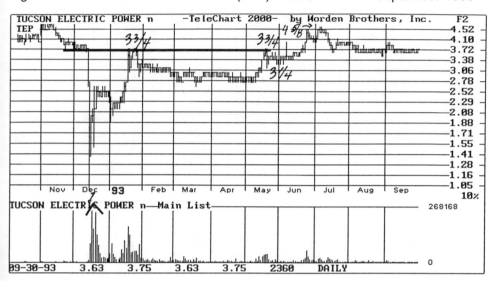

Chart courtesy of TeleChart 2000™ by Worden Brothers, Inc. Used with permission.

Arkla (ALG)

If investors would look at a mid-1993 listing of the Dow Jones Utilities they will see that the lowest-priced stock is Arkla, a natural gas distributor.

Arkla, until 1992, was largely a do-nothing stock. For nearly 10 years the stock traded between the mid-teens and the high 20s. The yield at around 6% was satisfactory, although there had not been an increase for six straight years.

All that changed in 1991. The stock went through the floor and the dividend was cut. A combination of high debt, low gas prices, and take-or-pay claims was putting substantial pressure on Arkla. Arkla was also tied up in the failed University Savings Association of Houston (see Figure 8-14).

By the time the selling panic was over, Arkla had fallen about 75% and was selling for less than book value.

Nearly all issues that have had panic selloffs share some common characteristics: The panic occurs, the stock rallies for a couple of months, and then the stock drifts back toward the panic lows.

There is no assurance that the stock will not decline to further lows, leading to another panic. On the other hand, many major advances have started after the

Figure 8 • 14 Arkla Inc. (ALG): March 1989 – December 1993

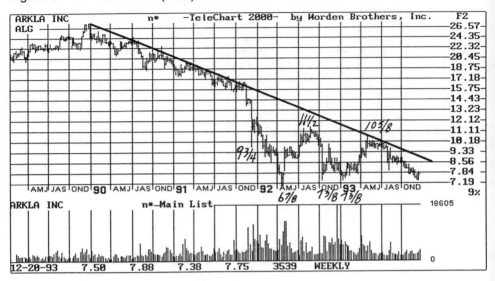

Chart courtesy of TeleChart 2000™ by Worden Brothers, Inc. Used with permission.

stock has drifted back to around the panic lows and becomes dead in the water, awaiting a new impulse. Investors need to act when that impulse is bullish.

Technically, the rebound rally from panic lows eventually carried the stock back to the declining trendline. In either a buying panic, or a selling panic, a stock pulls away from the trend. Subsequently, the stock works its way back to the trendline.

Arkla is currently operating within the trendline that has been in effect since late 1989, when the stock topped out at 27 3/4 on December 27.

Arkla first moved from a panic low of 6 7/8 on April 21, 1992, to a rebound high of 11 1/2 on August 31.

Subsequently, the issue moved lower. The stock was sagged at first, but the institutions who were looking to bail out on the rally sort of piled through the door all at once when they saw the stock starting to drop. A panic resulted on October 20 as the stock dropped 1 3/4 points to close at 7 3/4 on volume of 2.85 million shares. The intraday low was 7 3/8.

Arkla had a rally off the panic lows of 7 3/8, but two months later had settled in right above those lows.

During the first week of February 1993 Arkla started an advance, an advance in which the stock would come in closer contact with the down trendline. The issue as a result stopped rising at 10 5/8 in May and began to move horizontally. Had Arkla broken out of that trading range to the upside, Arkla would also have broken out of its larger downtrend in effect since December 1989.

As it was, the sellers still had the upper hand, and during the week ending August 6, Arkla broke to the downside, back down again to under 8.

Arkla has all the attributes of a low-priced, depressed stock. Investors just have to wait for the stock to breakout. But while the patterns of accumulation will differ in extent and duration, they all assume the same characteristics of give and take between resistance and support.

As for some other utilities, one natural gas firm, Columbia Gas, declared bankruptcy given the industry conditions, and other natural gas issues, such as Pacific Enterprises and Transco Energy, are reeling. Given the extensive declines in many of the natural gas issues, the best buying opportunity in a single group today may be in the natural gas utility issues.

The utilities usually can be counted to offer interesting opportunities in low-priced and depressed stocks. The firms periodically face financial strains, for a variety of reasons, but always manage to survive, rebound, and prosper once again.

The stocks, likewise, go through very predictable phases. If there is any one group which seems to fit best with Loeb's theory of buying depressed blue chips, to "always buy that which the majority thinks is speculative and sell it when the majority believes the quality has reached investment grade," it is the utilities.

•   •

Appendix I:
Sources of Information

When prospecting for low-priced and depressed issues, sources of information are important. An investor's ability to pick winners is often said to be a *knack,* but having a knack is largely dependent on having a sufficient, well-organized, intelligence-gathering network. History indicates that the Rothchild fortune was built largely because the family had a better intelligence network than the British Empire and could preempt the financial markets. While *Finding Winners* will not turn investors into Rothchilds, a degree of success will largely stem from the ability to tap and analyze existing information.

This Appendix will list and briefly describe important sources of information on low-priced and depressed stocks. The following sources are grouped by the organization providing the information.

General Publications

Standard & Poor's Corp.
345 Hudson Street
New York, NY 10014
1-800-221-5277

Standard NYSE Stock Reports

Standard NYSE Stock Reports publishes reports on *every* common stock listed on the Big Board. Many other sources cover NYSE issues, but they usually cover the most widely held or more popular ones, leaving out many of the low-priced and depressed. *NYSE Stock Reports* are the most complete and concise.

The *Reports* start with a summary section that lists specific statistics including price, yearly price range, P/E ratio, dividend yield, S&P Ranking, and Beta. The S&P ratings reflect earnings and dividend performance. As mentioned in an earlier Chapter, many low-priced and depressed stocks are rated B or less.

The *Reports* also include a monthly chart dating back 7 years showing price and volume enabling investors to get a pretty fair idea about the extent a stock is depressed.

The *Standard NYSE Stock Reports*, though, are largely fundamental. The *Reports* cover a Current Outlook and Important Developments; highlight Revenues and Common Share Earnings on a quarterly basis dating back 4 years; and, at the bottom of the *Report*, provide key Per Share Data for the past 10 years.

On the back page of the *NYSE Stock Reports* are 10 years of selective statistics, with Income and Balance Sheet Data in the top tables and Dividend Data and Capitalization in the lower half. A Business Summary is provided along with a brief review of Finances. Often, with low-priced and depressed stocks, these sections will be awash in red ink.

Every low-priced stock will have a *Report* periodically published on the company, and with very little time and effort investors can learn about the stock price and fundamentals of any company. The *Reports* may have few reassuring comments on these issues. However, investors are interested in knowing what the company does and just how much potential rebound it has.

The *Reports* are updated at least quarterly, and if significant news develops on any particular issue, a new report is published.

Many libraries and most brokerage offices carry the *Reports*. They are available on an annual subscription basis at $1,465, per year, are mailed first class, and are also available electronically.

The Stock Market Encyclopedia

The Stock Market Encyclopedia, is a quarterly publication made up of *Standard NYSE Stock Reports* covering two groups of stocks:

1. The 500 stocks making up the S&P 500;
2. The 300 most actively traded issues during the previous quarter.

The Encyclopedia is designed to cover the blue chips, the more widely held and more widely followed companies. For that reason, it targets few low-priced stocks. However, there are low-priced stocks among the S&P 500.

The Encyclopedia is useful because it covers many fallen blue chips, a primary focus of *Finding Winners*. One standard statistical feature of the *Encyclopedia* is its list of issues selling at $25 or less, with low P/E ratios and high rankings.

An annual subscription is $130. Individual copies are available for $55.

Watching Service

The quarterly *Watching Service* reports on up to 30 *Standard NYSE Stock Reports* of an investor's choice. The annual subscription price is $142 and is sent either first class mail or by fax. Ten additional reports are available for $66. Investors can change the stocks they receive at any time.

Stock Guide

The *Stock Guide* is a familiar investor reference, providing selected statistics on over 5,000 common stocks. While the monthly *Guide* does follow a large number of issues, it is not particularity useful in screening for low-priced stocks. The information is too brief because of space limitations. Nonetheless, the *Guide* can give investors a quick look at nearly every publicly traded company. An annual subscription is $128.

Moody's Investors Service, Inc.
99 Church Street
New York, NY 10007
1-800-342-5647 ext. 0435

Moody's Handbook of Common Stocks

Moody's Handbook of Common Stocks, published quarterly, provides one-page reports on over 900 NYSE stocks.

At the top of each report is a Long-Term Price Score, based on the stock's performance versus the NYSE Composite Index over the past 7 years, and a Short-Term Price Score, based on the stock's performance versus the Composite Index over the past year. For dividend buffs, stocks with at least 10 consecutive years of higher dividend payments are also given.

The reports include monthly high-low prices for the last 15 years.

The *Moody's Handbook* also provides significant statistical information and fundamentals such as Background, Recent Developments, and Prospects.

The principle drawback of *Moody's Handbook* is also its advantage. Moody's covers only 900 stocks with full-page reports, leaving many stocks without coverage. Many low-priced issues will not be seen in the *Handbook*.

On the other hand, if an issue is truly a depressed blue chip, the type of issue capable of significant rebound, and not just on a two-month fling, Moody's will probably cover it.

The charts in *Moody's Handbook* provide a handy review of many fallen blue chips, and they can help identify important major support and resistance levels. At the back of the *Handbook* are two additional features. The Condensed Statistical Tabulation provides selected statistical information on all stocks with no full-page coverage.

The second, more useful feature, is a section of long-term stock price charts on selected stocks showing high, short-term price scores. While the significance of Moody's Price Score system is not validated in the *Handbook*, it is most interesting that nearly half of the stocks listed are low-priced, depressed issues, where the high short-term price scores coincided with the stock breaking out of a base. While arbitrarily chasing after stocks with high short-term momentum runs the risk of buying high, the scores may also indicate a truly high-potential rebound situation in a depressed blue chip, highlighting a future buying opportunity.

An annual subscription to *Moody's Handbook of Common Stocks* is $235. Single copies are available for $80. The *Handbook* is available at most libraries.

Investor's Business Daily, Inc.
P.O. Box 66370
Los Angeles, CA 90066-0370
1-800-831-2525

Investor's Business Daily

Investor's Business Daily, published by William O'Neil & Company, is one of the best sources of information regarding technical analysis. However, major features in the newspapers are confined by price limitations.

For instance, the lead feature in the stock quote section, "60 NYSE Stocks With Greatest % Rise in Volume," is for stocks over $15 only. In the section "20 Most % Up in Price," and for the charts presented in "NYSE Stocks In The News" the cutoff price is $12. While *Investor's Business Daily* is one of the best sources for technical analysis of individual stock prices, it is confined to higher priced stocks.

Fortunately, *Investor's Business Daily's* chief columnist of "Inside The Market" column, Leo Fasciocco, generally has some interesting technical observations on selected low-priced stocks. "Inside The Market" reviews stocks of all price levels, moving up or down, breaking above or below bases and has periodic reports on lower-priced stocks not highlighted elsewhere in the newspaper.

For example, on July 15, 1992, Leo reported "M-A Comm Inc climbed 5/8 to 9 1/4 on triple its normal daily volume." On July 14, "Humana Inc rose 1 to

12 3/4 to move out of a six-week consolidation in heavy trading of 3.6 million shares." On July 9, "Sport Supply Group Inc climbed 7/8 to 14 1/2, a new high, and breakout from a ten-week base at 14." On July 8, "First Mississippi Corp surged 1 1/4 to 10 7/8 on six times normal daily volume." On June 28, "Diagnostek Inc spurted 1 to 8 7/8 on 11 times its normal volume."

Again, "Inside The Market" and its coverage of the technical action of individual stocks along with periodic commentary on lower-priced stocks is a useful feature of *Investor's Business Daily*.

A one-year subscription is $169. A 13-week trial $49. A helpful audio cassette, *100 Ways to Improve Your Investment Results,* is offered to new subscribers.

Dow Jones & Co.
200 Liberty Street
New York, NY 10017
1-800-221-1940 *(Wall Street Journal)*
1-800-544-0422 *(Barron's)*

The Wall Street Journal

As the country's leading business newspaper the *Wall Street Journal* carries a wealth of information. One of its most important features is the Price Percentage Gainers listed in the "Stock Market Data Bank" on page C2. Investors on the lookout for stocks on the move should always scan this section first. A properly analyzed large percentage move can be very helpful. Decisive breakouts occur with a large price increase on a large increase in volume. If any of the stocks listed in the Gainers column are breaking out of a base, it is important to know.

There are 20 stocks listed in the NYSE Price Percentage Gainers column. Typically three-quarters of the issues in a week's time will be stocks under $20.

Next to the Gainers column is the Losers column, where investors can glean some important information. For example, Stone Container, one of the weakest common stocks on the Big Board in 1993, slid steadily for over 18 months following a January 1992 high of $32 a share. In addition to a meltdown in stock price, the common dividend had been omitted during the third quarter of 1992. A heavy debt load was taking its toll on the company's bottom line and its ratings in the financial markets. Technically the stock showed a pattern of distribution.

When Stone Container's $1.75 Series E Cumulative Convertible Exchangeable Preferred stock showed up on July 26, 1993, at the top of the Losers list with a loss for the day of 21.9%, the preferred stock dropped 3 3/4, to 13 3/4. The firm had omitted its preferred dividend.

What had occurred? The pension funds were throwing in the towel. Simply, there was a selling panic among pension fund money managers who still held Stone stock issues as an investment. The action in the Stone Container preferred indicated that the stock issue was on the threshold of becoming truly depressed, not just low-priced, but depressed, with all investment holdings flushed out. The stock was entering a period of distress selling.

The Stone common showed some immediate weakness in light of the cut on the preferred dividend. The firm's financial outlook became increasingly weak.

However, at the time the common was above its April 8 lows of 6 3/8. The ability of Stone common to hold was bullish.

While a major rebound at Stone Container would most likely be poor for the next year, if not longer, the stock could also be expected to have a rally attempt during tax-loss selling. Overall, the "sell at any price" orders on the preferred was an indication that Stone Container was shaping up as a classic low-priced depressed issue offering significant rebound potential.

The *Journal* also has several standard features which highlight individual stock selections. John Dorfman runs the monthly "Investment Dartboard" contest and a column tracking brokerage house selections. I participated in and won one of the first of the contests. My stock, Citicorp, picked on technical as well as fundamental merit, was the only stock of the four participants to rise in a down market. All others' selections fell with the market. Since John interviews some of the leading analysts in the country, it is always interesting to hear the recommendations and why. Not many stocks are low-priced and depressed. However, some interesting stock selections appear from time to time.

The *Journal's* "Abreast of the Market" column sometimes features stock selections but is largely commentary on why the markets rose or fell the day before. A more important column for stock picking is "Heard On The Street."

While low-priced stocks are not regulars in "Heard On The Street," some interesting low-priced issues do appear there periodically. For instance, in one issue, there was a story on ADT Ltd., entitled "ADT Finds Investors Forgive and Forget."

ADT was low-priced at $8.25 and depressed. The stock sold at $34 in 1990. At $8.25 the stock was selling for less than book value.

The story reviewed the checkered history of ADT and reported on soured investments and questionable accounting methods. On a positive note, money managers seemed to be giving ADT the benefit of the doubt.

Finally, ADT technically was selling at support as it was developing at 7 3/4.

A one year subscription to the *Journal* is $149.00; for six-months $78.

Barron's

Probably all investors have read *Barron's* from time to time, as they should, since *Barron's* may be the leading publication offering "stock tips" and investment ideas.

Of particular interest are the fund managers interviews. In a regular section called "Mutual Choice," fund managers have an opportunity to tout their favorite stocks, some low-priced. For example, when Jerome L. Dodson of the Parnassus Fund was interviewed, he recommended Tandem Computers (NYSE: TDM). At the time, Tandem was selling in the low-teens, down from a high of over 37, certainly qualifying as a low-priced stock.

When Robert Martorelli of Merrill Lynch's Phoenix Fund was interviewed, in "Shaky Past, Stellar Future," he began by making reference to where he gets some of his ideas—the stocks which are making new lows. This fund manager likes to look for stocks which are trading for book value or less, for companies selling at 50% of sales or lower, for companies selling at the low end of their P/E ratios. Many low-priced and depressed issues, including ADT Limited around 8, appeared in the discussion.

Individual recommendations in *Barron's* articles often include stocks selling for under $20.

The annual subscription for this weekly is $119; for 13 weeks, $32.

Forbes, Inc.
60 Fifth Avenue
New York, NY 10020
1-800-888-9896

Forbes

Forbes may well be the best all-around publication for investors. It is edited extremely well, reflecting the steady hand of Managing Editor, James Michaels. *Forbes* also has few peers when it comes to investigative reporting.

Forbes is no-nonsense and hard-hitting. *Forbes* articles will periodically review some lower-priced stocks, and investors receive a thorough analysis of the firms.

Forbes also has several columnists who are worth reading. The "Streetwalker," reviews some of the recommendations of Wall Street research houses. While not a format for low-priced stocks, they do appear regularly. The Contrarian column is not a low-priced stock column, however, the column does cover out-of-favor stocks.

The *Forbes/Barron's* "Wall Street Review," edited by Eric S. Hardy, gives interesting statistical reviews. The "Review" recently listed 10 stocks with 1994 EST EPS between $0.01 and $0.07. Six were priced under $10.

An annual subscription is $54.

Value Line Publishing, Inc.
711 3rd Avenue
New York, NY 10017
1-800-833-0046

The Value Line Investment Survey

The Value Line Investment Survey is one of the most popular sources of information for investors. *Value Line* does not cover low-priced stocks per se. It covers 1,700 NYSE, AMEX, and over-the-counter stocks. In a recent issue, the Summary & Index section covered over 300 NYSE-listed stocks priced at less than $20 a share, one-third of which were under $10 a share. *Value Line's* low-priced stocks are added on the basis of merit not on the basis of price.

Like many services, *Value Line* covers the more widely followed issues. Issues like RJR Nabisco Holdings appear, but for the most part the low-priced stocks will be higher-priced stocks that fell in price. In other words, to be in *Value Line* and be low-priced, the odds are high that the stock was formerly blue chip or near blue chip but now is depressed—thus of particular interest for investors looking for winners.

The *Value Line's* individual stock write-ups contain informative graphic as well as statistical material. The charts at the top of the page cover market activity for at least ten years, enough to indicate whether a stock is just low-priced, or whether it is depressed.

The lesson with low-priced, depressed stocks is that in order to provide truly significant capital gains potential, earnings have to eventually rebound to match an advance in price. While a technical improvement in the price *may* precede a fundamental improvement, if the fundamentals do not follow suit, the stock will give up its gains.

Value Line's charts also reflect pre-split trading. A stock on occasion will have a reverse stock split. Instead of a 2-for-1 split, there may be a reverse stock split, usually 1-for-5 or 1-for-10. Companies reverse their stock to make it more appropriate to institutional investors.

A reverse stock split, however, is considered a new issue by some sources, and no mention is made of the preceding price history. Many services just reflect the price range of the stock post-split and do not indicate that a stock is selling far below previous highs. *Value Line* does report the pre-split trading history.

Value Line also publishes a host of tables for "bargain hunters." In a section entitled "High 3- to 5-Year Appreciation Potential," it lists 100 stocks with the top stock showing a potential of up to 615%. In a recent listing of the 100 stocks, 61 were less than $10 per share, and 30 were between $10 and $20. Only 9 were selling for more than $20. The top ten stocks with the highest potential were all under $10, with the average price of $3.94.

In a table called "Widest Discounts From Book Value" 100 stocks are listed. This listing also includes a large number of stocks selling under $20.

Is book value passe? Readers should reread my review of "The Anatomy of a Stock Market Winner" in Chapter 1 that credits "price-to-book ratio less than 1.0" as the number one characteristic of winning stocks that produced the highest median return.

Value Line does not state that stocks in these "bargain" tables will lead to superior returns. Indeed, many of these stocks rank poorly in the Value Line Timeliness ratings. In terms of performance, among the 100 *Value Line* recently ranked stocks ranked "1" for Timeliness, there were no stocks under $10. Only eight NYSE-listed issues were under $20. However, with so many of the huge capital gains coming from low-priced and depressed stocks, it would be interesting to track the future performance of the stocks in these tables.

Subscriptions are $525 a year. A 10-week trial offer $55. *Value Line Investment Survey* is probably the most widely distributed investment service through public libraries.

Chart Services

Technical analysis and charts go hand-in-hand. While technical analysis does not require the use of charts, charts do present the basic stock data—high-low-close and volume—in a convenient manner. As the saying goes, "a picture is worth 1,000 words," or perhaps, for *Finding Winners* 1,000 numbers.

Charts come in a variety of forms, but all are classified by time. The period of time a chart covers—long, intermediate, or short—has important uses. The longer-term charts allow investors to see the major trends in a stock plus major support and resistance levels. The intermediate to shorter-term charts narrow in on the intermediate and minor trends, plus intermediate and minor support and resistance levels.

The longer-term charts can give graphic representation of how seriously a stock may be low-priced or depressed. The shorter-term charts give investors the day-by-day to week-to-week patterns which invariably must be acted on when buying and selling.

William O'Neil & Company
P.O. Box 66919
Los Angeles, CA 90066
1-310-448-6843

Daily Graphs

Daily Graphs are available for NYSE and NASDAQ/AMEX-listed issues. *NYSE Daily Graphs* lists 1,600 common stocks. In any one week *NYSE Daily Graphs* prints and updates the majority of common stocks. Not all services that print weekly update their charts weekly.

Daily Graphs are concise, visually clear, easy to read, and have the most comprehensive information. The front part of the book covers the 700+ most actively traded and more widely held issues. High-priced, some low-priced, and the medium-priced issues are in the front section.

However, the majority of the lower-priced issues are normally found in the 800+ issues covered in the back section.

Since the stocks selected for the back section generally are showing some trading activity, they are usually in the process of moving up or moving down. Just by being listed in *Daily Graphs* increases chances of a stock being "in play."

On the other hand, some smaller issues, especially reflecting the January Effect, move so quickly that by the time *Daily Graphs* picks up the issues, a large percentage of the move is over.

Daily Graphs should be used along with other resources for finding winners among low-priced and depressed stocks.

William O'Neil's very readable book, *How To Make Money In Stocks*, contains many references on the use of *Daily Graphs* and technical analysis in general.

In addition, he publishes several other informative books and conducts "Advanced Investment" workshops across the country. Any investor using *NYSE Daily Graphs* should consider attending.

An annual subscription to *NYSE Daily Graphs* is $333. *Daily Graphs* is also available bi-weekly for $271 and monthly at $195. A 5-week trial is $14. Trial offers include "How to Select Stocks Using Daily Graphs" and "How and When to Sell Stock Short." As with many of the chart services, postage is a separate charge.

Long-Term Values

Long-Term Values provides 15-year charts on over 4,000 issues. The service is weekly, and each issue is updated every 1 1/2 months.

Long-Term Values is most useful in helping investors spot stocks that have had extensive declines and are trading at important support.

Long-Term Values is $227 per year. A two-week trial subscription is $10.

Trendline Charts
Standard & Poor's Trendline Dept.
25 Broadway
New York, NY 10004
1-800-221-5277

Daily Action Stock Charts

The *Daily Action Stock Charts* provide weekly charts for a 12-month period on over 700 of the most widely followed NYSE issues. All stocks with options are followed.

An annual subscription is $589; three months, $215; 8-week trial, $58. An informative report, "How Charts Can Help You Spot Buy and Sell Signals In the Stock Market," is provided as a bonus.

Current Market Perspectives

Current Market Perspectives, published monthly, provides weekly price and volume data on 1,476 NYSE listed stocks covering a period of approximately 3 1/2 years. Given the length of time, plus wide coverage, a depressed blue chip will most likely be highlighted in *Current Market Perspectives*.

Subscription rates are $225 for one year; the single issue price is $35.

Chart Guide

Chart Guide, covering over 4,400 issues, is one of the most comprehensive guide for stocks in terms of number of issues graphically presented. The *Chart Guide* covers NYSE, ASE, and NASDAQ.

Chart Guide's advantage is that it covers a large number of stocks that are "dormant" while other chart services cover stocks that are the most actively or widely traded. Many of the low-priced stocks that show the best gains in any given quarter, and especially reflecting the January Effect, will most likely be found in the *Chart Guide* before they start their move.

Subscription rates for the *Chart Guide* are one year, $160; three months, $50.

Securities Research Co. (SRC)
Babson-United Investment Advisors
101 Prescott Street
Wellesley Hills, MD 02181
1-617-235-0900

SRC Red Book

The *SRC Red Book of 5-Trend Security Charts,* covering 21 months, charts 1,108 leading stocks and is published monthly. The stocks charted are listed inside the front and back covers for easy reference.

SRC *Red Book* charts are printed on a semi-logarithmic scale. The space on the chart between a 10 and 20 rise will be equivalent to 20 to 40, and 40 to 80. In other words, the stock is graphed according to percentage move, not absolute dollar amount. Thus, stocks can be more accurately compared, individually, to one another, as well as to market indexes.

An annual subscription to the *SRC Red Book* is $124. A single issue is $17.

SRC Blue Book

The *SRC Blue Book of 5-Trend Cycli-Graphs,* published quarterly, covers 12 years and charts the same 1,108 stocks as the *SRC Red Book.*

Most investors probably use the *SRC* charts to buy stocks that have consistently rising prices, dividends, earnings, etc.

However, low-priced and depressed stocks are more likely to have the recessive or cyclical patterns as in the "Case Studies" shown at the bottom of the Legend page of the SRC chart books.

An annual subscription to the *SRC Blue Book* is $104. Single copies are available for $30.

Mansfield NYSE Chart Service
2973 Kennedy Blvd.
Jersey City, NY 07306
1-201-795-0629

The Mansfield stock charts may not be well known to many investors, but the Mansfield Stock Chart service is one of the most comprehensive.

The *Mansfield NYSE Charts,* published weekly, cover all NYSE common stocks. All stocks are listed alphabetically at the front of the service.

In addition, Mansfield has an ASE chart service and three OTC chart services: *OTC I* covering 1,200 most active; *OTC II* covering 1,300 second-tier; and *OTC III* covering 1,300 tertiary. In many aspects, Mansfield is one of the most complete chart services.

In addition to the weekly charts, Mansfield provides several interesting statistical tables, such as: 30 Best-30 Worst Performances, with a breakdown of 7, 3 week, and 1 week; Capital and Volume Trends; and Price Gaps.

Since breakouts are an integral aspect of technical analysis, a stock that has advanced decisively should be of interest. Rather than looking for breakouts from day-to-day, Mansfield summarizes the weekly activity. Investors can then refer to the background charts and verify that an advance was a valid breakout.

Stock Watch is a regular feature highlighting selected stocks including the low-priced. Each issue has technical comment.

The *Mansfield NYSE Chart Service* is $728 on a weekly basis. The service is also available on a bi-weekly basis at $447 and on a monthly basis at $232. A three-week trial is $48.

Chartcraft Point & Figure
Chartcraft
P.O. Box 2046
New Rochelle, NY 10801
1-914-632-0422

Chartcraft offers both the *Chartcraft Point & Figure* charting service and the *Investors Intelligence* newsletter.

The Point & Figure (P&F) may be the original method of stock charting but is probably the one least familiar to most investors. I don't intend to delve deeply into the subject because Chartcraft will send you a book on the mechanicals of P&F. However, the P&F method is very useful in identifying reversals in low-priced and depressed stocks, and some discussion here is warranted.

The P&F method uses price changes only. Only when a stock moves by a predetermined amount is an entry made in a box. Chartcraft requires three box moves in order to be recorded.

For stocks trading between $20 and $100, each box represents $1. For stocks trading between $5 and $20, each box represents $0.50. For stocks under $5, each box represents $0.25. For stocks over $100, each box represents $2.

When the stock moves up, an "X" is recorded. When a stock moves down, an "O" is recorded. No entries are made for unchanged prices.

Volume indications are ignored. P&F also ignores time to the extent that an indication is not made on a daily, weekly, or monthly basis, but only when there is a change in the stock price.

The Chartcraft Three-Point Reversal method focuses on reversals, where it takes three boxes to constitute a reversal. A Buy signal is given when an up (X) column goes above a previous (X) after an intervening down (0) column. A Sell signal is given when a down (0) column goes above a previous down (0) column after an intervening up (X) column.

Chartcraft takes P&F one step further. Reversals are not only based on price action charted, but also on relative strength.

The relative strength figures are computed weekly by dividing the price of a stock by the DJIA. By taking into account the overall market, Charftcraft eliminates any price action solely due to overall market activity. Investors are able to focus on stocks which are truly in the process of reversal.

P&F charting is, of course, applicable to any stock. However, since *Finding Winners* is focusing on low-priced and depressed stocks, a form of technical analysis such as the P&F 3-Box Reversal Method is tailor-made to provide investors with some additional insights.

We only scratched the surface of P&F charting. Chartercraft publishes a wide variety of materials and services.

Chartercraft's P&F monthly chart book offer 3,450 charts. Twelve issues, $360. Single copy $37. Chartercraft publishes a long-term P&F chart book on over 1,400 stocks. Single issue $49.50.

Investors Intelligence

Investors Intelligence is probably most familiar to investors because of their Advisory Sentiment Survey, compiled weekly from over 130+ services. However, *Investors Intelligence* offers much more than the Advisory Sentiment Survey.

First, at the top of every issue a market outlook is expressed and sometimes an overall investment philosophy. For instance, in a recent issue, editor Michael Burke quotes himself: "The stock market is the only business where people like to buy at high prices. It's as if an airline offered NY-LA Tix for $50 and people said something must be wrong with that line. I'll wait till it's $400."

In another recent issue he quotes James Fraser of the *Contrary Investor*: "When real value is out of favor, a contrarian moves in. Such an investor waits patiently. A contrarian speculator, on the other hand, tries to judge the psychological climate with other tools, as charts and technical indicators, that will cut (hopefully) down the waiting time. We do that at times, but would rather buy value peacefully rather than at a crowded starting gate."

One regular feature in *Investors Intelligence* is the Low-Priced Portfolio. All stocks in the Portfolio are low-priced. In fact, in a recent issue all were under $10, with 5 under $5. The *Investors Intelligence's* Long-Term Portfolio also has a fair share of low-priced stocks. The Bear Corner is one *Investors Intelligence* portfolio which tends to have higher-priced stocks. Mike Burke will also frequently highlight new stock recommendations which he feels are great "stock pickers." Many, of the stocks are low-priced in value or contrarian selections.

Investors Intelligence is not glossy. However, the service is all substance. Subscriptions are $175 per year.

General Sources

The Contrary Investor, Fraser Management
309 S. Willard Street, P.O. Box 494
Burlington, VT 05402
1-802-658-0322

The Contrary Investor

The Contrary Investor, edited and published by Jim Fraser, has been written for over 32 years. The newsletter is widely quoted, not only for its common sense approach to investing, but because the newsletter has a good record. At a time when most investors usually think of the day-to-day to week-to-week movements in the market and stocks, *The Contrary Investor's* perspectives more often than not help investors to "see the forest through the trees."

In terms of stocks, *The Contrary Investor* is not a low-priced stocks service per se, but low-priced stocks will make up many of the recommendations. In 1992, 20 out of the 25 recommendations were priced at or under $25.

A six-month trial is available for $45.

Dick Davis Digest
P.O. Box 9547
Fort Lauderdale, FL 33310
1-800-654-1514

Dick Davis Digest

The 12-year-old *Dick Davis Digest* is one of the best newsletters and sources of stock advice. The publication is concise, accurate, clear-cut, and comprehensive.

Each issue of the *Dick Davis Digest* begins with a Personal Note. For instance, in one recent issue, Steve Halpren, editor and publisher for eight years, prints excerpts from Warren Buffett's 1993 Berkshire Hathaway shareholders meeting. For those who think of investing as buying at the bottom "eight" and selling at the top "eight," Buffett always make refreshing reading.

Buffett is quoted: "Eight or 10 good investment ideas in a lifetime is all you need. You many not even need that many. If you stop and think about it, a 40-stock portfolio in 30 different industries is not an investment at all for most people. It's often twaddle sold by finance professionals and people, who, for a price, provide a steady dollop of frictional (trading) costs." The Personal Note section provides thoughtful perspective on investing.

The remaining pages of the 12-page *Digest* are packed with stock market opinions and recommendations. *Dick Davis Digest* uses over 450 investment newsletters, brokerage house research reports, industry publications such as *The Wall Street Transcript*, and annual reports as resources. While there is not a section on low-priced stocks per se, low-priced and depressed stocks always make their way into every issue. Low-priced stocks regularly appear in the *Digest's* leading feature article, Spotlight Stock.

Dick Davis Digest is published 24 times a year. A one-year subscription is $140. A 3-month trial is $39.

The Institute for Econometric Research
3474 N. Federal Highway
Fort Lauderdale, FL 33306
1-800-442-9000

The name of this organization, The Institute for Econometric Research, may sound a bit imposing, but the two principals of the firm, Editor Norman Fosback and Publisher Glen Parker, have ambitiously put together an array of excellent and highly readable newsletters and related items.

Market Logic and Other Newsletters

The Institute's flagship publication, Market Logic, is published twice monthly, and offers a range of advice, from market timing and indicator analysis to individual stock market and mutual fund recommendations. Periodic reports —Seasonality, the January Effect—and trading systems—Moving Averages—are discussed. The ideas, concepts, recommendations, etc., are all thoroughly researched and well thought out.

They also publish other newsletters. Stock newsletters: *New Issues, Investor's Digest, Stock Market Weekly,* and *The Professional Investor.* Mutual fund newsletters are: *Mutual Fund Forecaster, Fund Watch, Mutual Fund Buyers's Guide, Income & Safety,* and *Mutual Fund Weekly.* One newsletter of particular interest to low-priced stock investors is *Investor's Digest,* with its monthly "Featured Low-Priced Stock."

Investors should send for pricing information and an overview of the services provided by The Institute for Econometric Research.

The Hirsch Organization
Six Deer Trail
Old Tappen, NJ 07675
1-800-477-3400

Stock Trader's Almanac

Yale Hirsch is best known for his 27-year-old *Stock Trader's Almanac*, which is jam packed with useful stock market indicators and information, ranging from seasonal indicators to stock market lore and proverbs. The January Barometer, the Political Election/Stock Market Cycle, The Mid-December Lows–Only Free Lunch On Wall Street, are just a few of the enduring sections in the Almanac. Any investor who has not seen the *Almanac* should send for a copy.

Smart Money, Hirsch's flagship newsletter, has been published for over 20 years and provides a monthly dose of maxims and other interesting information from the *Stock Trader's Almanac* plus stock recommendations. *Smart Money* recommends, almost exclusively, low-priced stocks.

However, like another publication of The Hirsch Organization, *The Ground Floor*, the low-priced stocks are largely over-the-counter issues. Nonetheless, some NYSE issues appear from time-to-time.

Beating the Dow

Beating the Dow, a newer monthly publication, recommends higher yielding/lower-priced Dow stocks. Low-priced Dow stocks are more in line with the type of stocks which *Finding Winners* is looking to buy.

The Editor of "Beating the Dow," John Downes, teamed up with Michael O'Higgins in writing the book, *Beating the Dow, A High-Return, Low-Risk Method for Investing in the Dow Jones Industrial Stocks With As Little As $5,000.*

The premise of buying "cheap" Dow stocks is nothing new. *The Intelligent Investor* by Ben Graham quotes studies on the Dow 30. However, *Beating the Dow* takes the Dow analysis a step further, with the premise of the book being that not only buying the higher yielding Dow stocks has proven worthwhile over the years but that buying the lower-priced, higher-yielding Dow stocks generates even better returns.

Investors should read *Beating the Dow*; a copy of the book is available through most public library systems. *Beating the Dow*, the monthly, is available for $125 per year. For information on *The Stock Trader's Almanac, Smart Money, Beating the Dow*, and *Ground Floor Dow*, contact The Hirsch Organization.

New Generation Research, Inc.
225 Friend Street, Suite 801
Boston, MA 02114
1-800-468-3810

Turnaround Letter

The *Turnaround Letter* contains a wealth of information including selections on low-priced and depressed stocks. The letter's companion publications, *The Bankruptcy DataSource, The Bankruptcy Yearbook & Almanac*, and *The Troubled Company Prospector*, give information on troubled companies.

Each issue of the *Turnaround Letter* has a feature article covering such topics as "Going Against The Flow." In this article the editor first makes a case that while the most widely followed institutional method of investing, momentum, can offer some near-term rewards, individual investors can really get burned chasing the hot stocks. As an alternative, the *Turnaround Letter's* basic investment philosophy is summarized by the following paragraph:

"Instead we recommend an anti-momentum strategy. This consists of buying stocks that have already crashed after most of Wall Street has bailed out. These stocks have much less downside than their high flying counterparts and will eventually be rediscovered by mainstream investors (at which point it may be time for us to bail out)." These thoughts are classic G.M. Loeb and why investors in low-priced and depressed issues should make reading the *Turnaround Letter* a must.

The *Turnaround Letter* has three recommended portfolios: Aggressive, More Conservative/Income, and Moderate Risk. Each list of recommendations contains predominately low-priced stocks. A very well-researched resource for low-priced and depressed stocks, it's one-year subscription is $195. A single issue is $15.

The Plain Talk Investor
1500 Skokie Blvd., Suite 203
Northbrook, IL 60062
1-708-564-1955

The Plain Talk Investor

There is an expression in writing, to the effect that "you speak to express, write to impress." In other words, many writers junk up their writings with too much borrowing from *Roget's Thesaurus. The Plain Talk Investor*, however, lives up to its name in being extremely well written and is always refreshing to read. Editor Fred Gordon also recognizes value.

Fred's background, before he was in the newsletter business, was buying and selling scrap. In the scrap business, if you don't know how to buy low, and sell higher, you lose your shirt.

The tendency of many highly paid analysts on Wall Street is to buy the *Fortune* "10 Most Admired" and sell the *Fortune* "10 Least Admired," ending up buying high and selling low. Fred has the street smarts to do the opposite and a fine academic background—he is a fellow alumni of Northwestern University.

The Plain Talk Investor is not a low-priced stock service per se. However when low-priced stocks appear they are always worth a look. An annual subscription is $135.

Sources of Insider Information

In buying low-priced and depressed stocks few indicators can be as helpful as insider buying. While insider activity has been tainted to an extent—a la Boesky-type affairs—whenever an insider puts cash money either into stock or takes it out, it often is many, many times more meaningful than the "vapid aphorisms" typically found in the glossy annual reports.

The Wall Street Journal

The *Wall Street Journal* reports on insider activity in their monthly column "Inside Track". This column spotlights inside activity on a stock, and periodically a low-priced issue will be covered.

For example, Inside Track reported Boone Pickens and other insiders picking up a large number of shares of Mesa Inc. at between $5.75 to $6.75. The article then reviewed the basic business of Mesa, the firm's current financial profile, and the outlook for the natural gas business.

The article related a general feeling regarding Mesa on Wall Street as "wait and see," given its highly leveraged financial condition and the volatility of natural gas pricing. However, one statement in particular should have been of interest to readers of *Finding Winners:* "A number of securities analysts have stopped tracking Mesa because of the company's complex financial situation." Mesa had nearly all the ingredients of a depressed situation that had the potential to turn into a winner.

William O'Neill & Co. Daily Graphs

Daily Graphs also provides more comprehensive insider activity information in terms of the number of issues followed. *Daily Graphs* uses the symbolic forms "+"

and "o" on their stock charts to indicate buys and sells. While any one stock will periodically show a few buys and sells, a stock with a series of insider buys or sells is always a road worth further pursuit.

CDA/Investnet
3265 Meridian Parkway, Suite 130
Fort Lauderdale, FL 33331
1-800-243-2324

CDA/Investnet

Both the *Journal* and *Daily Graphs* use CDA/Investnet as their source of insider activity. Investnet offers a wide range of specialized reports, many of which are designed for institutional investors.

Watch List Service

Watch List Service is designed to highlight insider changes in a portfolio of stocks.

Insider Trading Monitor

Insider Trading Monitor, available on-line via personal computer.

Insiders' Chronicle

The *Insiders' Chronicle*, published weekly, is one of the most comprehensive resources for insider activity. Regular features include a lead commentary discussing the overall market and any particular note of insider activity; Highlights of Buy Side Activity and Sell Side Activity; and The Largest Insider Trades.

Many insider activity reports are biased toward the larger capitalized stocks. However, *Insiders' Chronicle* lists *each* and *every* insider transaction reported. A fair number of lower-priced issues are represented in any one report. Most of the activity is more or less random. However, a few will turn out to be incredibly important tips.

Not to diminish the importance of insider buying, but insider buying activity can be misleading. Buying activity of insiders can, in effect, just be holding up the price of the stock. Once the insiders run out of capital to pump up the price, a stock can go right down the drain. Insiders can be wrong!

Insiders' Chronicle, $375 annually; 8-issue trial, $80.